The life of Haydn

Presenting a fresh picture of the life and work of Joseph Haydn, this is the first biography of the composer to appear in over twenty-five years. In his lifetime Haydn achieved a degree of fame that easily surpassed that of Mozart and Beethoven. Later his historical significance was more restricted, regarded exclusively as the composer who first recognized the potential of the symphony and the quartet. However, Haydn had also composed operas, oratorios and church music with similar enthusiasm and self-regard. Too easily pigeonholed as a Viennese composer, he interacted consistently with the musical life of Vienna only during the earliest and latest periods of his life; London was at least as important in fashioning the composer's fame and legacy. To counter the genial view of the composer, this biography probes the darker side of Haydn's personality, his commercial opportunism and double dealing, his penny pinching and his troubled marriage.

David Wyn Jones is Professor of Music and Head of School at Cardiff University and has written extensively on music and musical life in the Classical Period. He is the author of *The Symphony in Beethoven's Vienna* (2006), *The Life of Beethoven* (1998), *Beethoven: The Pastoral Symphony* (1996) and is the editor of *Music in Eighteenth-Century Austria* (1996), all published by Cambridge University Press. His *Companion to Haydn* (2002) was awarded the C. B. Oldman Prize by IAML UK. He has contributed to several programmes on BBC Radio 3 and Radio 4.

Musical lives

The books in this series each provide an account of the life of a major composer, considering both the private and the public figure. The main thread is both biographical and musical, and discussion of the music is integral to the narrative. Each book thus presents an organic view of the composer, the music and the circumstances in which the music was written.

Published titles

The life of Haydn

DAVID WYN JONES

CAMBRIDGE
UNIVERSITY PRESS

CAMBRIDGE
UNIVERSITY PRESS

University Printing House, Cambridge CB2 8BS, United Kingdom

One Liberty Plaza, 20th Floor, New York, NY 10006, USA

477 Williamstown Road, Port Melbourne, VIC 3207, Australia

314-321, 3rd Floor, Plot 3, Splendor Forum, Jasola District Centre, New Delhi - 110025, India

79 Anson Road, #06-04/06, Singapore 079906

Cambridge University Press is part of the University of Cambridge.

It furthers the University's mission by disseminating knowledge in the pursuit of education, learning and research at the highest international levels of excellence.

www.cambridge.org
Information on this title: www.cambridge.org/9781107610811

First published in 2009
Reprinted 2010
First paperback edition published 2013

A catalogue record for this publication is available from the British Library

Library of Congress Cataloging in Publication data
Wyn Jones, David.
The life of Haydn / David Wyn Jones.
    p.   cm. – (Musical lives)
Includes bibliographical references and index.
ISBN 978-0-521-89574-3 (hardback)
1. Haydn, Joseph, 1732–1809.   2. Composers–Austria–Biography.
I. Title. II. Series.
ML410.H4W96 2009
780.92–dc22

ISBN 978-0-521-89574-3 Hardback
ISBN 978-1-107-61081-1 Paperback

CONTENTS

ILLUSTRATIONS

Illustrations are taken from the following sources: Galerie Lichtenstein, Vienna (10), Gesellschaft der Musikfreunde, Vienna (1, 3, 5, 7, 8 and 11), John Rylands University Library, Manchester (13), Österreichisches Staatsarchiv, Vienna (2), Royal College of Music, London (6, 9 and 12), Stadtpfarre, Eisenstadt (4).

Cover: portrait of Haydn by Ludwig Guttenbrunn, c.1791–2; private possession, London.

'Haydn was far from wanting to keep his life a secret; he responded with good humour to everything that I asked him about it.' These are the words of Haydn's first biographer, Georg August Griesinger, written a day before the final instalment of his biography appeared in the leading music journal of the day, the *Allgemeine musikalische Zeitung*, in August 1809, a mere three months after the composer's death. The author had known Haydn for ten years, shared the outlook of musical Europe that he was the greatest living composer and noticed that he not only enjoyed this status but also willingly promoted it. Alongside the pride there was a simplicity that captivated those who had met him and which informed a musical expression that was particularly distinctive and certain in its vision.

While Griesinger celebrated Haydn's universality the composer still held the title of Kapellmeister to the Esterházy family, a post he had occupied for nearly fifty years. From composing music for a single prince to addressing the whole of Europe constituted a musical life of unparalleled interest, made even more intriguing in that the local audience was never forgotten as Haydn discovered the larger one. Being a dutiful Kapellmeister and a free artist at the same time was something that was to trouble the Romantic era. It is only one of several creative paradoxes that characterized the composer's life and fascinate the biographer.

Haydn was recognized as the first composer to revel in the intellectual challenges of the string quartet and the symphony, yet he had spent much of his time at the Esterházy court composing and directing opera; even towards the end of his life, when the notion of a Classical School founded on the common achievement of Haydn, Mozart and Beethoven in instrumental music was slowly emerging, Haydn said that he wished he had devoted more time to vocal music. That Classical School was centred on Vienna, where all three had worked, but for much of his life Haydn's interaction with that city was either fitful or troublesome. He did not become a true Viennese until after his two visits to London, a city that had regarded him as one of their own, the 'Shakespeare of music', and which, in a matter of a few years in the 1780s and 1790s, had determined the composer's legacy as a master of instrumental music.

Posterity has always been reluctant to probe sympathetically another tension in Haydn's life: that a creative figure who so obviously, and intently, embraced Enlightenment values in his music – enquiry, reason, optimism and sensibility – should also be a devout, practising Catholic of the most traditional, unquestioning kind. As someone who headed his autograph scores 'In Nomine Domini' and concluded them with 'Laus Deo' Haydn has always been allowed his religious belief because it conveniently fuelled a simplistic view of his personality. This is unfortunate. Mid-eighteenth-century Austrian Catholicism shaped not only Haydn's formative years as a musician but aspects of his character that are better regarded as formidable than naïve, in particular an indivisible loyalty to state and church that enabled the composer to become a national icon in the Napoleonic period.

Two hundred years have passed since Haydn's death and Griesinger's biography, and the modern author has much more material to investigate, scrutinize and evaluate than Griesinger ever had, a good deal of it uncovered in the last thirty years or so. It was a long life, seventy-seven years, one of the longest of any major composer. If this biography captures some of the underplayed complexities and contradictions of that life, then it will be an appropriate tribute in this anniversary year: a man of the eighteenth century who speaks with a richly variegated voice to the twenty-first century.

It is a pleasure to record my thanks to many individuals who have assisted in the preparation of this biography, from providing information, answering queries, to reading proofs: Otto Biba, Anke Caton, Richard Chesser, Sarah D'Ardenne, Ingrid Fuchs, Simon Keefe, Else Radant Landon, Drew Maybey, Simon McVeigh, John A. Rice, Rupert Ridgewell, Pam Thomson, John Tyrrell, Mary Worthington and Charlotte Young.

1 God and country

When Beethoven lay bedridden in his apartment in the Schwarz-spanierhaus in Vienna in the last few months of his life he received regular visitors who brought him a variety of gifts. One of the most valued by the dying composer was a lithograph of Haydn's birthplace presented to him by an old friend, Anton Diabelli, whose publishing firm had just issued it. 'Look, I got this today. Just look at the little house, and such a great man was born in it.'[1] Beethoven had it framed and it hung on his wall for the last weeks of his life.

One could read Beethoven's comment as genuine recognition of his fundamental indebtedness to Haydn, a final accommodation of a relationship that had not always been an easy one. More directly Beethoven's remark on the lithograph image pointed to a stark difference in their respective lives: Beethoven had been born in the electoral town of Bonn, where his father was employed as a musician in the local court; Haydn had been born in the countryside, where his father was the local wheelwright and carter.

Haydn's birthplace pictured in Diabelli's lithograph, Rohrau, was a small, rather sprawling hamlet, 25 miles east of Vienna and next to the river Leitha that marked the boundary between the archduchy of Austria and the kingdom of Hungary. It was a flat area, prone to flooding, reflected in the place name, literally 'Reedmeadow'. Haydn's house was to be flooded several times in the nineteenth century and, on another occasion, the roof was badly damaged by fire. What survives

today is a rather sanitized reconstruction set alongside adjacent
properties that obscure the view to the distant Leitha mountains that
can be seen on the right of the lithograph. Haydn's father, Mathias
Haydn (1699–1763), was originally from the town of Hainburg, six
miles to the north on the Danube where his father, Thomas, too had
been a wheelwright. In Rohrau Mathias Haydn may have been the
builder of the small house in the 1720s; he certainly cultivated several
fields for fruit and vegetables, had a small vineyard and some animals.
Together with the specialist craft of a wheelwright and carter this led
to a secure standard of living characterized as much by bartering as by
the exchange of cash. German was the local language; to hear any
Hungarian one had to cross the river Leitha and even there it was
not the dominant language. In 1728 Mathias had married a local girl,
Anna Maria Koller (1707–54), daughter of a farmer, Philipp, a respected
villager who became the district magistrate. Before and during her
marriage Maria Koller worked as one of nine cooks in the palace of the
local landowner, Count Carl Anton von Harrach. Five minutes' walk
from the Haydn house in the direction of the distant mountains, this
summer palace was an imposing two-courtyard residence built in the
Renaissance style, surrounded by a defensive wall and a moat. Apart
from paying for a lute master from Vienna to teach his young daughter,
the reigning count did not particularly favour music as a recreation.

Mathias and Maria had twelve children in fifteen years, six of whom
survived childhood, three girls and three boys: Anna Maria Franziska
(1730–81), Franz Joseph (1732–1809), Johann Michael (1737–1806),
Anna Maria (1739–1802), Anna Katharina (1741–before 1801) and
Johann Evangelist (1743–1805). Joseph Haydn, the eldest boy, was
baptized on 1 April 1732 but there is no document that records his
birthdate. Later in his life Haydn maintained that it was 31 March,
telling one friend, Joseph Carl Rosenbaum, that it was at four in
the afternoon. Well into his forties Haydn thought he had been born a
year later, in 1733. Confusion about birthdates in Catholic countries
was not uncommon – Beethoven was similarly confused – since
celebrating the name day, the feast day of the saint after which the

child was named, was much more important than the birth date and, consequently, age. As was frequently the practice in Austria, Haydn's parents gave their children two Christian names, the second of which was routinely used. Haydn's names were taken from two proximate saints' days, Franz (Francis of Paola, 2 April) and Joseph (husband of the Virgin Mary, 19 March) and, following practice, Haydn hardly ever used Franz. The baptism records the names formally in Latin, Fransiscus Josephus. Later in his life Haydn often used the form Josephus instead of Joseph, especially on documents and letters, but much more common than either was the Italian form, Giuseppe, which he routinely wrote on his music.

The local church in Rohrau was situated five minutes away, in the opposite direction from the Harrach palace, in what is now Joseph-Haydn Platz. Holding no more than about fifty people or so and plainly decorated, the church and its services bound the community together, uniting body and soul in the Catholic liturgy. Although its musical provision was negligible, a reflection of Count Harrach's lack of interest, some of Joseph's earliest musical experiences would have occurred in the church, though nothing was vouchsafed to the composer's first biographers, Griesinger and Dies.

Joseph's mother is an elusive, unknown figure remembered, as befits a cook, for her neatness, industry and order, qualities she instilled in her children. More is known about the father, suggesting that his contented life was marked by a degree of ambition and pride, initially for himself and then for his children. Griesinger and Dies both pointed out that as a young man he had travelled 'as was customary for his trade', probably a reference to the long formal apprenticeship as a wheelwright, from apprentice (Lehrling), through journeyman (Geselle), to fully qualified craftsman. Certainly Joseph Haydn remembered his father recounting the time he had spent in Frankfurt where he learnt to strum the harp. Although Mathias never learnt to read music, singing songs to the accompaniment of the harp was a favourite pastime in the household. His own sense of self-worth was further enhanced in 1741 when, like his father-in-law before him, he

1. Birthplace of Joseph Haydn, Rohrau (Vienna, c.1820).

assumed the duties of district magistrate, which necessitated occasional visits to Vienna. None of his sons was to enter the family trade: Michael like Joseph became a court composer, working most of his life in Salzburg, and Johann was given a post as a tenor in the Esterházy court by his elder brother.

One occasional visitor to the Haydn household was Johann Mathias Franck (1708–83) from Hainburg. Married to a stepsister of Mathias Haydn he typically combined the duties of a head teacher of the only school in the town with those of choir director and sexton in the local church. During one visit to Rohrau he was treated to the customary homely singing by the Haydn family and noticed that Joseph was rhythmically accompanying himself on an imaginary violin, using a piece of wood as a bow; all this was to be fancifully captured in an early nineteenth-century depiction of Haydn's birth place (Figure 1). The general alertness and musicality of the five-year-old impressed Franck who suggested that he should be educated at his school in Hainburg. This was a more structured education than was available in Rohrau and the two hopeful parents may even, at this very early stage, have foreseen a career that was akin to that of Franck, teacher, musician, serving the church, or a mixture. In 1737 or 1738 Haydn moved to Hainburg to begin his formal education.

The town of Hainburg was a much more lively place than Rohrau, with plenty to feed the imagination of a young boy. Perched on a cliff on the south bank of the Danube it was a fortress town strategically placed between the Habsburg capital of Vienna and the Hungarian capital of Pressburg (Bratislava). Over the centuries it had been the scene of several bloody battles, as the name of the steep street from the church down to the river gruesomely suggests: Blutgasse. The last siege of the Turks had taken place in 1683, leaving a scarring folk memory; for some, like Haydn's grandmother (Mathias's mother), it was a living memory. The main street was the busy thoroughfare from Vienna to Pressburg and goods from as far as Constantinople were regularly carried through the town. The town gates were closed every night and Haydn's grandmother lived close to the Vienna gate. Down on the broad and swift Danube, Haydn would have seen the flat-bottomed boats that plied goods locally (the unregulated nature of the river downstream prevented it from being a major trading waterway until the nineteenth century). The winter of 1739–40 was one of the most severe in the century and the river was frozen solid from November to March.

Haydn lived as a paying lodger with Franck and his wife in the schoolhouse. One of his first, and lasting, impressions was the unkempt surroundings compared with home: 'It pained me to note that uncleanliness was the rule and, although I took great pride in my small person, I still could not prevent occasional spots on my clothing about which I was sensitive and ashamed.'[2] Although education in Austria at the time (that is before the reforms of Maria Theresia in the 1770s and Joseph II in the 1780s) was entirely haphazard and unregulated it did have the common characteristic of being tied to the

Catholic church. In Hainburg approximately seventy to eighty children attended the school, arriving at seven in the morning; they went to mass at ten before going home for lunch; at midday they returned to school where they stayed until three. Reading and writing was entirely based on religious matter, the Bible, the Catechism and the writing of Thomas à Kempis; arithmetic was perfunctory. Music was taught mainly after school hours and its immediate purpose was to serve the liturgy of the church, again organized and delivered by Franck. The church was larger than the one in Rohrau, richly decorated (especially the altar) and with paintings of the Fourteen Stations of the Cross on the walls. From the gallery at the back of the church the enveloping sound of music during the services of the Catholic liturgy would have been a major formative influence on the young Haydn, uniting music and religion. The central service of the mass was divided into two broad types. On most Sundays the musical forces of the choir of schoolboys and adults was accompanied by a basic ensemble of violins and organ; much more exciting, on important feast days the mass was accompanied by strings, trumpets and timpani, forces that drew on the wider musical resources of the town.

Haydn, naturally, received singing lessons that resulted in a voice that was noted for its musicality and confidence rather than its power and beauty. Violin and harpsichord lessons also turned him into a capable instrumentalist. More idiosyncratically, Haydn became a competent timpani player, the initial circumstances of which he fondly recalled in old age. Catholic services routinely spilled out into the streets of the town, for the Corpus Christi services, the election of the town councillors and the annual commemoration of the defeat of the Turks. Soon after his arrival in Hainburg another annual ceremony took place, Rogation, the Monday, Tuesday and Wednesday that preceded Ascension Day, characterized by public processions accompanied by the chanting of the Litany of Saints. Franck, as usual, was in charge of the music. His timpani player, however, had recently died. He turned to his new young lodger, taught him the basics of drumming and left him to practise. Haydn approached the task with enthusiasm, placing a breadbasket on an armchair as a substitute drum but failed to notice the residue of flour that covered the chair after the drumming. Franck was impressed with the boy's enterprise and facility, and ignored the flour. One problem remained. Haydn was too small to carry the drum and would not be able to reach it even if it was carried by an obliging adult. In the event it was carried by a particularly obliging hunchback, causing a good deal of merriment. Curiosity about timpani and timpani playing remained with Haydn throughout his life, his writing for the instrument revealing an individuality that is not apparent in the music of his contemporaries, including Mozart.

In 1739 Georg Reutter visited Hainburg, staying with his cousin the local priest. Reutter had just become Kapellmeister of St Stephen's Cathedral in Vienna and was looking for new choirboys. The priest recommended Haydn for an audition, during which the boy was asked whether he could sing a trill. He replied that not even Franck could do that. Bribed with some cherries – these allow the story to be placed in the early summer of 1739 – Haydn was taught to trill. Reutter was impressed but recommended that he should consolidate his technique through assiduous singing of scales, to develop accuracy of pitch and flexibility. Neither Franck nor, consequently, Haydn was familiar with the common Italian system of solfeggio (ut, re, mi etc.) but, once more, with determination and resourcefulness the young boy invented a system of his own using German pitch names, c, d, e etc. On a return visit the following year Reutter checked on Haydn's progress, declared himself happy and arranged for the boy to move to Vienna.

The two or three years that Haydn spent in Hainburg had transformed his personality from a lively boy from the countryside who could sing a little to an inquisitive, increasingly competent musician, one for whom music, education and even recreation were bound with the rich and regular patterns of the liturgical year. Haydn seems to have kept in touch with the Franck family, even after Mathias died in 1783; he owned a portrait of the schoolmaster which he left in his will together with 100 gulden to Franck's daughter and her husband. He told Griesinger: 'I shall owe it to that man, even in my grave, that he taught me so many things, although in the process I received more thrashings than food.'[3]

Vienna in 1740 was the most important city in German-speaking Europe, the administrative capital of the Austrian Monarchy, that is the territories over which the Habsburg family exerted direct rule, and, as a largely separate governmental process, the capital also of the Holy Roman Empire, an agglomeration of independent kingdoms, duke-doms, principalities, counties and even single cities that lay across central, German-speaking Europe. The complexity of the differentiated degrees of power was reflected in the formulation 'kaiserlich-königlich' ('imperial-royal'). It was also inherently unstable and was about to be put to the test. In the same year as Haydn arrived in Vienna, Maria Theresia, aged only twenty-three, succeeded her father, Karl VI, as Habsburg leader, the first woman ruler of the Habsburg dominions. Karl had spent the previous quarter of a century or so trying to ensure that the rest of Europe would accept a female ruler, but within weeks Frederick the Great of Prussia exploited the inevitable uncertainty and announced his intention of annexing Silesia, part of the Monarchy. The War of the Austrian Succession erupted at the end of 1740 and lasted eight years, followed a decade later by the Seven Years' War (1756–63).

As an eight-year-old choirboy newly arrived in the imperial-royal city Joseph Haydn would have been only dimly aware of this wider political unrest, but his entire existence, including much of the musical repertoire that he was required to perform, was a projection of char-acteristics deeply ingrained in the psyche of the Habsburg capital. As European politics became more agitated Vienna continually reasserted its identity as a seat of power.

For nearly 500 years it had been a heavily fortified city and this marked its personality as well as its topography (see Figure 2; north is towards the bottom of the map). The walls had four gates that opened out to the wider world and shut it out at night, the Kärntnertor to the south, the Schottentor to the west, the Rotenturmtor to the north, and the Stubentor to the east, four entrances that governed a similar

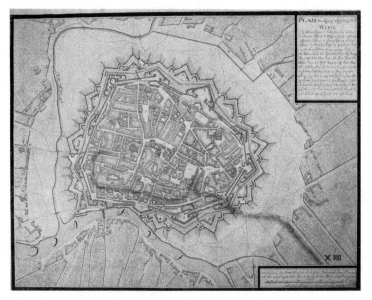

2. Map of Vienna, 1741.

division of the inner city into four quarters. To the north the Danube canal formed a convenient protection while in all other directions there was a wide area of open land, the Glacis. In contrast to the inner city, which was very compact, the suburbs beyond the Danube and the Glacis were more generously laid out and continually expanding. In 1740 the inner city and the suburbs between them contained a population of c.170,000.

Much of the inner city had been transformed in the earlier decades of the century by a spontaneous and self-confident building programme that defined its appearance for ever. Part of it was initiated by the imperial court, such as the imperial quarters themselves (the Hofburg), the court library and the Spanish Riding School. In a display of competitive loyalty to the Habsburg dynasty aristocrats built palaces close to the Hofburg, including many whose names were to figure prominently in the history of music, the Dietrichstein, Esterházy, Liechtenstein, Lobkowitz and Schwarzenberg families. Charles Burney, the English musician who visited Vienna in 1772 to gather material for his history of music, left a vivid picture of the compact nature of the city as well as its still modern splendour.[4]

> The streets are rendered doubly dark and dirty by their narrowness, and by the extreme height of the houses; but, as these are chiefly of white stone and in a uniform, elegant style of architecture, in which the Italian taste prevails, as in music, there is something grand and magnificent in their appearance, which is very striking; and even many of those houses with shops on the ground-floor, seem like palaces above. Indeed the whole town and its suburbs, appear, at first, glance, to be composed of palaces, rather than of common habitations.

Alongside the palaces Burney would have noticed the large number of religious buildings in the inner city, churches, monasteries, convents, nunneries and, if he had access, private chapels, many modernized or newly built. As leading proponents of the Counter-Reformation the Habsburg family had managed, in a very compelling and majestic manner, to bind the eternal truths of the Catholic faith with the power of the dynasty. When the Turks were repelled in 1683 this was not only a triumph of Habsburg secular might but of the Christian religion over the infidel. Almost in the centre of the city stood the cathedral of St Stephen's, the focus of Haydn's life for the next five years, its spire the highest in the city and acting as a watchtower, both emblematically and practically, for the inner city and the outer suburbs. It was one of the few churches that escaped modernization in the eighteenth century. Indeed in comparison with the sumptuous interiors of the Peterskirche, Schottenkirche and other Baroque churches, the interior of St Stephen's was thought rather gloomy by many commentators, including Burney: 'The church is a dark, dirty, and dismal old Gothic building, though richly ornamented; in it are hung all the trophies of war, taken from the Turks and other enemies of the house of Austria, for more than a century past, which gives it very much the appearance of an old wardrobe.'[5]

The imperial court had its own churches and chapels, notably the Hofburgkapelle and the Augustinerkirche, but it involved many others in the city through a carefully considered yearly cycle of visits in which the journey to and from the Hofburg was as much an affirmation of sacred and temporal power as the liturgical services themselves. St Stephen's was visited nine times during the year by the court, most notably on the first Sunday after 8 September, thanksgiving day, to commemorate the liberation of Vienna from the Turks, a much grander celebration than anything Haydn would have experienced in Hainburg. More rarely, in 1740 Haydn would have sung in the service in St Stephen's on 22 November that marked the culminating point of the Oath of Fealty procession that had weaved its way through the streets of Vienna to demonstrate its allegiance to the new ruler, Maria Theresia. Religious processions were daily occurrences, as Burney was to report for Sunday 6 September 1772.[6]

> In my way to the nuncio's whence I was to set off with the Abate Taruffi, to make Metastasio another visit, I was stopped by a procession of, literally, two or three miles long, singing a hymn to the Virgin, in three parts, and repeating each stanza after the priests, in the van, at equal distances; so that the instant one company had done, it was taken up by another behind, till it came to the women in the rear, who, likewise, at equal distances, repeated, in three parts, the few simple notes of this hymn; and even after them it was repeated by girls, who were the last persons in the process. When these had done, it was begun again by the priests ... I was told by an Italian at Vienna, that the Austrians are extremely addicted to processions, *portatissimi alle processioni*.

As Burney implies, music was an integral part of worship. Indeed it may fairly be said that the principal function of music in the city was to promote and celebrate the indivisibility of Catholic and Habsburg power, whether within the confines of the Hofburg itself or in the city generally. Most of the churches and the monasteries had regularly constituted orchestral and vocal forces as well as a Kapellmeister (sometimes a deputy too); one estimate from later in the century put the number of musicians that were dependent or partly dependent on religious institutions for employment at a staggering 2,000. The eight-year-old Haydn was now part of this all-encompassing social, musical and religious system, without its equal in the rest of Europe.

The man who had brought Haydn to Vienna was Georg Reutter (1708–72), Kapellmeister at St Stephen's, the twenty-seventh person to have held the position in a tradition that went back to the middle of the fifteenth century. Largely due to the disparaging remarks that Haydn later made about him, the standard image of Kapellmeister Reutter is a misleading one, crusty, unhelpful and rather set in his ways. But in 1740 he was a young man in his thirties with two small children, someone who just two years earlier had secured one of the key positions in Viennese musical life. For ten years before that he had composed mainly Italian opera, some twenty works, for the private court theatres in the Hofburg and the summer palace of Laxenburg, but he had always hankered after the more influential and prestigious position of a church musician. To mark his new post at St Stephen's he was ennobled in 1740 ('von Reutter') and soon began to accrue further church appointments that brought the musical establishment of St Stephen's and that of the court even closer together: second Kapellmeister at the imperial court in 1747, acting first Kapellmeister in 1751 and, finally, full Kapellmeister in 1769. He was the single most influential musician in Vienna.

As Kapellmeister in St Stephen's he had a retinue of thirty-one musicians as his disposal, five boys, twelve adult singers (male altos, tenors and basses), a subcantor, twelve string players and one organist. When trumpets, trombones and timpani were required they were engaged from outside, often from the court, and paid separately. Musicians from St Stephen's regularly supplemented those in the imperial court (the Hofkapelle) and vice versa. Most mass and vesper services were sung, and the official calendar of Sunday and feast days that required extensive use of music numbered eighty. Reutter's own output of church music reflects the heavy demands on the Kapellmeister and on his performers: about 80 masses, 6 requiems, 17 graduals,

31 offertories, 126 motets, 151 psalms, 53 hymns, 48 antiphons, 7 responses and 20 litanies. But while Reutter's music was probably the most frequently performed, as is evident from the sometimes very lengthy lists of performance dates on extant sources, other composers were represented too: Reutter's father, also Georg (1656–1738), Giuseppe Bonno (1711–88), Franz Tuma (1704–74) and, the most esteemed of all, Johann Joseph Fux (1660–1741). The bulk of the repertoire was accompanied by orchestral forces, from works that required two or three string players plus continuo to much grander works dominated by the insistent sound of trumpets and timpani, always in C major. This repertoire constituted a continually unfolding tradition that is poorly served by the familiar division of the century into Baroque and Classical. During Lent and Advent a cultivated legacy of an older, Renaissance tradition was evident, vocal music without independent instrumental support; the music of Allegri (1582–1629) and Palestrina (1525/6–94) figured as well as music by contemporary composers, including Fux and Reutter, that offered a modern updating of the style.

Reutter and his family lived in the Capellhaus, which is where Haydn and the other choirboys lived too. Directly in front of St Stephen's it obscured the view of the cathedral and, for that reason, was demolished in 1803, but in Haydn's youth it enabled the Kapellmeister and his charges to get to the cathedral in a matter of minutes. Given the demands on Reutter's time and on that of his choristers, it is not surprising that Haydn's formal education was rather patchy, perhaps less regular than it had been in Hainburg. Instruction in reading, writing, arithmetic and some Latin was given while on the musical side Haydn's sight singing was improved still further through the use of Kapellmeister Fux's *Singfundament*, vocal exercises that used the standard Italian note names rather than the German names he had invented for himself. In addition Haydn remembered useful singing lessons from one of the tenors, Ignaz Finsterbuch, and violin lessons from the double-bass player, Adam Gegenbauer; keyboard lessons were given as a matter of course and the aspiring musician is known to have acquired a portable clavichord. When Haydn was pressed about whether Reutter had done any teaching, his reply was that he could recall only two lessons; in 1745 Michael Haydn joined his brother at the Capellhaus and his memory of Reutter's commitment was the same. However, Michael Haydn did recollect participating regularly with his fellow pupils in mock tribunals to assess their youthful compositions. When it came to his own first attempts Joseph Haydn remembered Reutter being very dismissive, though the story became rather misleading in the telling.

Griesinger writes of the young Haydn writing sacred compositions in eight and sixteen parts ('acht- und sechzehnstimmige Komposi-tionen') while Dies is more specific, a Salve regina in twelve parts ('ein zwölfstimmiges Salve regina'), all ridiculously ambitious it seems.[7] But multi-choral writing in twelve or sixteen parts was not a typical part of the Viennese tradition and 'parts' here almost certainly means the number of performers required, not the number of har-monic lines; surviving performance material from the period often indicates the total number of instrumental and vocal parts on covering title pages (sometimes using the Latin 'partes') as part of a rudimentary cataloguing process. Given this usage Reutter's alleged reply that Haydn should concentrate on music for two performers rather than eight or more – Dies has 'You silly boy, aren't two parts enough for you' – was perfectly reasonable. The mention of an early attempt at a Salve regina is significant. It was the most frequently set Marian text in the period (Reutter composed nineteen) and a natural first text for Haydn to tackle. Settings typically used one or two soloists, chorus and strings plus continuo, an ensemble that could easily result in sixteen participants, the highest number quoted in the anecdotes.

Haydn spent nine years as a working choirboy in St Stephen's. While there is no record of him returning to his family in Rohrau at any point, it is difficult to imagine that he did not; certainly, Mathias Haydn made periodic visits to Vienna in his capacity as magistrate and would have renewed acquaintance with one or both sons. It would be easy to paint a picture of Haydn living in a self-enclosed world bounded by the practices of the church year, occasionally relieved by performances outside Vienna, in Klosterneuburg, Schönbrunn and Laxenburg, but this was not a rarefied world but a key part of a wider, sympathetic culture. In narrowly musical terms too it provided a realistic base for a career in music. That career nearly took a very particular direction when Reutter and his colleagues contemplated ensuring a future for Haydn as a male alto or soprano through having him castrated. Castrato singers were still common in mid-century Vienna in church music and in the more private world of the court opera and, though the operation was not always successful, Reutter's ambitions on behalf of a very musical treble were perfectly in keeping with practices of the time. Haydn's version of the story, which like many others improved with the telling, has Mathias Haydn arriving in the Capellhaus unsure whether the operation had been carried out and relieved to learn that it had not.

Haydn's voice began to break in 1748 at the age of sixteen and for a particular service in the abbey of Klosterneuburg his brother had to replace him in the solo section of a mass setting. By the end of the following year, 1749, he had left, a departure almost certainly hastened by the mischievous prank of cutting off the pigtails of the wig of a fellow chorister.

From the age of seventeen to twenty-five Haydn was to live a more unstable life, as a jobbing musician in Vienna. He himself described it as a 'wretched existence',[8] characterized by uncertainty and periods of comparative poverty. Yet it was also a period when Haydn broadened his experience of music and music making, though church music always remained at the core. Some of these various activities are known, even if the chronology and the duration are often uncertain, but many remain hidden.

After his dismissal from St Stephen's Haydn almost certainly went home to Rohrau, if only for a short period, where his mother, in particular, raised the idea of her eldest son pursuing a career in the Catholic church. This was not just the submissive wish of a caring mother, since a career as a music director, a Regenschori, at a major abbey, for instance, would have happily united musical ambition with a life devoted to God. Haydn resisted and returned to Vienna though the idea resurfaced almost immediately when, through hunger, he contemplated joining the Servite Order in Rossau, in the suburbs to the north-west of the city. It was almost certainly in the summer of 1750 that Haydn joined a pilgrimage to Mariazell, a destination much favoured by the Viennese; St Stephen's itself organized an annual pilgrimage and it is possible that Haydn went with people from the cathedral. Walking and singing the popular pilgrim songs, the journey would have taken them five or six days, first westwards along the Danube before turning south and making the steady climb through the Styrian hills to Mariazell. The town received over 100,000 pilgrims per year, from all ranks of society. The particular object of veneration was a rustic carving of the Virgin Mary and the infant Jesus, some twenty inches high, placed ostentatiously in a surround of solid silver designed by Fischer von Erlach. Griesinger and Dies both tell the story of Haydn wanting to sing in the choir, being refused permission, sneaking into the choir loft during a service, snatching a part from a chorister at an opportune moment and singing a solo section to the delight of everyone.

Some of the incidental details given in the anecdote are significant. Dies has Haydn announcing that he is from the Capellhaus in Vienna which suggests that he did, indeed, travel with a group from St Stephen's; and Griesinger states that Haydn sang the part of a boy alto, indicating that his voice at the age of eighteen had still not settled in register. More substantially, both relate that Haydn showed the local music director some compositions. One of the earliest authentic compositions by Haydn to have survived is a Mass in F, rediscovered by the composer in his old age when he gave it the significant date of 1749, the year when he left St Stephen's. Haydn may well have had a few church compositions available that he hoped to persuade churches in Vienna and elsewhere to take on; the Mass in F is a very practical work that would not tax most church ensembles of the time, four-part chorus with solo parts for two trebles, and an orchestra of two violins and continuo. There are a number of extant eighteenth-century sources in Austria for this work, which suggests that Haydn's policy worked; the mass led its own independent life until the composer became reacquainted with the work half a century later. One coincidence of the Mariazell visit that is not reported by Griesinger and Dies is that Haydn's future employers, the Esterházy family, were substantial benefactors of the church. Over ten years were to pass before they became Haydn's benefactor too.

Back in Vienna, Haydn had already secured lodgings, as a subtenant of Johann Michael Spangler in the attic of the Michaelerhaus, in the middle of Vienna between the Hofburg and the Graben. It was right next door to the Michaelerkirche where Spangler was a tenor and it is difficult to imagine that Haydn did not, at some point, sing or play in that church, though there is no evidence. In the middle floors of the Michaelerhaus where, as was the custom, the rooms were much more commodious, two persons of note lived: the dowager Princess Maria Octavia Esterházy, mother of Paul Anton and Nicolaus, who were to be the first two of Haydn's patrons, and Pietro Metastasio (1698–1782). While nothing came of any contact with the first, the second proved fruitful, introducing Haydn to the hitherto wholly unfamiliar world of Italian opera, Italian composers and Italian singers. For over twenty years Metastasio had been imperial court poet in Vienna, the author of nearly thirty librettos, many of which were repeatedly set by composers throughout Europe. When Burney met him in Vienna in 1772 he found him insufferably grand, someone who preferred silence to conversation. There is no record of what Haydn thought about him, but he was certainly the most distinguished man of letters that the young musician had ever encountered.

Metastasio was overseeing and paying for the education of a young girl, Marianna Martines (1744–1812), daughter of an official in the papal nuncio in Vienna. On his recommendation Haydn taught her singing and harpsichord for three years until her tenth birthday; as an adult she was a respected composer, pianist and society hostess and could no doubt claim that she was the first of many distinguished pupils of

Haydn, but there does not seem to have been any contact between the two in later life. In the 1750s she was one of many female pupils from polite society whom Haydn taught and for whom he wrote his first keyboard sonatas, individually tailored to advance the technique and musicianship of the pupil. As compositions, Haydn did not lay great store by them and many were lost after they had served their immediate purpose.

It was through Metastasio that Haydn met the renowned composer Nicola Porpora (1686–1768), now living in semi-retirement in Vienna but much in demand as a singing teacher. He himself had trained in the operatic hotspot of Naples and had taught the famous castrato Farinelli. As a composer he wrote nearly fifty serious operas, several on texts by Metastasio. His career took him to London in the 1730s, where he was a serious rival of Handel, to Dresden in the 1740s, and Vienna in the 1750s, where he later died at the age of eighty-two. Haydn was engaged by Porpora as an accompanist for his singing lessons, combining those duties, as was often the case in eighteenth-century Austria, with the duties of a general servant. It is not difficult to imagine the impact that tales of operatic life, regaled with the highly coloured imagination of someone who had worked in opera houses all his life, had on the young Haydn. He obviously held him in great affection, both as a teacher and a personality. Griesinger quoted Haydn directly: 'There was no want of *Asino, Coglione, Birbante* [ass, idiot, knave] and pokes in the ribs, but I put up with all of it because I greatly profited from Porpora in singing, in composition and in the Italian language.'[9] Through Porpora, Haydn's musical circle was further extended when he accompanied his master in private concerts in the palaces of Prince Joseph Maria von Sachsen-Hildburghausen; Gluck (1714–87) and Wagenseil (1715–77) are specifically named by Griesinger. The prince's musical retinue included a gifted teenage violinist named Carl Ditters (later Dittersdorf, 1739–99) and it must have been then that Haydn first met someone who was to become a close friend.

Haydn's comment that Porpora assisted his development as a composer raises the perplexing problem of his musical education after

St Stephen's, what he learnt, when, and whether it was through instruction or self-instruction. Both Griesinger and Dies report that Haydn studied two standard, widely read treatises, Fux's *Gradus ad Parnassum* and Mattheson's *Der vollkommene Capellmeister*. While there is some overlap in their coverage in the area of basic theory, the two treatises are different in their overall content and suitably complementary for any pupil.

As a choirboy Haydn would have recognized Johann Joseph Fux (1660–1741) as the central figure in the Austrian musical tradition in the first half of the century and his treatise was a permanent testimony to that authority, one that was maintained for decades after his death. Fux had served three successive Habsburg emperors, reaching the position of imperial Kapellmeister in 1715 and virtually all his music, over 400 items of church music, twenty-two operas and some instrumental music, was written for the court, promoting its religious and temporal values. By the time Haydn entered St Stephen's, Fux had effectively retired, weakened by arthritis but he was a figure of great esteem and reverence. His treatise, *Gradus ad Parnassum* (Steps to Parnassus) had been published in Vienna in 1725 and was dedicated to the Holy Roman Emperor, Karl VI. In the same way that the Habsburgs as Holy Roman Emperors assumed the mantle of promoting the Catholic faith, Fux in the treatise sought to link contemporary church music with the great Roman tradition of the Renaissance, specifically Palestrina. The text of the treatise is laid out as a dialogue between the master, Aloysius (that is Palestrina, the 'light of music') and the eager pupil Josephus (Fux himself), and moves progressively through theory, species counterpoint, fugue, invertible counterpoint, before concluding with a survey of contemporary musical style. Lavishly illustrated with music examples, the text also requires considerable fluency in the Latin language to appreciate the many subtle points of technique that are expounded, also the dry wit that surfaces from time to time, not least the many complimentary references to Fux's own music even though he is nominally the pupil. Haydn's knowledge of Latin was clearly up to the task and presages a lifetime of occasional recourse to aphorisms in that language, in a slightly self-conscious manner. It is possible also to see a connection between Fux's wit and irony and that of the adult Haydn. But the most compelling indication of Haydn's regard for Fux is that his copy of the treatise was heavily annotated and formed the basis of his own teaching.

As these considered annotations suggest, the treatise does need a teacher to interpret and promote the pedagogical approach and it is difficult to imagine that Haydn, however curious, could have gained much from reading it as a choirboy in St Stephen's. By the 1760s, however, his music often reveals the legacy of training in species counterpoint and that knowledge was most likely gained in the intervening years, the 1750s, from a mixture of self-instruction, assistance from other musicians and, most fruitfully (as any teacher will recognize), from having to teach it himself.

While Fux's treatise asserted the values of Haydn's own heritage, Mattheson's *Der vollkommene Capellmeister* (The complete Kapellmeister) belongs to a wholly different tradition, that of the north German Baroque. Johann Mattheson (1681–1764) was born in Hamburg, where he spent most of his working life, first as a singer, then as a composer and prolific writer on music; *Der vollkommene Capellmeister* was published in the city in 1739. With over 500 pages (including index and postscriptum) it is a different work from Fux's treatise, a compendium of information on the knowledge and aptitude needed to be a successful Kapellmeister, rather than a serial work of instruction in composition, a volume that Haydn could have read with profit before, as well as alongside, Fux. Some of the content would have been alien to Haydn, such as the discussion of music associated with the Lutheran liturgy, the consequent emphasis on the organ and the admiration for the 'three H's' as Mattheson termed them, Handel, Heinichen and Hasse. Mattheson's remark that nothing is to be gained from beating a recalcitrant student would have amused the pupil of Franck and Porpora; his view that a Kapellmeister should have knowledge of four languages apart from his own, Latin, Greek, Italian and French, was in the process of being partially realized by Haydn (he never learnt

Greek); and Mattheson's scepticism of the fashionable view that all musicians should visit Italy in their formative years might have provided some succour to one who was never to do so. This did not mean that Mattheson devalued singers and singing. On the contrary, from the early injunction 'Everything must sing properly', there is continual emphasis on knowledge of singing, both as a technique in itself and as the foundation of good composition, something that Haydn had experienced from childhood, was now being consolidated and expanded by Porpora, and was to remain an ideal all his life. Diligence and industry are stressed too. If Haydn in his old age ever looked at the copy of Mattheson's treatise in his library he might well have thought that in this aspect, at least, he had measured up to the prescriptions of the north German.

Alongside this emerging sense of self-improvement and ambition there is evidence of wider participation in the musical life of Vienna in the 1750s, prompted by the need to make money but fuelling a curiosity too. In the summer in particular, often well into the autumn too, there was an active tradition of serenading in the compact streets and courtyards of the inner city. Unlike Italy, serenading in Vienna hardly ever took the form of singing, rather instrumental music for anything from one player to ensembles of eight or more. Name days, birthdays and other special occasions would enable individuals living on the first floor (or higher) to open their windows and be greeted by a group of musicians in the courtyard or the street below, a scene that, in turn, attracted a casual audience of onlookers, much as buskers do today. In his old age Haydn remembered composing a work for two violins, two violas and bass in 1753, probably the Cassation in G (Hob.II:2), which is very likely his earliest surviving instrumental work. As many as a dozen similar compositions for mixed ensembles were written in the 1750s; one has the subtitle 'Der Geburtstag' (The Birthday: Hob. II:II). As well as composing such works Haydn was a frequent participant and, almost certainly, organizer.

One particular serenade led to the writing of music for a German opera company. Unlike Italian opera, which was performed only in the private theatre in the Habsburg court, German opera was performed by travelling companies in which the impresario was also the leading actor-cum-singer; it was an unsophisticated form of entertainment in which spoken dialogue was interrupted by some simple musical numbers. In Vienna, Joseph Kurz's company had long been popular and regularly performed in the Kärntnertortheater; as a performer he often assumed the role of the lovable oaf, Bernardon, and was widely known as Kurz-Bernardon. His wife was eleven years younger, attractive, with a good voice and a talent for comic acting. It was probably in 1752 that Kurz arranged for her to be serenaded in the local manner; Haydn was a participant and the composer of the music, possibly a trio for two violins and bass. Pleased with the music and the performance (not to mention the response of his young wife) Kurz got to know Haydn and asked him whether he would be interested in writing music for his travelling company. Stretching himself across several chairs in imitation of a drowning man he invited Haydn to respond with some appropriate music; seated at the harpsichord the young man responded immediately with an improvisation in a lurching 6/8 time, an early instance of a fondness for musical pictorialism that was to culminate over fifty years later in The Creation and The Seasons. On the strength of this eccentric audition Haydn provided the music for Der krumme Teufel (The crooked devil) for which neither the libretto nor the music has survived. As was the practice in early German opera there was a sequel, or perhaps just a slightly revised second version, Der neue krumme Teufel (The new crooked devil), that was extensively performed in the following decades in Pressburg, Nuremberg, Warsaw, Laibach (Ljubljana), Berlin, Innsbruck, Munich as well as Vienna, performances that frequently identify Haydn as the composer. But, again, not a note of the music survives. It is particularly unfortunate since the tally of performances made it the most frequently performed of all Haydn's stage works.

Although Haydn was well paid by Kurz, 20 to 25 ducats (about 112 gulden), there is no evidence that he worked further for him. Instead for much of the decade other forms of employment, particularly those associated with the performance of church music, provided the mainstay of Haydn's existence. While it was not as well paid, church music held the promise of a career in a way that Kurz's company did not and there were plenty of opportunities for someone who could sing, play the violin and organ, and compose.

Reutter was now in charge of all music making at the imperial court except opera, the summit of his career. Yet it was a difficult time to be in charge since the protracted War of the Austrian Succession (1740–8) had already caused a review of all court expenditure, including that devoted to music. Prompted by Pope Benedict XIV's encyclical 'Annus qui' on the propriety of music in the church, Empress Maria Theresia had requested a review of church music at court, suggesting that it should focus on music 'alla Romana', that is unaccompanied music as presented in the Sistine Chapel in Rome, conveniently reducing the need for expensive instrumentalists. For a particular part of the church calendar, Lent, this seemed a small adjustment to the traditional Viennese practice of a cappella music supported by organ or doubling instruments, but Reutter seems to have found the Hofkapelle singers incapable of performing without the customary instrumental support and had to admit that some of them were too old, infirm or unreliable. For Lent and Holy Week in 1754, 1755 and 1756 Reutter engaged between eight and fourteen extra singers to assist in the services; Haydn sang in sixteen services in 1754, twenty-five in 1755 and sixteen in 1756, renewing professional contact with his former teacher. All the services took place in the Hofburgkapelle and, as well as music by Reutter himself, included Allegri's Miserere and Palestrina's Stabat mater, the latter a work for double chorus, a particularly pressing reason to have a complement of capable, young singers. The court records do not specify which voice Haydn sang, probably tenor.

Reutter's duties at the imperial court extended also to instrumental music. The 1750s was a decade when the imperial palace was the home to no fewer than fourteen Habsburg children, sons and daughters of Maria Theresia: the eldest was Maria Elizabeth, born in 1737, the youngest was Maximilian Franz (Beethoven's future patron in Bonn), born in 1756. During Carnival when the court took part in a series of private balls, special balls were organized for the children and those of the aristocracy. Often the children were in fancy dress, such as flowers, and the dance music was provided by an orchestra of some two dozen players specifically hired for the occasion. Haydn was engaged as a violinist for four of the children's balls in 1755 and seven in 1756. It is not known who wrote the music for these balls and any number of composer-players could have done so, including Haydn. His earliest surviving dances are the 'Seitenstetten' minuets (named after the only extant source in Seitenstetten Abbey) and it is possible that they were played at court, or it may have been some minuets that have not survived.

Haydn's contacts with the imperial court between 1754 and 1756 were discovered only in the 1990s. The fact that they were not mentioned by either Griesinger or Dies may be significant, suggesting that they were not regarded as particularly important in the broader narrative of their biographies. On the other hand Griesinger does document a clutch of other freelance activities as a church musician, possibly because of the hectic timetable involved and because they featured Haydn as a violinist, organist and singer.[10]

> Haydn also in this period was lead violinist for the Order of St John of God [Barmherzige Brüder] in the Leopoldstadt, at sixty gulden a year. Here he had to be in the church at eight o'clock in the morning on Sundays and feast days. At ten o'clock he played the organ in the chapel of Count Haugwitz, at eleven he sang at St Stephen's. He was paid seventeen kreutzers for each service.

Leopoldstadt was the largest of Vienna's suburbs, to the north of the city. The Order of St John of God had a monastery there with a church dedicated to John the Baptist. Located on the main street and with a spire that still constitutes a local landmark the church had been rebuilt after the Turkish invasion and extended in the 1730s, an indication of its role in an area of Vienna that was growing rapidly. The order was esteemed throughout the Austrian Monarchy for its medical services to the community and, to this day, the hospice prepares and dispenses medicines. It also believed strongly in the palliative powers of music which, consequently, featured prominently in its services. Haydn's position is described as a 'Vorspieler', that is, the leader of the orchestra, the person who shared responsibility with the organist and a member of the choir for directing the performance. The church of the Barmherzige Brüder in the Leopoldstadt is the most likely venue for the first performance of two items of church music that Haydn composed in the mid-1750s, the Salve regina in E and the Ave Regina in A, both readily revealing Italian vocal mannerisms picked up in Porpora's circle. This was Haydn's most satisfying job to date, though at 60 gulden per annum it was not particularly well paid and had to be supplemented by, at least, the two other jobs mentioned by Griesinger.

It is very unlikely that any service at the church in the Leopoldstadt lasted more than ninety minutes, giving Haydn enough time to pack his violin, walk down the main street, cross the wooden drawbridge over the Danube canal, enter the inner city through the Rotenturmtor and criss-cross his way to Wipplingerstrasse for his next duty at ten o'clock. Count Friedrich Wilhelm Haugwitz (1702–65) was an influential adviser at the court of Maria Theresia and at the time held the post of director of the imperial-royal Bohemian Court Chancellory, that is the government department responsible for administering Bohemia, from land registration to taxation. Haugwitz lived in the chancellory in Wipplingerstrasse. In 1756 he was granted permission to have a private chapel in the building, occupying a discrete corner on the first floor; the empress provided a trust fund of 10,000 gulden and the chapel was appropriately dedicated to St Therese. It was in this newly established private chapel that Haydn was employed as an organist. It is possible that some of the five or six organ concertos that he composed in the 1750s were first performed here, though the role of music could not be as lavish as in public churches in the city.

Walking from the Bohemian Court Chancellory to St Stephen's would have taken the young Haydn about five to six minutes, which suggests that services in the private chapel lasted little more than forty-five minutes. At St Stephen's, his duties as a tenor were less onerous and, if he was delayed, he could probably have slipped into the choir unnoticed. Reutter was by now first and second Kapellmeister at St Stephen's and his former pupil was no doubt seen as a valuable participant in the precarious business of maintaining appropriate musical standards at the cathedral, as he had been at the court. For Haydn it was the final stage of a long morning; having started at eight o'clock his duties were not complete until 12.30. The date of the foundation of the Haugwitz chapel, 1 February 1756, and the year when Haydn is thought to have become Kapellmeister to the Morzin family, 1757, provide the timeframe for these three duties, though it is entirely likely that the Leopoldstadt post and the freelance singing in St Stephen's were already taking place before the Haugwitz job was added to them.

The picture of a young man in his twenties walking hastily around Vienna in order to earn a living is in keeping with later observations that Haydn was someone with darting physical movements. But beyond other physical characteristics, that he was short in stature, habitually wore a wig and had brown eyes, there is little from these early Viennese years that gives an impression of a human personality. Next to nothing is known about his personal life. His mother died in 1754 and a surviving letter from Mathias Haydn to Michael Haydn, in which he informs the brothers of a carriage that he has arranged to bring them to Rohrau, may be linked to this sad event; the letter mentions two young women who are to travel in a second carriage, Nänerl and Lossl; whether these were particular friends of Joseph and Michael or just family acquaintances is not known. Inevitably visits to Rohrau were characterized by the reliving of childhood memories but when Mathias sang his harp songs, the two musically educated sons now sneered.

Like all single people in Vienna dependent on insubstantial and erratic income Haydn moved accommodation several times during the decade, though few details are known. He borrowed small amounts of money from acquaintances and sometimes slept on the floors of others. Especially unnerving was an occasion in the early 1750s when Haydn was living in the Seilerstätte, in the inner city to the south-east of St Stephen's. All his possessions were stolen and he had to write to his parents asking for some linen for shirts. His father came to Vienna, gave him some money coupled with a paternal reminder of the eternal truth 'Fear God, and love thy neighbour', a Christian outlook that was rewarded when friends gave him a new dark suit and some underclothing.

One of Haydn's musical friends was the violinist Georg Ignaz Keller, who played in St Stephen's and in the Hofkapelle. He introduced him to his brother, Johann, who lived with his family in the Ungargasse, a long fashionable street in the suburb of Landstrasse to the east of the city where Johann worked as a wig maker. He had two daughters, Maria Anna (1729–1800) and Therese (1732–1819). Haydn gave the younger daughter, who was the same age as him, keyboard lessons and was taken into the house as a welcome guest. In their early twenties Joseph and Therese fell in love but, as Haydn wistfully remembered for the rest of his life, the parents had already determined that Therese should become a nun. She joined the Franciscan order of the Poor Clares in 1755 and it has been conjectured that Haydn played one of his organ concertos at an associated ceremony a year later. When the order was dissolved in the 1780s Therese returned to civilian life and renewed polite acquaintanceship with Haydn; he remembered her in his will, leaving her 100 gulden. She died of tuberculosis in 1819.

Haydn's fondness for the Keller family was matched on their side by subtle pressure on him to turn his affection towards Maria Anna who was three years older. His reluctance can be judged by the fact that it was to be a further five years before the two were married.

Board and lodge in return for musical services led directly to the composition of Haydn's first string quartets. Baron Carl Joseph Weber Fürnberg (c.1720–67) was a member of the imperial household in Vienna who had particular responsibility also for the administration of Lower Austria. His summer palace was in Weinzierl near Weissenkirchen in the Danube valley. A keen music lover, he invited performers to stay in his palace to participate in informal musical evenings. As a violinist Haydn was a frequent visitor; as a composer his string trios were probably played at the palace, and perhaps first composed for Fürnberg. Certainly Haydn recalled that his first quartets were written for him, something that understandably loomed large in Griesinger's biography. The author even quotes the musical incipit of the work that was later to be known as op. 1 no. 1, and there is the distinct implication that the genre had been accidentally invented there and then, in Weinzierl in the mid-1750s. But music for two violins, viola and cello (or double bass) was not a new combination; it would have arisen naturally when any four-part music for orchestra such as concertos and early symphonies was performed with one player per part. At the same time, the way in which the medium is exploited by Haydn in these first examples already shows his characteristic control of detail.

Haydn credited Fürnberg with introducing him to the Morzin family for whom he became Kapellmeister in 1757 (perhaps later). In a parallel case to the first quartet, Haydn remembered writing his first symphony for Morzin, and Griesinger duly emphasized the significance of this historical moment too and in a similar manner, by quoting the incipit of the work that became known as Symphony no. 1 in D. But it is worth shifting the perspective back fifty years, from the early nineteenth to the mid-eighteenth century, to ponder what this particular employment might have meant to the composer at the time.

Haydn was certainly gratified. Dies quoted him directly: 'My good mother, who had always the tenderest concern for my welfare, was no longer living, but my father experienced the pleasure of seeing me a Kapellmeister.'[11] He may have been surprised too, for the duties of the post were quite different from those that Haydn had experienced in Vienna. Thoroughly immersed in the life of a church musician he would have regarded instrumental music as less important and, certainly, the environment in which it was played, typically a private palace, was not as familiar. In this respect he was quite a different young musician from his friend Dittersdorf who had little or no experience of church music but had worked since the age of eleven in the court of Prince Hildburghausen. Dittersdorf was a violinist of stature, an ability that led naturally to the composition of concertos and symphonies; Haydn, on the other hand, was not a soloist and had not yet composed a single violin concerto or a single symphony. Becoming a Kapellmeister at a secular court must have been a challenge that was both new and unexpected. It signalled a turning point for Haydn and, ultimately, the whole course of music history.

Oddly, Haydn himself remembered very little about the Morzin years and the efforts of scholars across two centuries have not added much. The Morzin family had a summer palace in Lukavec (Dolní Lukavice), south of Pilsen in a predominantly Czech-speaking part of Bohemia. The family probably had a palace in Prague too (which Haydn could have visited), though in Vienna they usually sought accommodation in the Batthyany palace. The reigning count in the 1750s was Franz Ferdinand Maximilian but it is uncertain whether he was Haydn's employer or whether it was his son, Carl Joseph Franz. The father was a widower but the son's wife, Wilhelmine, was someone whom Haydn did remember because her neckerchief came undone as she lent over him when he was playing the harpsichord. This was another story that improved over the years. 'It was the first time I had seen such a sight: it embarrassed me, my playing faltered, my fingers stopped on the keys. "What is it Haydn, what are you doing?" cried the countess. Full of respect I responded, "But, your grace, who would not be upset?" '[12]

The palace at Lukavec had been built in the early part of the century, beautifully proportioned with a central portion that led to two short, balancing wings, the whole looking out across the fertile Bohemian landscape. It was in this landscape that Haydn fell off a horse, with the result that he hardly ever rode again. There was a chapel in one of the wings and across from the main entrance there was a small church. While it is possible that Haydn was responsible for church music, Griesinger's emphasis on symphonies is understandable, but how many is uncertain; a generous estimate would be fourteen. Nothing is known about the orchestra. It is unlikely to have numbered more than about fifteen and is very likely to have included players who were also, even primarily, household servants. Even more of a mystery is what happened to Haydn and the musicians when they went to Vienna in the winter; were they put up too in the Batthyany household, were they left to their own devices or, indeed, apart from Haydn, were they employed for the summer months only? If Haydn did some teaching at the court then some of the keyboard sonatas and works for keyboard and ensemble (variously called concertino and divertimento) may have been written at this time. Finally, Haydn's salary is not clear: Griesinger writes 200 gulden, Dies has 600 gulden; the former seems a little low, the latter too high.

The winter of 1760–1 was spent in Vienna and provides the next events of certainty in Haydn's biography. On 9 November the marriage contract between Haydn and Maria Anna Keller was drawn up with the twenty-eight-year-old Kapellmeister promising to provide a substantial dowry of 1,000 gulden, more than Dies indicated he earned at the Morzin court, much more if Griesinger's figure is correct. Haydn could have borrowed the money or he may have saved it, an early indication of the thrift that was to be evident in later life and that, eventually, led to a comfortable existence. The marriage itself took place on 26 November in St Stephen's, almost exactly twenty years after Haydn had first entered the church as a choirboy; the register duly records his occupation as music director ('Musik-Direktor') to Count Morzin. This was about to change.

The life of a Kapellmeister, instrumentalist or singer at a secular court in the middle decades of the eighteenth century was by no means a secure one. Financial difficulties, merger of courts on marriage, the devastation of war and lack of interest were common reasons for the abrupt termination of employment, though the number of courts that wished to maintain a musical retinue meant that new posts were reasonably easy to find; Dittersdorf, for instance, was made redundant three times in his life, but found new employment each time. During the winter of 1760–1 the first of these circumstances, financial difficulties, forced the Morzin family to disband its musical retinue. Even though Haydn's period of service at the court had been only three years at the most, his music, including his early symphonies, had already become well known in aristocratic circles, and he was a prominent figure in what was a fashionable surge of interest in the new genre around 1760, as revealed in the careers of other Austrian composers such as Dittersdorf, Gassmann, Michael Haydn, Leopold Hofmann, Vanhal and Wagenseil. This new musical fashion for the symphony, the particular ability of the young composer and the personal recommendation of Count Morzin (who, presumably, vouched also for his administrative skills as a Kapellmeister) led to Haydn being offered the post of Vice Kapellmeister at the court of the Esterházy family. As Haydn himself often remarked, this was the greatest single stroke of fortune in his life; he was to remain in the service of the family until his death in 1809, a total of fifty-eight years, serving four successive princes. Even within the practices of the time it was a remarkable relationship, in the entire history of Western music even more so. There is nothing that matches the musical riches that resulted, directly or indirectly, from this patronage.

The Esterházy family was one of the richest in the Austrian Monarchy, owning large swathes of land in northern Hungary and Bohemia, accumulated through the spoils of the wars with the Turks and dynastic marriages. Recognized as the leading noble family in Hungary, it had always been staunchly loyal to the Habsburg dynasty. German, not Hungarian, was their language of choice, they had played a full part in assuming the virtual dominance of the Catholic religion in their territories, had willingly raised troops for the imperial cause (as in the War of the Austrian Succession) and many family members had active careers in the military. As long ago as 1687 Emperor Leopold I had awarded the family the hereditary title of Prince of the Holy Roman Empire.

The reigning prince was Paul Anton (1711–62) who had succeeded to the title at the age of ten. Later as a young man he studied jurisprudence in Vienna and Leyden and learnt Italian and French. Literature and music were consuming pastimes and he amassed a large collection of books and music from France and Italy, as well as from German-speaking Europe. Following family custom he served in the imperial army, raised a local regiment to fight in the War of the Austrian Succession and in the early years of the Seven Years' War was given the rank of Field Marshal. Between these two wars the prince, accompanied by his wife, Maria Anna, served as ambassador for three years at the court of Naples. A competent player of the flute, violin and lute, he was able to indulge his musical interests in one of the most heady musical cultures in Europe, one in which opera was central. Back in Austria Paul Anton had his own Kapellmeister, Gregor Werner (1693–1766), who had served the court loyally for over thirty years. Engaging Haydn as Vice Kapellmeister was meant to provide assistance to Werner but there was a clear sense too that Paul Anton wanted musical entertainment at court to be more up to date, to reflect his European experience rather than the increasingly limited one of the resident Kapellmeister.

The Hungarian estates of the Esterházy family were administered from their palace in Eisenstadt. They also had a palace in the Hungarian capital, Pressburg, and a summer palace across the Danube from Pressburg, in Kittsee, a few miles east of Hainburg. Symbolically, however, the most important palace for Prince Paul Anton was the one in Vienna, in the Wallnerstrasse, a few minutes' walk – less by carriage – from the Hofburg. Haydn would have passed it on numerous occasions and as a youth in the 1740s would have noticed the extensive building work that was going on to ensure that both the exterior and the interior reflected the most recent taste. The palace followed the fashionable Viennese pattern of an enclosed courtyard with principal rooms on the first and second floors. It was here, at the age of twenty-nine, that Haydn signed his contract on 1 May 1761.

2   Serving princes

Haydn's contract with the Esterházy court consisted of fourteen clauses written across five pages. Two copies were prepared, one for the new employee, one for the Esterházy administration. Some of the clauses are routine ones for court musicians of the time, others reflect the particular circumstances of Haydn's employment. It is worth considering them in turn for they were to determine Haydn's life for decades and to mould certain aspects of his personality for ever.[1]

Convention and rules for the behaviour of the Vice-Kapellmeister
This day, according to the date hereto appended, Joseph Haydn, native of Rohrau in Austria, is accepted and appointed a Vice-Kapellmeister in the service of his Serene Princely Highness, Herr Paul Anton, Prince of the Holy Roman Empire, of Esterházy and Galantha Tit. etc. etc. in this manner; that whereas

1st. There is at Eisenstadt a Kapellmeister named Gregorius Werner who, having devoted many years of true and faithful service to the princely house, is now, on account of his great age and the resulting infirmities that this often entails, unfit to perform the duties incumbent on him, it is hereby declared that the said Gregorius Werner, in consideration of his long service, shall continue to retain the post of Chief Kapellmeister, while the said Joseph Haydn, as Vice-Kapellmeister at Eisenstadt, shall in regard to the Choir Music depend upon and be subordinate to said Gregorius Werner, as Chief Kapellmeister; but in everything else, whenever there shall be a musical performance, and in all required for the same in general and in particular, said Vice-Kapellmeister shall be responsible. Continuing.

The prestige and self-regard of the Esterházy court is immediately apparent. Only the very largest musical establishments, such as the imperial one in Vienna or that in which Michael Haydn and the Mozart family served in Salzburg, could afford to designate an official deputy to a Kapellmeister. Unlike those two courts, however, this was to be a temporary post designed to ensure continuity and expansion of the musical provision during the declining years of its Kapellmeister, Gregor Werner. Now aged sixty-eight, Werner had been a faithful servant of the Esterházy family and the contract diplomatically presents the appointment of a young deputy, more than half his age, as a gesture of support. Werner himself had lived and studied in Vienna in the 1720s and was steeped in the musical traditions of Catholic church music. When he joined the Esterházy court in 1728 he immediately set about improving the provision of liturgical music at court and during the course of the next thirty years composed prolifically in this area, over 150 Marian antiphons, 92 masses, 18 vespers and 4 requiems. Although this music travelled very little and Haydn may have known very few works by his colleague, the new Vice Kapellmeister would have valued such an exemplary career devoted to God and man. For his part Werner probably knew even less of the music of his young deputy. Instrumental music occupied a very small part of his musical output and he was now too old to appreciate the rapidly developing fashion for symphonies, quartets and keyboard sonatas, genres in which Haydn was already acquiring a name for himself. While the gulf in age was to provoke tension, the real problem was the difference in musical outlook, the old-fashioned versus the modern, a division enshrined in the first clause of the contract.

Werner was to continue to look after church music and, though Haydn was to assist him if necessary, the Vice Kapellmeister was to look after what the contract rather blithely terms 'everything else', that is secular music, vocal and instrumental, for the entertainment of the court. Here was the hidden reason for the new appointment. Through his travels in France, Germany and especially Italy Prince Paul Anton had become acquainted with a range of music, often at the cutting edge of style and of a kind that Werner could never have supplied. As well as this large library of foreign music Paul Anton also regularly required scores of operas and ballets given at the imperial court in the 1740s and 1750s, again music that Werner would hardly have known. All this music was systematically catalogued in the 1750s, a library that demonstrated musical sympathies that were wholly alien to the Esterházy Kapellmeister. The prince clearly wanted a musical figure at court who reflected the 1760s rather than the 1720s.

The division of sacred and secular that is implicit in the contract was made explicit in the subsequent administrative practice of the court, two separate music establishments, one called 'Chor Musique', the other 'Cammer Musique', the first headed by Werner and including other long-standing personnel, the second headed by Haydn and with personnel that was almost entirely new. While the labels were wholly conventional and, for that reason, inoffensive, the particular circumstances of the court meant that there was a systemic edginess between, on the one hand, the old and faithful and, on the other, the new and fashionable.

For Haydn the particular provision of the contract with the Esterházy family confirmed a gradual drift away from the likelihood of a career as a church musician to one that was now to be devoted, almost entirely, to secular music. As Vice Kapellmeister Haydn was to compose only one new item of church music, a Te Deum in C (Hob.XXIIIc:1).

2nd. The said Joseph Haydn shall be considered and treated as a house officer. Therefore his Serene Highness is graciously pleased to place confidence in him that, as may be expected from an honourable house officer in a princely court, he will be temperate, and will know that he must treat the musicians placed under him not over-bearingly, but with mildness and leniency, modestly, quietly and honestly. This is especially the case when music will be performed before the high master, at which time the said Vice-Kapellmeister and his subordinates shall always appear in uniform; and the said Joseph Haydn shall take care that not only he but all those dependent upon him shall follow the instructions that have been given to them, appearing neatly in white stockings, white linen, powdered

and with either a pigtail or a hair bag, but otherwise of identical
appearance. Therefore

3rd. The other musicians are responsible to the said Vice-
Kapellmeister, thus he shall the more take care to conduct himself
in an exemplary manner, so that the subordinates may follow the
example of his good qualities: consequently the said Joseph Haydn
shall abstain from undue familiarity, from eating and drinking, and
from other intercourse with them so that they will not lose the
respect that is his due but on the contrary preserve it; for these
subordinates should the more remember their respectful duties if it
be considered how unpleasant to the master must be the consequence of any discord or dispute.

Though Haydn's function was to provide musical entertainment for the
court he was not classified as a servant; along with his musical colleagues
he enjoyed the rank of a house officer, one level above the servants,
cleaners, cooks and caretakers, and on a par with the doctor, the librarian,
the master of the stables and the grenadier guards, a status that carried
certain expectations of behaviour, as the second sentence indicates. The
clause goes on to characterize such behaviour using phraseology that
would have reminded Haydn of similar sentiments in Mattheson's *Der
vollkommene Capellmeister*: 'He should in no way be offensive or scandalous
in his living and conduct, for commonly the greatest contempt arises from
that' and 'Affability is considered a most favoured and rewarding virtue
by people in all ranks: a director, then, should of course strive for it'.[2] Such
attributes were to become second nature to Haydn, earning him the
respect and affection of his colleagues and laying the foundation of the
fatherly disposition that led them to call him Papa.

As well as being contented, the musicians had to be neat and
orderly, and Haydn had to ensure that their appearance was appropriate. To this end he and they were given two uniforms each, one for
the winter and one for the summer, typically renewed in alternate
years; immediately previous uniforms were to be kept for travelling and
if any musician left the court all uniforms had to be surrendered. On a
visit to the Esterházy court sometime in the early 1760s Haydn's father

drew enormous pleasure from seeing his son smartly dressed in a blue uniform with gold trimmings. Haydn too would have found this requirement entirely conducive, feeding a concern about personal appearance that lay somewhere between the proud and the vain.

Behaviour and disposition are the concerns of the third clause too. While it was only natural that a contract of employment should lay down strict social boundaries between the Vice Kapellmeister and his musicians Haydn was able to traverse these without compromising his authority. He and his wife were repeatedly asked by them to act as witnesses to marriages and godparents to children, suggesting that they readily participated in the social celebrations that followed the church services; however, there were never to be reports of the excessive drinking that characterized Salzburg gossip about Joseph's brother Michael. In Eisenstadt Haydn lived with the other musicians in the Old Apothecary at first, circumstances that led Werner to suspect that he was too lenient with his charges. In 1766 Haydn purchased his own house, perhaps more a matter of status (he was now full Kapellmeister) than a desire to be separated from his colleagues.

4th. The said Vice-Kapellmeister shall be under permanent obligation to compose such pieces of music as his Serene Princely Highness may command, and neither to communicate such new compositions to anyone, nor to allow them to be copied, but to retain them wholly for the exclusive use of his Highness; nor shall he compose for any other person without the knowledge and gracious permission of his [Serene Princely Highness].

Approached from the Romantic standpoint of the free artist who composed according to inner compulsion and who, accordingly, set an example to society, this clause seems highly restrictive, even suppressive. But its measured clauses are wholly in keeping with custom and practice in Haydn's time and are included merely to reinforce expectations rather than to imply that working for the Esterházy family meant that particular limitations were in force. It was a normative code of behaviour: if the prince provided the facilities and the income, then he owned the result, the music. While there were to be instances when new pieces were specifically commanded, notably baryton trios and certain operas, most works, especially concertos and symphonies, were initiated by Haydn and written in the expectation that they would be well received by a trusting, musically appreciative patron.

All the music was to remain the property of the court, and scores and manuscript parts were not to be distributed outside. In practice, as everyone must have known, this particular provision was difficult to police and many works by Haydn did find their way to the outside world, laying the foundation of his future fame; some of these manuscript parts were supplied by the composer, others were distributed by performing musicians. The whole business was not unlike the modern practice of photocopying, strictly controlled in legal theory but casually observed and impossible to monitor.

The final sentence, that Haydn was not allowed to compose for anybody else without permission, was easier to enforce. There is no known instance of Haydn asking permission but he must have done so for large-scale works such as the 'Applausus' cantata, written for Zwettl in 1768, the oratorio Il ritorno di Tobia, written for the Tonkünstler-Societät in Vienna in 1775, and the opera La vera costanza in 1778 (if there is any basis in the story that it was first intended for the imperial court in Vienna).

> 5th. The said Joseph Haydn shall appear daily (whether here in Vienna or on the estates) in the antechamber before and after midday, and enquire whether a high princely order for a musical performance has been given; to wait for this order and upon its receipt to communicate its contents to the other musicians; and not only himself to appear punctually at the required time but to take serious care that the others do so as well, specifically noting those who either arrive late or absent themselves entirely. If nevertheless . . .

Given the vast number of documents that survive that chronicle how the Esterházy court functioned in the eighteenth century it is surprising that very little of detail is known about its concert life, when musicians performed and what they played. The precise circumstances surrounding the composition and first performance of the vast majority of Haydn's instrumental works, notably symphonies, are simply unknown. The fifth clause of the contract suggests that Haydn could be expected to provide some kind of musical entertainment every day. This could be a formal concert with one or more items, especially if there were guests, but they might be less formal, involving some selected performers and for the pleasure of the prince alone. The contracts of some of the players make it clear that music was often expected at mealtimes.

The central role of the symphony in Haydn's creative life over the next three decades has encouraged a view of musical performance at the court that is probably too restricted. As well as symphonies Haydn himself composed a number of concertos in the 1760s; extracts from vocal works were played; and while Haydn's music was the most frequently encountered, the repertoire would have embraced a range of contemporary music, by Dittersdorf, Gassmann, Pichl, Vanhal and others. Haydn's quartets might well have featured too. All these genres – operatic arias, quartets, concertos and symphonies – were embraced by the term 'Cammer Musique' (literally music for the chamber or the salon) and Haydn was expected to organize performances as required. The daily meetings in the antechamber must have had an element of forward planning too; the prince could demand immediate entertainment but equally likely was some indication of future requirements.

6th. Contrary to rightful expectations there should arise between the musicians quarrels, disputes or complaints, the said Vice-Kapellmeister shall endeavour to arrange matters, so that the high master be not incommoded with every trifle and bagatelle; but should a more serious matter occur, which the said Joseph Haydn is not able himself to set right or in which he can not act as intermediary, then his Serene Princely Highness must be respectfully informed.

This clause returns to the subject matter of the second and third clauses, the behaviour of the musicians under Haydn's control. At the

age of twenty-nine Haydn already had valuable experience of what
would now be called personnel management, the niggles, the petty
jealousies and the personality clashes of working life. Over time he
became an astute manager of them; nevertheless, there were to be a
few serious incidents that had to be referred upwards. Haydn's
immediate superior was the Estates Director, responsible for the
smooth working of the entire court and who acted on behalf of the
prince. From 1763 that post was held by Peter Ludwig von Rahier, a
self-regarding model of bureaucratic efficiency but also unyielding and
brusque. Sometimes Haydn found himself siding with his musicians in
disciplinary matters and was able to capitalize on his favoured status
with the prince to persuade Rahier not to act unreasonably.

No doubt the most serious incident occurred in June 1771. Two of
Haydn best musicians, the oboist Zacharias Pohl and the cellist Xavier
Marteau, were playing dice in the inn near the palace in Eszterháza,
first for money and then for a jug of wine. Competitiveness, pride and
alcohol led to a scuffle during which Pohl was punched in the face by
Marteau, the stone in his ring causing Pohl to lose his right eye. It took
six months for Pohl to recover and for Rahier to present his conclusions: in the presence of Haydn, who was anxious to maintain the
services of both musicians, Pohl and Marteau were forced to sign an
agreement that required the latter to pay Pohl's medical expenses
together with some financial compensation. Marteau worked for a
further seven years at the court, Pohl, the one-eyed oboist, until 1781,
with Haydn having to manage the lingering guilt of the one and the
resentment of the other.

> 7th. The said Vice-Kapellmeister shall take careful care of all the
> music and musical instruments, and shall be responsible for
> ensuring that they are not ruined and rendered useless through
> carelessness or neglect.

Music libraries that are devoted to performance material are busy
and complex ones. One Te Deum by Werner or one symphony by
Haydn could involve fifteen or more separate parts, some unique,

some duplicate. Parts were easily lost, misplaced or damaged and had to be replaced. When the court moved between its various residences, Vienna, Kittsee, Pressburg, Eisenstadt and Eszterháza, performing parts for individual compositions had to be carefully assembled, distributed, re-collected and, finally, returned to the correct position on the shelves. There is some evidence too that material from the Esterházy library was lent to other institutions. During one working week at court, therefore, the number of parts (as opposed to single works) that were in circulation could easily run into over 100; at the same time new material was constantly being added, whether of works by Haydn or other composers. Keeping control of a busy working library was a difficult task and Haydn, even if he could manage to delegate most of the duties, was the person charged with overall responsibility. Within a few years it was to be a duty that Werner was to accuse the new Vice Kapellmeister of neglecting.

Haydn was responsible for the musical instruments also. As was common practice at the time, the Esterházy court owned most of the instruments played by its employees, violins, violas, cellos, double basses, flutes, oboes, bassoons and horns, as well as the keyboard instruments. When new performers arrived with their own instruments they were purchased from them and the court was responsible for buying reeds for the oboes and bassoons, new crooks for the horns, replacement strings for violins, violas, cellos and double basses, and running repairs on everything. Usually these services were provided outside the court, mainly in Vienna, and Haydn dutifully countersigned (and, on occasions, no doubt queried) hundreds of invoices.

8th. The said Joseph Haydn shall be obliged to instruct the female vocalists, in order that they may not forget, when staying in the country, that which they have been taught with much effort and at great expense in Vienna, and inasmuch as the said Vice-Kapellmeister is proficient on various instruments, he shall take care to practise on all those with which he is acquainted.

Although the singers of the Chor Musique came under Werner's jurisdiction he was obviously no longer capable of ensuring that new, young female singers, in particular, maintained their technical standard, and this duty was passed on to Haydn, a practised singer of the liturgy. These singers also took part in concert performances with their colleagues from the Cammer Musique, so it was entirely appropriate that the Vice Kapellmeister should look after them. Indeed by July 1761 three singers from the Chor Musique were transferred formally to Haydn's retinue, though they could still be called upon to sing in church services.

Having detailed Haydn's duties as a composer, manager, librarian, administrator and vocal teacher, the contract finally turns to the Vice Kapellmeister's responsibilities as a performer. As is indicated in Mattheson's treatise, proficiency rather than virtuosity was expected, in Haydn's case on the violin, harpsichord and organ. These three instruments fed naturally into the unstated responsibility of the Vice Kapellmeister, rehearsing and directing the performance, whether as a violinist or a continuo player. Accordingly he played the violin in symphonies and other instrumental music, harpsichord in secular vocal music such as cantatas and operas, and the organ in church music. Although he was never the equal of Mozart and Beethoven as a keyboard player there are a couple of works from the 1760s, 'Qual dubbio ormai' (the cantata written to celebrate the prince's name day in 1764) and the Missa in honorem BVM ('Great Organ Solo Mass', c.1768), that place the harpsichord and organ, respectively, in the limelight.

9th. A copy of this Convention and Rules for Behaviour shall be given to the said Vice-Kapellmeister and to all the musicians subordinate to him, in order that he may hold them to all their obligations therein established. Moreover,

10th. It is considered unnecessary to set forth on paper all the duties required of the said Joseph Haydn, more particularly since the Serene Master is pleased to hope that he shall of his own free will strictly observe not only the above-mentioned regulations but any others – in whatever circumstances – which the high master might issue in the future; and that he shall place the musical establishment on such a footing, and in such a good order, that he shall bring honour upon himself and thereby deserve further princely favour; to which his discretion and zeal are relied upon. In confidence of which...

Clauses 9 and 10 point out that no contract can stipulate all duties and that to succeed Haydn should expect to perform over and beyond the call of duty. Towards the end of the tenth clause there is a further hint of the hidden sensibilities of the situation in which Haydn found himself: if the musical establishment is improved – by which is implied modernized – the Vice Kapellmeister will be discretely rewarded. Just over a year later such a reward was forthcoming, affecting the salary mentioned in the next clause.

11th. A yearly salary of 400 florins [gulden] Rhine value to be received from the office of the Chief Cashier in quarterly payments is hereby agreed. In addition

12th. When on the estates, the said Joseph Haydn shall board at the officer's table or receive half-a-gulden in lieu thereof.

Haydn's initial salary as Vice Kapellmeister was 400 gulden, the same as Werner though the Kapellmeister received, in addition, allowances for accommodation, food and drink, and the printing costs of the librettos for his oratorios. In June 1762 Haydn's salary was raised to 600 gulden, more than Werner's income, even after taking allowances into consideration. As well as accommodation Haydn was entitled to eat at the table reserved for the house officers of the court; if he chose not to, he could claim half a gulden a day, a generous sum equivalent to 178 gulden a year. In future years these entitlements were sometimes supplemented by ex gratia payments of anything up to 30 ducats (c.135 gulden) for duties well executed on particular occasions.

13th. This Convention with the said Vice-Kapellmeister is agreed to on 1 May 1761 and is to be valid for at least three years, in such a manner that if the said Joseph Haydn at the end of that period wishes to seek his fortune elsewhere, he shall inform the master of his intention by half-a-year's notice. Similarly,

14th. The master undertakes not only to retain the said Joseph Haydn in his service during this period, but should he provide complete satisfaction, he may look forward to the position of Chief Kapellmeister. On the other hand, his Highness is free at all times to dismiss him from his service, also during the period in question. In witness whereof two identical copies of this document have been prepared and exchanged. Given at Vienna this first of May.

Joseph Haydn mpria

The position was a probationary one for three years but in a final, direct indication of the nature of the appointment the contract indicates that Haydn could look forward to being chief Kapellmeister. The court allowed itself maximum room for manoeuvre: while Haydn could be dismissed with immediate effect, he was bound for three years and had to give six months' notice if he wished to leave at the end of that period.

Although Haydn signed his contract on 1 May he had already been working for the court for several weeks. The central purpose of his employment was to set up a new entourage of musicians, the Cammer Musique, primarily located in Vienna while Werner and the church musicians were based in Eisenstadt. As Vice Kapellmeister he would have played a part in selecting these players and since the first contracts were signed on 1 April that process must have begun before that. By June, Haydn's orchestra consisted of twelve core players, one flute, two oboes, two horns, five violins/violas, one cello and one double bass, an ensemble that could be supplemented if necessary by players from Werner's retinue in Eisenstadt or perhaps on an ad hoc basis by extra players in Vienna. Not enough is known about the names and careers of instrumentalists in Vienna at the time but it is safe to assume that Haydn knew many of them already and it is possible that some may have served with him at the Morzin court.

While Haydn had to satisfy himself on the musical capabilities of his new colleagues, details of the contracts were left to the Esterházy administration with some flexibility to suit personal circumstance. The standard salary was 240 gulden, substantially more than their colleagues in the Chor Musique. Most were engaged, like Haydn, for three years but many did not receive the daily allowance in lieu of any meals provided by the court and one, the bass player and violinist Melchior Griessler, chose to have a lower salary in order to have an annual supply of victuals (wheat, corn, millet, lentils, beef, salt, lard, candles, wine, cabbage, beetroot, pork and firewood).

One player was an entirely new acquaintance, Luigi Tomasini, soon to become a trusted colleague and friend, someone who was to work alongside Haydn at the Esterházy court for over forty years. Born in Pesaro in 1741 he had entered the service of Prince Paul Anton Esterházy in Italy as a servant musician. His talents as a violinist were nurtured by the prince, who paid for a period of instruction in Venice in 1759 and in the following year he studied with Leopold Mozart in Salzburg. It was only natural that he should become a key member of the new ensemble and he was accordingly transferred from the servants' payroll to the musicians' payroll. As well as being a more proficient violinist than Haydn he was also more experienced, and he soon assumed the position of leader.

Haydn's first compositions for the court were three symphonies evoking different times of day, Le matin, Le midi and Le soir (nos. 6–8). He told Dies that the idea for these programmatic symphonies came from Prince Paul Anton, and there is no reason to doubt this claim since programmatic symphonies were not yet part of the tradition in Vienna and there is nothing in the composer's musical background that would have prompted him to write such works. As the French titles imply, they reflect the prince's knowledge of music from that country, including the specialist collection recently catalogued, in particular the propensity of the French Baroque for pictorial instrumental music, whether as part of the lavish operas of Rameau or as independent compositions by Boismortier and Corrette. From being an Austrian musician Haydn was suddenly a French musician manqué, a fashion statement by the prince that was even more impressive than the new uniforms worn by the players. This tapped into a broader Francophile mood in Vienna, prompted by the Habsburg desire to reach an understanding with the Bourbon family, a diplomacy that was cemented by the ill-fated marriage of the empress's daughter, Maria Antonio (henceforward Marie Antoinette), to Louis XVI. Gluck composed a series of French operas for the court theatre and Haydn, with great flair, based the entire first movement of *Le soir* on an air from Gluck's *Le diable à quatre* about a woman who takes snuff in order to annoy her husband. The prince's discrimination was further flattered by the extensive concertante writing in all three works, with solos, duets, trios and quartets for flute, oboes, bassoon, horns, violins, cello and double bass, a perfect demonstration of the capabilities of the new retinue.

While Paul Anton and his guests enjoyed the topicality and flair of the music of the new Vice Kapellmeister in the Wallnerstrasse in Vienna, a large building project was taking place in the summer palace in Eisenstadt, the construction of a theatre for the performance of operas and plays. It was no doubt the intention of the prince that Haydn and his colleagues should participate in the operatic repertoire of the theatre and, given that he had paid for Tomasini to study in Italy and had himself lived for several years in Naples, it is possible that he contemplated sending the new Vice Kapellmeister to that country to familiarize himself with the latest operatic fashion. But Paul Anton's ambitious plans for musical life at court were never to reach fruition. During the winter of 1761–2 he became ill and died on 18 March, aged only fifty.

Paul Anton had no children and he probably anticipated that, after a long life, he would be succeeded by his nephew, Anton. In the event it was Anton's father (Paul Anton's brother), Nicolaus, who inherited the title (see Figure 3). This early death allowed the most lavish of Haydn's Esterházy patrons to determine the development of the composer's career for nearly forty years; ironically, when his son did eventually succeed, in 1790, he turned out be the least committed of Haydn's patrons.

Only three years younger than his brother, Nicolaus (1714–90) had followed a similar career, legal studies at the universities of Vienna and

3. Prince Nicolaus Esterházy (engraving by G.F. Schmidt, c.1760).

Leyden, extensive travelling and a distinguished career in the imperial army, seeing active service as an officer in the War of the Austrian Succession and in the Seven Years' War; in between the two wars he had played an influential part in the reform of the imperial army. He was one of the first recipients of the Order of Maria Theresia and he and the imperial court no doubt anticipated continuing service on behalf of the Habsburg dynasty, whether in Vienna itself or, like his brother, as a diplomat abroad. While the relationship between the two Esterházy brothers had always been a cordial one, Nicolaus's lifestyle had always been rather carefree and Paul Anton, as head of the family, had on occasion to curb some extravagant expenditure. His assumption of the title of Prince Esterházy changed the direction of his career for ever.

He left the army and assumed his new responsibilities with enthusiasm, energy and maturity, without losing a predilection for extravagance and ostentation that was to earn him the nickname of 'der Pracht-liebende' ('the lover of splendour', usually rendered in English as 'the magnificent'). He remained an active and faithful supporter of the Habsburg dynasty, representing the Bohemian nobility at the election in 1764 in Frankfurt of Maria Theresia's son, Joseph, as Prince of the Holy Roman Empire (the Esterházy family owned land in Bohemia too) and in the same year assuming the honorary position of captain of the Hungarian Guard, a select group of 120 men who acted as a personal bodyguard to the empress on public occasions. He was a key ally of Maria Theresia in nurturing Hungarian loyalty to the throne, a loyalty that was to be tested to the limit in the 1780s when Joseph II's administrative reforms rode roughshod over Hungarian sensibilities. It was this loyalty that earned the family the automatic right from birth, rather than from accession, to be called 'prince' and 'princess' rather than 'count' and 'countess'. Away from the army in the 1740s and 1750s Nicolaus and his wife, Marie Elisabeth, spent the summer months in Süttör, a small palace in the Hungarian countryside to the south of the Neusiedlersee. As a youth he had learnt the cello and at Süttör his musical interests were indulged by the occasional concert, perhaps even some makeshift opera.

Given his personality and interests there was no danger that Nicolaus would question the new musical structure that Paul Anton had just put in place. Indeed as someone who felt little or no loyalty to Werner, within a few months of assuming the title it was Nicolaus who increased the salary of the nominal Vice Kapellmeister to 600 gulden. Moreover, to an even greater extent than his brother, he revealed that his musical priorities lay with Haydn's domain, secular vocal music and instrumental music, to the slow but steady detriment of church music.

In particular Nicolaus shared Paul Anton's enthusiasm for developing opera at Eisenstadt. For a few years a troupe of Italian musicians and actors had visited the town in the summer months. In

July 1762 its director, Girolamo Bon together with his wife, Rosa, and daughter, Anna, both singers, were engaged directly by Nicolaus to provide theatrical entertainment. That summer Haydn provided the music for a comedy entitled La marchesa nespola (The marchioness of the loquats) and, over the next few years, three further comedies, now lost, Il dottore (The doctor), La vedova (The widow) and Il scanarello (The butcher). As the short titles hint, these comedies were probably comic plays with musical numbers rather than fully sung operas.

It was very likely during the summer of 1762 and for the new prince that Haydn made his first extended visit to Eisenstadt, the principal summer palace of the family and the seat of its administrative power. He would have made the 26-mile journey from Vienna through flat, fertile countryside, passing the imperial summer palace of Laxenburg. Approaching Eisenstadt from the north he would have noticed the landscape becoming more undulating and the vineyards, established in Roman times, more numerous. The town itself was not ruled by the Esterházy family but had the status of a free town directly responsible to the Hungarian crown. Undoubtedly, however, it owed its prosperity to the family, an unequal relationship that is exemplified in the size and location of the town hall and the palace: the former, the Rathaus, is a Renaissance building in the broad main street with colourful frescos on the first floor that still catch the eye, temperance, fortitude, justice, love, hope and faith; but a few minutes' walk westwards and up a gentle hill lies the much more imposing Esterházy palace with, in the 1760s, an uninterrupted view southwards across the countryside. This commanding aspect had been occupied since the thirteenth century but had been transformed in the seventeenth century when a Baroque palace was erected, a palace that survives to this day though the modifications of the nineteenth century have made it less visually of a piece than all the other palaces that figured in Haydn's life. It is built around a square courtyard, emphasized by seven symmetrically placed windows on each side. To the right were the principal living quarters, to the left the palace chapel, the focus of Werner's energies for over thirty years. Immediately in front, and occupying a more elongated space than the standard seven windows imply from the outside, is a spacious hall, now called the Haydnsaal. Though the presence of such a hall was not unusual in aristocratic palaces of the time its size certainly was, capable of seating several hundred people in comfort and with a lofty ceiling rising up to the third storey of the rest of building, producing a particularly lively acoustic. Mural and ceiling paintings represent scenes from Ovid's *Metamorphoses*, the myths of Cupid and Psyche and the Golden Apples of the Hesperides, interspersed with the various coats of arms of the Esterházy family. This opulent hall was used for banquets as well as for concerts and could easily be converted into a temporary theatre also. Behind the hall, when Haydn first arrived, was the new theatre instigated by Paul Anton and where the four comedies with music were first performed. The northern aspect of the palace then opened into gardens laid out in a mixture of Italian and French styles.

Returning to the front entrance Haydn would have crossed a moat – more decorative than functional – before turning right to walk further up the hill towards the musicians' quarters in the Old Apothecary. Along the way he would have passed several landmarks. First was the Jewish area, marked by a chain across the road; over 400 strong, the community constituted the backbone of the commercial life of the area and Haydn and his wife, like everybody else in Eisenstadt, would have purchased all manner of goods here, from ribbon and lace to pots and pans. In return for a tax, the *Schutzgeld* (literally 'protection money'), and some services to the Esterházy family, the community enjoyed the protection of the family and, through them, of the remainder of the townspeople.

A few minutes further on stood the local church of the Barmherzige Brüder with a small statue of Saint John of God on the outside. As in Vienna there was a hospice and an apothecary and it was here that Haydn received potions for chest infections and stomach complaints, as well as his tooth-cleaning powder. Just before the Old Apothecary was a small church endowed by the Esterházy family, the Bergkirche. But Haydn's pious nature would have been particularly fired by the

4. Jesus is divested of his clothes. From the Kalvarienberg, Eisenstadt.

Kalvarienberg near by, the Mount of Olives, a grotto erected in the first decade of the eighteenth century and the regular destination of pilgrims. Walking through its carefully built rocky tunnel Haydn would have viewed and reflected on the life of Christ, depicted in life-sized carvings and vividly, even garishly painted figures (see Figure 4). It was regarded as the eighth wonder of the world.

It was in the sparse rooms of the Old Apothecary that Haydn composed in the early 1760s. From the comic stage work, *La marchesa nespola*, he turned next to serious opera, the story of Acis and Galatea.

In fact it may have been re-turned since there is evidence to suggest that *Acide* had been initiated in Paul Anton's time, possibly intended for a formal opening of the new theatre in Eisenstadt in 1762. His death and the engagement of Bon's troupe by Nicolaus put the project on hold; it was revived as part of the lavish three-day celebration associated with the wedding of Count Anton with Countess Marie Therese Erdödy that took place in the palace in January 1763, when it was performed on the afternoon of the second day followed by a masked ball in the great hall. The pastoral story of two shepherds, Acis and Galatea, whose love is threatened by the monster Polyphemus, its comparative brevity (thirteen scenes only) and its allegorical association with the happy couple place it firmly in the long tradition of the *festa teatrale* and Haydn responds idiomatically and knowledgeably to the musical characteristics of the genre, large-scale da capo arias, vocal virtuosity prompted by particular words such as 'accende' (inflames), 'paventar' (fear) and 'pompa' (pomp), some comedy in Polyphemus's music and agile musical responses to the changes of mood in the recitatives.

Within a matter of a few months in 1762–3 Haydn had demonstrated an entirely new side to his musicianship, the ability to compose Italian operatic music, both comic and serious, that was thoroughly up to date. For a musician who had grown up in the musical practices of Austrian Catholicism and then developed a particular facility in modish instrumental genres, this was a notable achievement, all the more so when one considers that Italian opera was not easily encountered in Vienna at the time. Certainly Haydn would have known individual arias from accompanying Porpora's lessons or participating in any concerts that included them, but opera in French (*opéra comique*) dominated the performing repertoire of the Burgtheater in the 1750s, not Italian opera. Also Haydn's duties at the Morzin court in Lukavec would have minimized still further the opportunity to attend any performances of Italian opera in Vienna. At least some of his knowledge of the style came from personal study rather than direct experience in the theatre. Shortly before taking up his post at the Esterházy court he had recommended Galuppi's highly fashionable *dramma giocoso*, *Il mondo alla roversa*, to a pupil named Robert Kimmerling, 'because of its good lyricism'.[3] That particular opera was never performed in Vienna and Haydn and Kimmerling studied it from a keyboard reduction issued by the firm of Breitkopf in Leipzig; perhaps other Italian operas, by Hasse and Piccinni, masters of the serious and comic styles respectively, were studied in this way too.

At the time Piccinni lived in Naples but between 1760 and 1773 Johann Adolf Hasse (1699–1783) lived mainly in Vienna, a revered figure who had dominated operatic life throughout Europe for nearly forty years. In the imperial city he continued to compose, including several works of the *festa teatrale* type. Haydn almost certainly met him in the early 1760s and, though it never became a close personal relationship, he retained his enthusiasm for the man and for his music for many years.

A much more unexpected musical interest that became evident in the 1760s, again through personal study, was C.P.E. Bach (1714–88). He belonged to a wholly different musical environment from Haydn, also from Hasse: he was employed as a keyboard player in the Prussian court of Frederick the Great in Berlin (Austria's constant enemy in the 1740s and 1750s), he was a Protestant, someone who was never to write an opera of any kind and who composed symphonies only fitfully. Nevertheless, Haydn, in challenging, almost defiant tones, told Griesinger that 'whoever knows me thoroughly must discover that I owe a great deal to Emanuel Bach, that I understood him and have studied him diligently'.[4] While Haydn's music provides appropriate echoes of Dittersdorf, Hasse, Porpora, Reutter, Wagenseil and other composers from the Viennese environment, there is little that actually sounds like C.P.E. Bach. However, Haydn's already evident interest in creating a strong sense of thematic continuity in his music and, more particularly, incorporating embellishment within the compositional process, rather than as an accidental aspect of extempore performance practice, would have been nourished by the study of Bach's music. Bach was the author of an influential treatise, *Versuch über die wahre Art das Clavier zu spielen* (Essay on the true art of playing the keyboard), published in two parts in 1753 and 1762. Haydn owned a copy and, like the writings of Fux and Mattheson, it played a formative part in his musicianship. As a result of reading its particular precepts Haydn changed his notational practice for appoggiaturas and figured bass in the 1760s. In the long term Bach's celebration of the expressive power of instrumental music, very unfashionable in the middle of the century, would have provided continuing appeal for Haydn, and it was this aesthetic as much as the compositional rigour that went with it that prompted his enthusiastic tribute.

Haydn had a rich and varied life in the early 1760s. Based mainly in Vienna with visits to Eisenstadt, he was able to keep abreast of musical developments in the capital, compose symphonies and concertos for an ensemble that he had personally selected and respond to the new challenges that his employment offered. It was tinged by sadness when his father died in September 1763; at the age of sixty-four he had remained active as a wheelwright but a pile of wood fell on him, breaking several ribs, and he died shortly thereafter.

Kapellmeister Werner was six years older than Mathias Haydn, increasingly frail and increasingly irritated by the behaviour of his deputy. The fault line that characterized the division of responsibilities in Haydn's contract was laid bare by the very evident success of the new musical life at the Esterházy court. In the autumn of 1765 simmering resentment coupled with a display of residual authority culminated in a strongly worded letter of complaint from the Kapellmeister addressed directly to Prince Nicolaus.

Werner's complaint is about immaturity and the failure of responsibility, and there is no attempt to avoid the personal: Haydn is the target. The opening sentence even indulges in the weary pun on his name, 'a good heathen' ('eines guten Heyden').[5]

> I am forced to draw attention to the gross negligence in the local
> castle chapel, the unnecessary large princely expenses, and the lazy
> idleness of the musicians, the principal responsibility for which
> must be laid at the door of the present director, who lets them all

get away with everything, so as to receive the name of a good
Heyden: for as God is my witness, things are much more
disorderly than if seven children were around.

He then goes into extensive detail, sometimes referring to the same
issue more than once: the church musicians are absent for lengthy
periods without permission; performance standards are consequently
poor; many instruments have been lost; the library is in disorder with
no record of material that has been lent 'to all the world'; a promised
catalogue has not materialized; and the former practice 'under the late
lamented prince' of two-hour concerts on Tuesdays and Thursdays in
the officers' quarters should be reinstated to keep the musicians
occupied. Having discharged his duty, as he saw it, Werner finally
asks, rather incongruously, whether some additional firewood could
be added to his victuals for the winter.

While these specific complaints were probably well founded, they
were also the inevitable result of Haydn being a master in his particular
domain and an assistant to Werner in another. Haydn could quite
legitimately claim that he was giving full attention to duties associated
with the Cammer Musique and that spending his time between Vienna
and Eisenstadt made it difficult for him to assume continuing
responsibility for the musicians of the Chor Musique. Haydn probably
felt that it was more important to please Prince Nicolaus than to please
Werner (an impossibility anyway), an attitude fuelled by the knowledge
that Nicolaus was less interested in the church music establishment
than his predecessor, Werner's 'late lamented prince', had been.

Nicolaus's reaction was accordingly a mixed one. Werner almost
certainly got his additional firewood but Haydn was never required to
give a written response and the matter was passed to Rahier for
his attention. He produced a document that simultaneously clarified
Haydn's responsibilities for the church musicians in Eisenstadt
and gave him some assistance: catalogues of the music and of the
instruments were to be prepared; Joseph Dietzl (tenor and organist)
was to make certain that all performing material was returned to its

proper place and ensure that repairs to the instruments were carried out; performing duties were to be strictly observed by everybody with regular fortnightly reports; and the Tuesday and Thursday concerts were to be resumed.

While Haydn would have welcomed this clarification he would have been surprised by the postscript that was added to the letter, in effect a new complaint, this time from the prince.[6]

> Finally, said Kapellmeister Haydn is urgently enjoined to apply himself to composition more diligently than heretofore, and especially to write such pieces as can be played on the gamba, of which pieces we have seen very few up to now; and to be able to judge his diligence, he shall at all times send us the first copy, cleanly and carefully written, of each and every composition.

This was a sharp rebuke. In just under five years at the court Haydn had composed one serious opera (*Acide*), four comedies with music, five celebratory cantatas, a Te Deum (to help out Werner), over twenty symphonies, three or more violin concertos, one cello concerto, one double-bass concerto, one flute concerto and two horn concertos, hardly the output of someone who lacked diligence. He was now being reminded to write music for the 'gamba', not the viola da gamba but an unfamiliar, eccentric instrument, the baryton, that Nicolaus had taken up only the previous summer. It was a gamba in the sense that its seven strings were strung above a fingerboard with frets, enabling Nicolaus the cellist to become reasonably proficient in a short time, eccentric in that there was a parallel set of ten strings behind the fingerboard that resonated in sympathy with the bowed notes or, more deftly, could be plucked by the thumb of the left hand. Very few people played the instrument and this command from the prince must rank as one of the most indulgently self-interested in the history of musical patronage. Haydn duly obliged. Between 1765 and the late 1770s, when the prince's interest waned, he composed 126 trios involving the baryton, presented in five elegantly bound volumes, plus some three dozen further works that featured the instrument.

Having survived most of the winter Gregor Werner died on 3 March 1766, aged seventy-one. Following a service in the palace chapel in which Haydn, presumably, directed the music, he was buried in the palace cemetery; in his will Werner had stipulated that each of his musical colleagues be provided with a wax candle for the procession. Despite the trouble that Werner had caused over the previous months, there was never any real doubt that Haydn would assume the senior position and he duly did so. As full Kapellmeister Haydn now had responsibility for the complete range of musical activities, both sacred and secular.

A very different instruction from the prince, issued exactly two months before Werner died, on 3 January, was to have an equally marked influence on Haydn's musical future. It came from Rahier and was addressed to the entire Esterházy administration.[7]

> You are herewith informed of the formal decision of his highness that the castle at Süttör is henceforward to be called Esterház; accordingly the correct form of the address in future is determined as Eszterház by Süttör.

Süttör had been Nicolaus's summer residence for over ten years and he retained his affection for the castle after he assumed the title of prince in 1762, now signified by a formal change of name to that of the family. While 'Süttör' fell into disuse 'Eszterház' was more commonly rendered as Eszterháza or Esteraz while Haydn himself normally used 'Estoras'. The castle was located 26 miles south-east of Eisenstadt near the southern tip of the Neusiedlersee in Hungary which, unlike Eisenstadt, was a predominantly Hungarian-speaking part of the country. A detailed description of the castle drawn up for Count Nicolaus in 1760 showed that it had forty-one rooms on three floors, including two halls and a room that served as a chapel, and that it was located in extensive gardens. There were plans to enlarge the palace and these were made more extensive when the count became the prince. Between 1762 and 1784 the palace was transformed into one approximately three times the size and further

5. The palace of Eszterháza from the gardens (engraving by F. Landerer, 1784).

buildings were built in the gardens. In a century that had seen extensive building in the Austrian territories Eszterháza was recognized as particularly grand, second only to the transformation of the summer palace of Schönbrunn for the imperial family outside Vienna, and was variously referred to as 'the Hungarian Delight', 'the Hungarian Paradise' and 'the little Versailles of Hungary'. By January 1766 the building work was sufficiently advanced for the transformation to be signalled by the new name (see Figure 5).

The palace sits on a west–east axis with the main entrance to the north and the south façade surveying extensive parkland. From the central palace, which incorporates the previous smaller one, two wings project in a gentle curve towards the main gate. Reaching out at a right angle from both wings were a winter gallery (to the east) and an art gallery (to the west). The principal room on the ground floor, the Sala Terrana, opened directly into the garden, hot in summer on the garden side but cooler, with a marble floor, the further one moved into the palace. Summer banquets took place there and probably some concerts. The private quarters of the prince were to the east of the Sala Terrana, those of the princess to the west. Reaching from the ground floor through the entire three storeys was a chapel, circular in shape and holding no more than twenty people; there was a small organ but only the smallest of Haydn's church pieces could have been performed there. The principal feature of the first floor, and of the palace as a whole, is the Prunksaal, a large salon with a commanding view of the French ornamental gardens, the straight paths taking the eye easily towards four symmetrically placed church spires that rise from a distant hill. The ceiling is decorated with a fresco depicting Apollo on a sun chariot, the walls are demarcated by six large mirrors and two fireplaces, and the four corners house life-size statues depicting the four seasons. At the front of the building above the staircase is the music room, more intimate but with the same high ceiling; any music performed here would have drifted easily into the Prunksaal. While the Prunksaal has five large chandeliers the adjacent music room has wall brackets that hold a total of sixty-four candles.

The principal indulgence of the palace were two purpose-built theatres, located in the gardens so as to facilitate the broadening vista from the palace. To the south-west was the main opera house, completed in 1768, to the south-east a smaller marionette theatre, completed in 1773. Next to the main opera house was a Chinese Ballroom (sometimes called the Bagatelle), a dance hall that was also used as a garden house. To the west of the opera house, a couple of minutes' walk, were the living quarters of the musicians and any visiting troupes of actors. Though habitable from the same year as the opera house was completed, changes were still being made in the following decade. It had seventy-six rooms on two storeys built round six courtyards and with communal kitchens. While most musicians were allocated one or two rooms, Kapellmeister Haydn had a four-room flat, as did the apothecary and the court librarian. The prince built an inn of seventeen rooms near by that provided some additional accommodation, recreation for his employees and, on special occasions, acted as a refectory. Although servants, musicians and actors were discreetly kept away from the main palace they could all roam the extensive gardens that led, via the formal alleys, to a game reserve and a swine reserve.

Until the opera house and musicians' accommodation were completed in 1768 any visits to Eszterháza by Haydn would have been very brief but there was already a sense in 1766 that the locus of the Kapellmeister's work would shift from Vienna and Eisenstadt to Eisenstadt and Eszterháza; certainly more of that year and the following one was spent in Eisenstadt than had been the case hitherto. As tangible evidence of Haydn's new status and the fact that less time was being spent in Vienna, he purchased a house in Eisenstadt in 1766, unusual for a man of his means, doubly so since he was not an official resident of the town; he paid the previous owner in instalments and borrowed the remaining money. The property was located to the east of the palace down the hill in Klostergasse (now Haydngasse), half the distance from the palace in comparison with the Old Apothecary buildings. It had two floors. On the ground floor were six rooms, including cellars and a stable for four horses; on the first floor were the two principal rooms with stucco decoration that overlooked the street, plus one further room, a kitchen and a hallway. It also had several various substantial pieces of land on the outskirts of Eisenstadt, which Haydn may have sublet, and a smaller kitchen garden on the eastern boundary of the village. According to local lore Haydn would sometimes compose in the hut in the kitchen garden in order to get away from his wife; of course this need have happened only once for the story to have started, and there is certainly no mention of it in any of the early biographical sources. Maria Anna Haydn, for her part, would have been as pleased as her husband at the new purchase. Alas, in what is a poignant parallel to the unhappy marriage, the house was to be plagued with problems, from awkward neighbours to two fires, and was sold after only twelve years to an accountant at the Esterházy court, Anton Liechtscheidl.

In 1766 Haydn composed symphonies, baryton music and one short opera, *La canterina*, an intermezzo in two parts that lampoons a gullible singing teacher. Almost certainly the musical highlight of the year for the composer was an ambitious setting of the mass text, the Missa Cellensis; this was the first time that Haydn had composed a mass for over sixteen years and, at over sixty minutes, it was destined to be his largest work in the genre. While it is tempting to link the work with

Haydn's new responsibilities for church music at Eisenstadt the title, written by the composer himself on the autograph, points elsewhere, to an occasion associated in some way with the pilgrimage church of Mariazell (Cellensis = of Zell). Haydn had maintained his contact with church musicians in Vienna and it is possible that it was written for the annual service in the Augustinerkirche in Vienna on 8 September 1766 (a Marian feast day) organized by the Styrian confraternity and devoted, in particular, to celebrating the icon of the Blessed Virgin Mary in Mariazell. As a former pilgrim himself Haydn would have been inspired by the commission and Prince Nicolaus, reflecting the long association of the family with the pilgrimage church, would have readily agreed. The Augustinerkirche was an imperial church, much frequented by the Habsburg family, and the following anecdote related to Vincent Novello in 1829 may well refer to the Missa Cellensis; certainly Hasse's prediction is more comfortably located in the mid-1760s than later.[8]

> At the first mass which Haydn produced in Public, the Empress Maria Theresa was present – Hasse stood by her and she asked his opinion of the young composer.
>
> Hasse told the Empress that Haydn possessed all the qualities that are required to form the highest style of writing, viz. beautiful and expressive melody, sound harmony, original invention, variety of effect, symmetrical design, knowledge of the powers of the different instruments, correct counterpoint, scientific modulation and refined taste. Hasse also predicted that Haydn would become one of the greatest Composers of the Age.

The following couple of years saw a series of major items of sacred music that further enhanced Haydn's reputation as a church composer. For the traditional para-liturgical service on Good Friday 1767 he set the demanding, penitential text of the Stabat mater, subsequently forwarding the work to Hasse for his approval; that composer sent a generous letter of praise which Haydn retained for the rest of his life, though it then disappeared. The Stabat mater was to become the most widely distributed sacred work by the composer in his lifetime, featuring in the concert life of Paris and London as well as in religious services of Catholic countries such as Austria, Italy and Spain. Once more Haydn used his contacts in Vienna to present two performances, at the church of the Barmherzige Brüder in Leopoldstadt in 1768 and the Piaristenkirche in 1771. In 1768 the Viennese church music network, and Haydn's reputation within it, resulted in a commission from the abbey of Zwettl in Upper Austria for a work to celebrate the golden jubilee of the taking of the vows of its abbot, Rainer Kollman, a large-scale work with a laudatory text in sustained allegory, set for soloists, chorus and orchestra, the 'Applausus' cantata. Since by its nature this was a one-off work that could not be appropriately performed elsewhere, Haydn plundered it as a source for liturgical offertories and motets, substituting sacred texts for the original allegorical texts; in this secondary format much of the music found its way around the churches and monasteries of Austria.

The year 1768 also saw the composition of two masses. The first was a work for unaccompanied chorus and continuo in the style described by Fux in his *Gradus ad Parnassum* as 'stylus a cappella', associated primarily with Lent; Haydn was dissatisfied with the work, abandoned it and added the wry remark to the autograph, placed as if it were part of the title, 'sunt bona mixta malis' (the good mixed with the bad). The second mass, in E flat, adds a concertante organ part to the already colourful orchestral fabric of two cors anglais, two horns, strings and continuo; the 'Grosse Orgelsolomesse' was probably first performed in the palace chapel in Eisenstadt in 1769.

In the months between the 'Applausus' cantata and the 'Grosse Orgelsolomesse' Haydn had to turn his hand once more to Italian opera. The opera house at Eszterháza was completed in 1768 as was the living accommodation for the musicians and, two years on from the formal change of name, the musical ambition of Eszterháza was now to be made apparent by a new opera from the resident Kapellmeister. Rather than a strait-laced serious opera the prince wanted a highly fashionable comic opera, a *dramma giocoso* of the kind fashioned in Italy in the 1750s by the poet Goldoni and the composer Galuppi.

Eight years earlier Haydn had recommended a *dramma giocoso* by Galuppi, *Il mondo alla roversa*, to a pupil; now he had the opportunity to compose one and the choice fell on Goldoni's libretto *Lo speziale* (The apothecary). But the vocal resources at the Esterházy court were barely up to the task and many of the salient characteristics of *dramma giocoso* were emasculated or distorted. Goldoni's libretto typically divided the singers into two groups, serious (*parti serie*) and comic (*parti buffe*), whose interaction through clearly differentiated musical styles was a fundamental part of the appeal of the genre. But Haydn did not have enough singers and had to resort to excising the serious group altogether and refashioning the work for the comic group only. Also there was a mismatch between the expertise of Haydn's singers and the casting conventions of *dramma giocoso*: the comic part of Sempronio, the old apothecary, would normally be taken by a bass or baritone, but Haydn had to give it to a tenor; and the serious role of the ardent suitor, Volpino, who was expected to be a tenor, was given to a soprano. Despite these brutal adjustments the first performance greatly pleased Prince Nicolaus, who immediately presented the composer and the singers with a monetary gift, a bonus in modern parlance.

Two years later, in mid-September 1770, Eszterháza was the venue for the wedding of Prince Nicolaus's niece, Countess Lemberg, with Count Pocci. Two performances of a new opera by Haydn were given, *Le pescatrici*, a second setting of a *dramma giocoso* by Goldoni, though this time Haydn's vocal forces enabled him to meet the conventions of the genre without injury. Once more composer and singers were rewarded with a bonus.

To the extent that imprecise dates permit safe conclusions, the number of symphonies that Haydn composed in the years immediately after he assumed the senior position of Kapellmeister decreases a little, perhaps fewer than ten across the period 1766–70, a natural consequence of the extension of his duties into sacred and operatic music. The chore of baryton music continued, on average one new trio a fortnight; he even spent six months secretly learning the instrument in order to impress the prince, only to be told, dismissively, that such expertise was to be expected. Much more musically rewarding, Haydn found time in 1769 to return to the medium of the quartet, thereafter completing three sets of six in three years, op. 9 (1770), op. 17 (1771) and op. 20 (1772).

In his mid-to late thirties Haydn had explored a vast range of music in a short period of time, probably the most intensely demanding and challenging few years in his life. Some genres, like *dramma giocoso*, were being explored for the first time, others, especially church music, he had long hoped to explore; while baryton trios, for instance, could be written on automatic pilot (though one prone to creative computer error), his symphonies and quartets were demonstrating an ever more penetrating fascination with musical language and the expressive power of instrumental music. He was a driven man. But who did the driving? To what extent was he obliged to write this quantity of music? Baryton music was expected as were the two particular operas. There was probably less pressure to produce new symphonies since the concerts in Eisenstadt and Eszterháza could be filled with existing works and symphonies by other composers. Given that the prince was less interested in church music perhaps it was Haydn's decision to write so many major items in the late 1760s. Finally, the return to the string quartet after an absence of nearly ten years was almost certainly the composer's idea, though there was ample opportunity for them to be played and appreciated at the court. For Haydn duty was something that was indivisible: duty to his art, duty to his faith and duty to his prince were one and the same thing.

It came at a price, however. His marriage seemed to be founded on mutual indifference, probably exacerbated by the fact that Maria Anna could not bear children; acting as godparents was some consolation, at the same time a reminder. Maria Anna may have been the first to stray when in the early 1770s she became the lover of Ludwig Guttenbrunn, a painter working at the Esterházy court.

There is also evidence that Haydn's health suffered a little towards the end of the 1760s, even though his constitution was essentially a robust one. He told Griesinger that he remembered defying the orders of his doctor to stay in bed, rising to write a keyboard sonata while his wife was in church; typically the memory was also a musical one, triggered by the unusual key of the sonata, B major (only the opening bars are known). In the winter of 1770–1 Haydn was so ill that his brother Michael was summoned from Salzburg. He recovered and composed a setting of the Salve regina, performed in the chapel in Eisenstadt with four vocal soloists and Haydn himself playing the concertante organ, a deeply personal act of devotion and thanks. This illness seems to have prompted an element of reassessing his working life. Although he was never to be anything less than busy and the curiosity and integrity of individual works were constantly evident, the prolonged fixated nature of his compositional energy in the late 1760s was not to be as evident in the following decade.

After ten years of service at the court Haydn's position as director, confidante and spokesperson on behalf of his musicians was well established. Simmering disquiet in 1772 resulted in the most imaginative display of Haydn's diplomatic skills, the 'Farewell' symphony (no. 45).

Early in January, in preparation for the annual move to Eszterháza, probably on 1 May, Rahier informed the musicians that, with the exception of Haydn, Tomasini, and three of the singers, families would not be allowed to accompany them to the summer palace. In itself this was not unexpected since the limited accommodation had to house visiting actors as well as musicians, but it had by now become an irksomely regular practice. It was aggravated by well-founded rumours that the prince wanted to save some expenditure, probably by reducing the already minimal amount that was being spent on maintaining music for the church services in Eisenstadt when the court was spending more and more time in Eszterháza. Long summer months in Eszterháza clearly captivated the prince but for the musicians, especially the ones without their families, there was an element of tedium: as well as the usual concerts they provided any incidental music for the theatre performances given by visiting troupes but regular opera performances were not yet a feature of court life. Indeed in 1772 it is quite likely that there were no opera performances. In August no fewer than five musicians, Christian Specht (bass, also viola), Carl Schiringer (double bass), Johannes Hinterberger (bassoon), Joseph Dietzl (horn) and Andreas Lidl (baryton), became so ill that they had to return to Eisenstadt for treatment. A brief absence by the prince had allowed Xavier Marteau (cello), Carl Chorus (oboe) and Johann May (horn) also to return to Eisenstadt to their families. But in September it was being made clear that all were expected back in Eszterháza. Resentment, illness and tedium were aggravated when the prince announced his intention to stay until December, two months longer than was then customary. The musicians approached Haydn, who instead of going to Rahier, or even the prince directly, came up with the idea of a symphony that hinted at their disaffection.

First performed in the late autumn of 1772, when the nights had long drawn in, probably in the customary venue of the music room, the symphony would have seemed for much of its course to have been another work in a familiar idiom, now usually called *Sturm und Drang*, one that Haydn had exploited in earlier works, notably no. 39 in G minor and no. 44 in E minor. But the players' knowledge that there was to be an unexpected conclusion would have been heightened by the experience of playing this particular symphony in the highly unusual key of F sharp minor (it remains the only example in the entire history of the genre). Like those of no. 39 and no. 44 the finale is intensely atmospheric. The movement seems to be moving towards its appointed close when it is deflected in a manner that would have suggested to the musical prince that something important was to ensue: the music turns to the major key and to a slow tempo for an extended section of luxurious orchestration and warm lyricism. Throughout the 1760s Haydn had often characterized his symphonies with concertante solo writing. Here it is put to a novel purpose, as each solo heralds the disappearance of that instrument from the fabric of the music, until only two violins are left, emphasized – and there is no reason to doubt the anecdote – by the appropriate player (or players) blowing out the candle on the music stand, getting up and leaving the music room. The first to go were Zacharias Pohl, the one-eyed oboist, and Johann May (horn); next was Johannes Hinterberger the bassoon player, followed by Carl Chorus (oboe) and Joseph Dietzl (horn); a longer, inevitably lugubrious solo heralded the departure of the double-bass player, Carl Schiringer; the cello player Xavier Marteau was followed, in turn, by Carl Franz, Joseph Oliva and Franz Pauer (violins), and Christian Specht (viola). Two muted violins only, played by Tomasini and Haydn, were left to conclude the symphony in the increasing gloom, *pianissimo*. Prince Nicolaus, who would have marvelled at the masterly control of unwinding tension as well as the theatre, understood its purpose immediately. He walked to the anteroom where Haydn and his players had assembled and announced that they would be returning to Eisenstadt the following day.[9] Haydn's masterly evocation of the likely consequences of disaffection, combined with the inherent sense of resolution that is achieved in the music, had had the desired effect. Long absences away from the family remained a running sore, however, partly ameliorated in 1775 when the prince provided an additional allowance of 50 gulden per annum per musician (about a sixth of the salary of most players), but only fully resolved when the musicians' quarters were enlarged to accommodate wives and children.

The summer after the 'Farewell' symphony, 1773, was a more active one for Haydn and his musicians in Eszterháza. For the name day in July of Princess Maria Anna, the widow of Paul Anton, a new Italian comic opera, *L'infedeltà delusa*, was commissioned from Haydn, his first for three years. The marionette theatre was finally ready, smaller than the main theatre and built in the fashionable form of a rococo grotto. Its completion along with that of the Chinese Ballroom was hastened by news that later in the summer Empress Maria Theresia would be paying a state visit to Eszterháza. Musical entertainment beyond the normal routine was an occasional highlight of life in Eszterháza and Haydn and his musicians had previously participated in the celebrations associated with the wedding of Countess Lemberg and Count Pocci and the visit of Prince Louis de Rohan, the colourful French envoy at the imperial court; this state visit was to be particularly lavish, and steeped in cultural and political meaning.

As Queen of Hungary, Maria Theresia had always displayed sensitivity to that part of the Habsburg dominions, recognizing its identity while simultaneously cultivating its loyalty. A new public holiday, 20 August, was proclaimed in honour of Stephen I, the founder of the Hungarian kingdom, she encouraged the administrative development of Buda and Pest alongside that of the capital Pressburg, promoted a tolerant attitude amongst the aristocracy to any peasant unrest, and rewarded their loyalty with titles and honours. State visits to the palaces of the leading members of the Hungarian aristocracy were a further way of demonstrating and nurturing an identity that was both Hungarian and Habsburg. She had paid formal visits to the Esterházy court before, in 1754 (during the reign of Paul Anton) and in 1770, on both occasions to the small summer palace of Kittsee. Eszterháza, deep in the Hungarian countryside and newly civilized by Prince Nicolaus, captain of the Hungarian Guard and the most loyal and influential of aristocrats, was much more significant. Haydn and his music played a prominent part in this display of munificence and loyalty.

To prepare for the visit Haydn spent three days in Vienna in August 1773, though particular details are not known. Archduchess Marie Christine and her husband Prince Albert of Sachsen-Teschen (governor of the Austrian Netherlands) arrived at Eszterháza on 31 August so that they could be part of the welcoming party the following day. On 1 September Prince Nicolaus rode on horseback to the nearby town of Ödenburg (Sopron) to escort the imperial party. At about 10.30 Maria Theresia, Queen of Hungary, arrived at Eszterháza accompanied by three of her children, Archduchess Maria Anna, Archduchess Marie Elisabeth and Archduke Maximilian; their official greeting by Prince Albert and Marie Christine was witnessed by a gathering of leading members of the Hungarian aristocracy. Late in the afternoon a formal walk and drive in the gardens preceded a visit to the opera house, where Haydn's newest Italian opera, L'infedeltà delusa, by now well rehearsed, was given. The assembled guests and their entourages numbered over three hundred and everyone was given a copy of the libretto; copies for the imperial family were printed on damask silk and a further fifty were printed on gold brocade paper. Described as a 'burletta per musica' the opera offered straightforward comic entertainment with no allegorical content. After the opera the guests moved to the Chinese Ballroom for a masked ball, the music provided by the Kapellmeister and his colleagues, all dressed in Chinese costume. An enthusiastic dancer in her youth, in her mid-fifties Maria Theresia preferred to witness the colourful event from a raised dais; she stayed for one and a half hours, others stayed until 5.30 in the morning.

A formal lunch on 2 September combined the meal with a lengthy parade of guests presenting their compliments, all accompanied by Tafelmusik, almost certainly including one or more symphonies by Haydn. The so-called 'Maria Theresia' symphony (no. 48) had been composed c.1768, and may have gained its nickname as a result of this occasion. There was a walk in the gardens in the late afternoon that preceded a visit to the marionette theatre. Haydn and his colleagues were on duty again, presenting the first performance of his first marionette opera, Philemon und Baucis. It is a fable of moral example and enlightenment as two gods, Jupiter and Mercury, leave Olympus, travel to earth in disguise, and are given shelter by Philemon and Baucis, who are mourning the death of their son, Aret, and his beloved, Narcisa. Moved by their plight the gods bring the two lovers back to life, before returning to Olympus. As the gods departed, the allegory was made explicit: the Habsburg coat of arms was presented on stage surrounded by figures representing glory, clemency, justice and valour, and the Hungarian nation, that is marionettes clothed in native costume, moved towards it with all the humility and loyalty that inanimate puppets could muster. During the final chorus (Haydn's music is unfortunately lost) a figure representing happiness clasped the coat of arms with one hand and showered beneficence on the Hungarian people with the other.

A public dinner followed that led to the final, climactic event, a spectacular fireworks display in the garden that went on for hours, strategically interrupted by a display that showed the Hungarian coat of arms above the letters VMT (Vivat Maria Theresia), illuminated pictures after Van Dyck and local peasants singing and playing indigenous music, a noisy and unending extravaganza that involved several thousand participants. Some of the festivities, now in an uncoordinated manner, were still going on when the imperial party left Eszterháza at 10.00 on 3 September.

Haydn remembered two things about the visit. He was presented to Maria Theresia and, as well as thanking her for the gift of a snuffbox (the common currency of largesse), related the story of how as a young boy he had been caught clambering scaffolding at Schönbrunn and been given a thrashing on the express orders of the empress. The second memory, also particular, points to a rarely documented part of Haydn's life in any period, recreation. He liked to shoot on foot and at one of the meals during the state visit the empress was served three hazel hens that the Kapellmeister had recently shot while out with the court huntsmen. So proficient was the Kapellmeister as a huntsman that local Croats coined the phrase: 'To je lovac-ribar kao Haydn' ('He is a hunter-fisher like Haydn').

A week before the visit of Maria Theresia to Eszterháza, Franz Novotni, the organist of the small church ensemble based in Eisenstadt, died unexpectedly a few months before his thirtieth birthday. That ensemble was never a priority for Prince Nicolaus and it took the court until December to sort out the vacancy. There were two candidates. The first was Simon Kölbel, born in Eisenstadt, a former pupil of Werner, a composer, someone who enjoyed the patronage of Prince Lobkowitz and Countess Zinzendorf, and was already known to the court as a teacher of the favoured page, the dwarf Johann Sidler; for the last six years he had been the organist in the Augustinian monastery of St Dorothea in Vienna and was anxious to return to his home town. The other was Johann Georg Fuchs, who for fourteen years had been schoolmaster and organist in Forchtenau, a village to the south-west of

Eisenstadt and part of the Esterházy estates. Haydn was asked to audition the two. According to Rahier's subsequent report to the prince, the Kapellmeister found Kölbel not competent enough, Fuchs even less so; he was also worried that neither candidate could play other instruments (Kölbel, in fact, was a violinist and double-bass player) and doubted Kölbel's sincerity since he had indicated that he could earn more in Vienna than in Eisenstadt. Clearly Haydn had ulterior motives. He wanted the job himself and having first besmirched both candidates made the clever proposal that the court schoolmaster in Eisenstadt, Joseph Dietzl, should play the organ in the summer when, presumably, his teaching duties were less demanding and Haydn was in Eszterháza, and that Haydn should play in the winter months when he was in Eisenstadt and Dietzl was busy teaching; Dietzl was to receive the salary, Haydn was to receive the victuals that went with the job. The prince agreed, but he was at least as wily as his Kapellmeister and added the stipulation that Dietzl should play in the winter too if Haydn was not available.

Why did Haydn manoeuvre himself into a job that only added to his already busy schedule and which, moreover, was not one in which the prince was particularly interested? The motives were twofold. The victuals were useful, wheat, rye, lentils, barley, millet, beef, salt, grits, candles, wine, cabbage, turnips and firewood, amounting to a year's allowance for six months' work. Haydn's wife was alleged to be a spendthrift and these victuals, unlike money, could not be used for any other purpose. If Maria Anna was a spendthrift then Haydn was certainly frugal and this arrangement appealed to that aspect of his personality. There was also a genuine attraction to the job, an unpressurized post away from the scrutiny of the prince, one in which Haydn the devout Catholic rather than Haydn the Kapellmeister could play the organ surrounded by a handful of like-minded colleagues, precisely the circumstances that had characterized the first performance of the Salve regina in G minor two years earlier.

Haydn was able to undertake these spiritually rewarding duties immediately and, apart from one visit to Vienna, remained in Eisenstadt until early May 1774. Even though the prince was to be largely absent from Eszterháza that summer, a full programme of entertainment was given. The visiting theatrical troupe gave performances of over a dozen works including Shakespeare's *King Lear*, *Macbeth* and *Othello*, bowdlerized and drawing maximum melodramatic impact from the many scenes of violence and horror. Haydn provided incidental music for some of these plays but it is in the nature of such music that it was easily lost; the only example to have survived is that to Jean-François Regnard's play *Le distrait*, which Haydn converted into a symphony (no. 60), though other symphonies from this time may well contain recycled theatre music. The marionette theatre remained popular with one performance per week and, again, Haydn would have directed the music. At the main opera house four works are known to have been performed, Haydn's *Acide*, *La canterina* and *L'infedeltà delusa* plus, unusually, a work by an outside composer, Piccinni's *La contadina in corte*. With no new major stage or liturgical work dating from the year, Haydn was able to concentrate on composing symphonies, at least four (nos. 54–7), and maintaining the supply of baryton music.

Towards the end of the year Haydn received a surprise but welcome request from Vienna to compose an oratorio, an entirely new challenge. Under the leadership of Gassmann (1729–74), a musicians' benevolent fund, the Tonkünstler-Societät, had been formed a few years earlier to provide pensions for the widows and orphans of former members. The principal means of raising funds was a pair of concerts on consecutive (or near consecutive) evenings at Christmas and Easter, for which the Viennese musicians gave their services free of charge. Since philanthropy went hand in hand with solidarity, the number of participants in these concerts, even in the early years of the society, was unusually large, over a hundred. As well as being the traditional seasons of Christian charity, Christmas and Easter were chosen because the theatres were closed and their musicians could more easily contribute to the common cause. All the performances to date had taken place in the public theatre near the Kärntner city gate, the Kärntnertortheater, and the chosen composers were mainly establishment figures associated with Vienna, Gassmann and Hasse in 1772, Hasse and Dittersdorf in 1773, and Bonno and Hasse in 1774. Haydn would have been particularly pleased to follow in Hasse's footsteps.

For these public occasions the Tonkünstler-Societät had appropriated the long private tradition in the imperial court of presenting oratorios in Italian, usually drawing on biblical subject matter of a narrative rather than a contemplative nature that allowed composers to create music that drew on the stylistic characteristics of serious opera, a sequence of recitatives and da capo arias plus the occasional duet and chorus. Haydn was presented with a libretto written by Giovanni Gastone Boccherini (brother of Luigi), imperial theatre poet at the time, drawn from the book of Tobit in the Apocrypha; it focuses on the plight of Tobias's blind father, cured by the bold action of his son. Since Haydn was composing the work in Eisenstadt rather than Vienna he used his own singers as soloists rather than ones from the Viennese theatres, who would have been unfamiliar to him. Likewise, for the associated practice of presenting instrumental items in the interval between the two parts of the oratorio, he turned to his Esterházy colleagues; Tomasini played a violin concerto at the first performance, on 2 April 1775, Marteau a cello concerto at the second performance two days later. Haydn directed the forces from the harpsichord. The performances were a great success and the court newspaper, the *Realzeitung*, gave its imprimatur: 'the entire, very numerous public was delighted and Haydn, once again, was the great artist whose works are loved throughout Europe, and in which foreigners find the original genius of a master.'[10] For someone who spent most of his time in Eisenstadt and Eszterháza these remarks were tantamount to official recognition from the imperial court and must have been as unexpected as they were gratifying.

By the end of April Haydn was back in Eszterháza. Even though the prince was absent for most of the summer, visiting estates in Poland, the visiting theatrical troupe was once more engaged and the marionette theatre was in operation. But unlike 1774 it was not to be a summer of comparative routine. Another imperial visit was planned for the end of August, by Archduke Ferdinand, and Haydn was expected to provide a new opera, his second large-scale work of the year, L'incontro improvviso. The subject matter was the highly fashionable one of an indulgent peep at the strange world of the Orient, heightened as always in *dramma giocoso* by being viewed through the eyes of clearly differentiated social classes, a prince and princess, a servant, a slave, the sultan and his harem. The text was based on one of Gluck's most popular French operas, *La recontre imprévue* (1764), and was probably chosen by the prince himself. Aged only twenty-one, Archduke Ferdinand had been the Habsburg governor in Lombardy for five years and had married Maria Beatrice d'Este, the occasion of the first performance of Mozart's *festa teatrale*, *Ascanio in Alba*. An escapist comedy in Italian, based on a work he probably already knew, and performed in a summer palace away from Milan and Vienna was the ideal entertainment for a young man.

Haydn's opera was performed on the second night of a four-day visit, from 28 August to 1 September. Certain aspects of the entertainment followed the pattern of the visit in 1773 by Ferdinand's mother, sisters and brother: banquets, a marionette opera (a work by Ordonez, *Alceste*, directed by Haydn), a theatre performance of Regnard's *Le distrait* (with Haydn's music), guided walks in the park, a masked ball and fireworks. But throughout there was due attention to the more relaxed protocol appropriate to an archduke and some indication, beyond Haydn's opera, of entertainment that was suited to a young man. There was a deer hunt, which the archduke might have expected, but more imaginative was a mock village fair with a commedia dell'arte theatre, peasant music, a dentist who menacingly approached his victims on stilts, a singer who held up paintings of gruesome scenes while singing equally gruesome songs, and a pedlar who arrived on a cart drawn by monkeys, lions and tigers.

Although there was, almost certainly, more than one performance of L'incontro improvviso in 1775 it was an opera that was never revived at the Esterházy court, despite its fashionable 'Turkish' ambience. The prince would not have been bothered by its inordinate length, though he may well have thought that his Kapellmeister did not quite have the theatrical slickness of leading composers of Italian comic opera such as Anfossi, Paisiello and Piccinni. Haydn was too valuable and central a figure at the Esterházy court to send him to Italy to rectify this weakness; at the same there was a fully functioning opera house at Eszterháza that was underused. Rather than sending the Kapellmeister to Italy he may well have thought it would be more beneficial, and generally entertaining, to do the reverse, bring Italian opera to Eszterháza. From 1776 the theatre became a full-time opera house with a schedule that soon rivalled any private or public opera house in Europe and with Haydn as its de facto music director. The Kapellmeister had spent fifteen years at the court, during which opera had assumed an ever more substantial part of his duties. For the next fourteen years, until 1790, it was to be central.

Images of Haydn: 1776

Letter by Haydn addressed to Mademoiselle Leonore. D. Bartha (ed.), *Joseph Haydn: Gesammelte Briefe und Aufzeichnungen* (Kassel, 1976), pp. 76–8; H. C. Robbins Landon, *Haydn: Chronicle and Works.* [vol. 2]: *Haydn at Eszterháza* (London, 1978), pp. 397–9.

Estoras, 6 July 1776

Mademoiselle!

You will not take it amiss if I hand you a hotchpotch of all sorts of things as an answer to your request; to describe such things properly takes time, and that I don't have; for this reason, I do not dare write to Mons. Zoller personally, and therefore ask for forgiveness.

I send only a rough draft, for neither pride, nor fame, but solely the great kindness and marked satisfaction that so learned a national institution has shown towards my previous compositions, have induced me to comply with their demand.

I was born on the last day of March 1733 in the market town of Rohrau, Lower Austria, near Bruck-an-der-Leitha. My late father was a wheelwright by trade, served Count Harrach, and was by instinct a great lover of music. He played the harp without knowing a note of music, and as a boy of five I correctly sang all his simple little pieces; this led my father to entrust me to the care of my relative, the schoolmaster in Hainburg, in order that I might learn the foundations of music as well as other youthful necessities. Almighty God (to whom alone I owe the most profound gratitude) endowed me, especially in music, with such proficiency that even in my sixth year

I was able to sing some masses with the choir, and to play a little on the harpsichord and violin.

In my seventh year the late Kapellmeister von Reutter passed through Hainburg and quite accidentally heard my weak but pleasant voice. He immediately took me to the Capellhaus where, apart from my studies, I learnt the art of singing, the harpsichord and the violin from very good masters. Until my eighteenth year I sang soprano with great success, not only at St Stephen's but also at court. Finally I lost my voice, and then had to eke out a wretched existence for eight whole years, by teaching young pupils (NB: many geniuses are ruined by having to earn their daily bread because they have no time to study): I experienced this, unfortunately, and would have never learnt what little I did had I not, in my zeal for composition, composed well into the night; I wrote diligently but not quite correctly until, finally, I had the good fortune to learn the true fundamentals of composition from the celebrated Herr Porpora (who was at that time in Vienna); eventually, by the recommendation of the late Herr von Fürnberg (from whom I received many marks of favour), I was engaged as Director at Herr Count von Morzin's, and from there as Kapellmeister of His Highness the Prince, in whose service I wish to live and die.

Amongst others of my works the following have received the most approbation:

The operas	*Le pescatrici*
	L'incontro improviso
	L'infedeltà delusa, performed in the presence of Her Imperial-Royal Majesty.
The oratorio	*Il ritorno di Tobia*, performed in Vienna
The Stabat mater	about which I received, through a good friend, a testimonial from our good great composer Hasse, containing quite undeserved eulogiums. I shall treasure this testimonial all my life, as if it were gold; not for its contents, but for the sake of such an admirable a man.

In the chamber style I have been fortunate enough to please almost all nations except the Berliners; this is shown by the public newspapers, and in the letters addressed to me. I wonder only that the

Berlin gentlemen, who are otherwise so sensible, have no balance in their criticism of my music, for in one weekly paper they praise me to the skies, whilst in another they dash me sixty fathoms deep into the earth, and this without explaining why; I know very well why: because they are incapable of performing some of my works, and are too conceited to take the trouble to understand them properly, and for other reasons which, with God's help, I will answer in good time. Herr Kapellmeister von Dittersdorf in Silesia wrote to me recently and asked me to defend myself against their harsh ways, but I answered that one swallow doesn't make a summer; perhaps one of these days some unprejudiced person will shut their mouths, as happened to them once before when they accused me of monotony. Despite this, they try very hard to get all my works, as Herr Baron van Swieten, the Imperial-Royal ambassador at Berlin, told me only last winter, when he was in Vienna: but enough of this.

Dear Mademoiselle Leonore: You will be good enough to give this present letter, and my compliments to Monz. Zoller for his consideration: my greatest ambition is simply the following, that all the world regards me as the honest man that I am.

I offer all my praises to Almighty God, for I owe them to Him alone: my sole wish is to offend neither my neighbour, nor my gracious Prince, nor above all our merciful God.

> Meanwhile I remain, Mademoiselle, with high esteem,
> Your most sincere friend and servant
> Josephus Haydn.

This autobiographical draft, dating from 1776, is the only occasion when Haydn wrote at length about his life and outlook as a composer. It is particularly valuable since it gives a picture of the composer in his mid-forties, whereas references to this period in the biographies of Griesinger and Dies are not only filtered through the respective authors but reflect Haydn's recollection of events that had happened several decades earlier. Here there is a seriousness of purpose coupled with an absence of the anecdotal that give it a different flavour.

He had been asked to provide the material for a volume entitled *Das gelehrte Oesterreich*, prepared by Ignaz de Luca, effectively a short dictionary of national biography that appeared between 1776 and 1778. De Luca (1746–99) was a political scientist who had studied at the university of Vienna and from 1771 worked at the Lyceum in Linz, before returning to Vienna in 1783–4. A prolific author of essays on government administration, politics, statistics, literature and geography, he was a valued servant of the Habsburg dynasty. This sense of loyalty is evident in the preface to Das gelehrte Oesterreich, headed 'Dem Vaterlande gewidmet' (Dedicated to the Fatherland), where he bemoans the fact that in comparison with many European countries, notably France and England, Austria has not managed to create a national identity through its authors. The dictionary was intended to list intellectual achievement in order to promote a sense of Austrian nationhood. Its reach was a wide one, including lawyers, doctors, teachers, priests and translators as well as artists, authors and musicians. At the same time it is rather haphazard, both in who is included and the relative length of entries. The musical coverage is particularly erratic. Gluck is included but not Hasse; two composers at the Habsburg court have entries, Salieri and Steffan, but not Bonno, the Kapellmeister; Franz Dussek and Johann Antonin Kozeluch, who worked in Prague, have very brief entries yet Dittersdorf, now in Johannisberg in Silesia, is absent; and one of the longest musical entries is that devoted to the blind Wunderkind, Marie Therese Paradies. The absence of Mozart, a successful composer at the age of twenty, is to be expected, however; he was a citizen of the ecclesiastical principality of Salzburg that belonged to the Holy Roman Empire rather than to de Luca's Austria.

De Luca was obviously dependent on acquaintances and friends of friends to submit material and the fact that the Haydn entry turned out to be the largest for any musician was an accident rather than a matter of editorial judgement. Haydn forwarded his material to Mademoiselle Leonore, who was known in Esterházy circles, who then sent it to the man named by Haydn in the first paragraph as Zoller, who evidently worked for de Luca but is otherwise unknown. Haydn's draft was reworked to make it suitable for a dictionary, preserving the factual content but also devitalizing the human being who had supplied it.

Apart from the fact that Haydn believed that he was a year younger than he was, the account of his early years is unremarkable, from Rohrau, to Hainburg, to Vienna. Porpora is given priority over other formative teachers such as Franck and Reutter, crediting him with imparting 'the true fundamentals of composition'. When it comes to his own compositions Haydn is particularly proud of five major works composed in the previous nine years, three operas, an oratorio and the Stabat mater, the last receiving the cherished approval of Hasse. None of these works is part of the modern standard repertoire and, indeed, only the oratorio and the Stabat mater achieved widespread distribution in Haydn's lifetime; the three operas were never performed outside Eszterháza. As well as pride in the composition of large-scale works, Haydn is reflecting contemporary attitudes to composition: Italian opera and oratorio formed the currency of excellence and Haydn wished to be judged by these standards. Instrumental music in the middle decades of the century did not have that sense of status and while, as the following paragraph indicates, Haydn's instrumental music had already circulated beyond Austria, his ambitions in the middle 1770s were ones that were firmly in keeping with the times. He may have wished to become another Hasse, even though he was composing a good deal of music, particularly quartets and symphonies, of a kind that Hasse never composed. It was to take a further ten years or so for Haydn even to begin to realize that he had set a historical process in motion as a pre-eminent composer of instrumental music.

In the mid-1770s the relative value of vocal and instrumental music was made additionally difficult for Haydn because his instrumental music – he uses the phrase 'in the chamber style' – was receiving a mixed response, a situation that angered as well as perplexed him. The musical press was an active one in northern Germany, the 'Berliners', and had frequently criticized Haydn's quartets and symphonies for their lack of seriousness, highlighting in particular his fondness for presenting melodies in octaves, like 'father and son begging' as one commentator put it. It was because of this critical ambivalence as well as the more general status of instrumental music that Haydn did not list a single symphony or quartet. This three-way tension between achievement, ambition and expectation clearly exercised Haydn, even if he also pretended to rise above it.

Other aspects of his personality that emerge in this document may appear complacent, even naïve. Modesty, piety and a sense of duty run right through it, qualities that are all too easy to appropriate for a genial, unsophisticated view of the composer and which seem out of step with more progressive thinking in the Age of Enlightenment. But for Haydn these were real strengths, a reflection of the society in which he had grown up where social mores, political loyalties and religious belief merged imperceptibly. That society had already coined a term for this outlook, *pietas Austriaca*, Austrian piety, a clear national identity. When Haydn indicates that he wishes 'to live and die' in the service of the prince and, in the penultimate paragraph, praises Almighty God and seeks forgiveness if he has offended his neighbour, his prince or his God, these were sentiments of someone who personified *pietas Austriaca*. In that sense he clearly belonged to a volume that aimed to project a national consciousness.

3 Italian opera at Eszterháza

In 1776 Haydn was in Eszterháza as early as January rehearsing Gluck's *Orfeo ed Euridice*, the first work given as part of the new plan for an extended season of opera. In the damp and cold climate of winter he would have made the short walk from his flat in the musicians' house to the opera house several times a day. As a building in the Classical style the opera house had uneven proportions, 60 feet wide but 200 feet long, its elongated structure determined by practicalities, but with its width cleverly stretched by ornamental gates on either side. From the foyer, two balancing staircases on either side led to the large oval box on the first floor where the prince and his principal guests viewed the stage head on and, in the typical manner of eighteenth-century theatre, at a distance that placed them in a perfect, balancing perspective. Adjacent to the box were several lavishly furnished rooms that could be used before, after, and even during the performance for relaxation, dining and billiards. Two further boxes were placed closer to the stage, right and left, and were reached by flights of open stairs from the adjacent gardens. Principal guests in the first-floor boxes sat on individual chairs. On the ground floor, however, guests sat on long pews, eleven rows in all, separated by a wide aisle and with some standing room at the back. Altogether, as the report on the visit of Empress Maria Theresia in 1773 suggests, the theatre could hold some 400 people, though in practice performances must often have been given in front of a relatively small number of people. In public opera houses of the time audience members often came and went as they pleased, sampling the opera rather than listening to a complete dramatic experience. At Eszterháza that practice might have been compromised by deference to the prince; if he stayed, so did everybody else, and since Nicolaus is known to have enjoyed even the most prolix of operas, some audience members might well have felt trapped. It would be a mistake, however, to regard the opera house as being for the sole benefit of the prince; performances were planned in advance, continued when Nicolaus was away from Eszterháza and were regarded by the many people who were employed by the court – actors, architects, gardeners, guards, officers, servants and so on – as their entertainment too.

Aristocrat and servant alike looked towards a notably large stage, approximately 40 feet wide and 60 feet deep; the depth was responsible for the narrow nature of the building as a whole and to enable the audience to view the action at the back of the stage it was gently raked. The wings contained six (possibly eight) sets of flats on castors, each one housing up to four changes of scenery. Since many operas featured stock scenes, such as a garden, a cave, a domestic interior or a baronial hall, sets were normally reused rather than devised for each new production. Beneficent gods, chariots and clouds were lowered from the flies and evil spirits could disappear through trapdoors.

The orchestra was on the same level as the auditorium, the players sitting on both sides of a long music desk that ran the width of the auditorium. Seated at the end playing the continuo Haydn had a good view of the stage to his left, his players in front of him (Tomasini in particular), the audience to his right and, if he glanced upwards and further to his right, the prince in his box. Spirit lamps rather than candles provided most of the light in the auditorium and on stage, deflected as necessary by mirrors. In the autumn and winter months, everybody's comfort was ensured by eight large stoves, some of which were placed in the basement so that the heat could rise through grilles into the auditorium. Near the stage, for maximum accessibility, was the store cupboard for the music, yet another library that Haydn was expected to keep in order. Changing rooms for the singers were underneath the stage and costumes were housed in a large room behind it. Unlike the scenery, costumes were more likely to be designed for individual operas (and singers), though there is evidence that some costumes, too, were reused. Adjoining the opera house was the Chinese Ballroom (the Bagatelle), a dance floor overlooked by a gallery. A heating stove in the building caused a major fire in 1779 that could have brought operatic life at Eszterháza to an end, only four seasons after it had become a permanent feature of court life.

The year 1779 had been a long operatic season for Haydn, beginning in March with two comic operas by Paisiello and Astarita, *Le due contesse* and *I visionari* respectively, continuing with the first performance of his own *La vera costanza*, and followed by no fewer than seven further first performances of works by Anfossi, Franchi, Gazzaniga, Naumann, Piccinni and Sarti. Haydn and his musicians were still at Eszterháza in November, preparing for the musical entertainment that was to feature in the celebrations associated with the wedding of Count Antal Forgách and Countess Grassalkovics. The Chinese Ballroom was to be used and a few days before the event staff began to heat the room. As well as the customary large stoves built for the purpose they mistakenly used two Chinese stoves that were intended for decorative purposes only. At 3.30 in the morning of 18 November one of the Chinese stoves exploded, the richly varnished ballroom caught fire and the flames spread quickly to the adjoining opera house. Despite the wet weather the fire was a fierce one that destroyed the building and much of its content, the costumes, several orchestral instruments (including Tomasini's violin), the harpsichord that Haydn played and most of the operatic library.

The wedding went ahead as planned on 21 November with the performance of Felici's *L'amore soldato* transferred from the opera house to the more cramped surroundings of the marionette theatre. Apart from ensuring that the wedding went ahead the prince issued an immediate instruction that the main opera house should be rebuilt and on 18 December, a month to the day of the fire, the foundation stone to the new theatre was laid. An absurdly ambitious date of 15 October 1780 was set for the reopening of the theatre, a date that proved impossible despite the valiant efforts of architects and builders; it finally opened on 25 February 1781 when Haydn's La fedeltà premiata was given for the first time. In the interim the stage of the marionette theatre had been enlarged a little so that a normal season of Italian opera could take place in 1780, ninety-three performances of eight works: four new operas (two by Anfossi, one each by Gazzaniga and Salieri) and four revivals (Felici, Gassmann, Haydn and Sarti).

One of the uncertain aspects of operatic life at Eszterháza is who chose the operas that were to be performed. The wider European practice in commercial theatres was for the impresario, sometimes with the guidance of a resident librettist, to make the choice. Philip Georg Bader was Director of the Theatres at Eszterháza for one year, in 1778–9, but his duties were organizational rather than entrepreneurial. Another figure, Nunziato Porta, held the title of Opera Director between 1781 and 1790 and exerted a strong guiding influence on the repertoire since he was also an experienced, if not particularly gifted librettist who had recently worked in Prague. Haydn's role in choosing the repertoire was probably minimal, not only because it was unusual for composers to get involved in such matters but because his own knowledge of the wider repertoire was a limited one. The prince certainly had the final say and may well on occasions have had the first say too. The choice of repertoire for the very first season, 1776, was certainly that of a connoisseur.

In a manner that was clearly intended to make a statement about operatic ambition, the season featured two operas that were admired throughout Europe, Gluck's Orfeo and Piccinni's La buona figliuola, one serious (an azione teatrale), one comic (a dramma giocoso). Since their first performances in, respectively, Vienna in 1762 and Rome in 1760, these two works had set the agenda for the continuing development of serious and comic opera. For the new venture at Eszterháza both the prince and, after him, Haydn would have been aware of the significance of presenting such works in the very first season of a permanent company.

Four further works were given in 1776. Sacchini's *dramma giocoso*, *L'isola d'amore*, had been given its premiere in Rome in 1766 before being heard in several other Italian cities and, in 1769, in Vienna, though what motivated the prince to choose or sanction its performance at Eszterháza in 1776 is unclear; later, many people at Eszterháza would have remembered the work not for its particular merits but because Barbara Dichtler, who had served as a singer at the Esterházy court since 1757, died on stage during a performance. Alongside these works were three comic operas composed by Haydn's old friend Dittersdorf for performance in the courts of Grosswardein and Johannisberg. Always a lively promoter of his own music Dittersdorf had written directly to the prince offering the works; as well as Haydn's friendship he would have been able to evoke that of the tenor Vito Ungricht who had worked with him in Grosswardein and Johannisberg and who had just joined the musical retinue at Eszterháza.

If fashion and opportunism had characterized the first full season of Italian opera at Eszterháza, the following one saw the emergence of other characteristics. Five new works were presented, Dittersdorf's *L'Arcifanfano*, Gassmann's *L'amore artigiano*, Haydn's *Il mondo della luna* and Paisiello's *Il marchese villano* and *La frascatana*, and two operas, Dittersdorf's *Il barone di rocca antica* and Sacchini's *L'isola d'amore*, were revived from the previous season. With this mixture of the old and the new a company repertory was being formed, one that became much more familiar to the Eszterháza audience than would have been the case in public theatres of the time since the membership of that audience was overwhelmingly the same from evening to evening; alongside the novelty of the new there was the comfort of the familiar. Within the repertoire there was another consistency, a predominance of comic works, more specifically of *dramma giocoso* with its delineated character types, contemporary setting, mocking of social conventions and light moralizing, all of which was preferred to the self-regarding, sometimes very laboured progress of serious opera. Rather than glorifying a prince, this was court opera that expressed wider Enlightenment values with verve and naturalness.

While the unfortunate destruction in the 1779 fire of many of the musical sources (scores, vocal and orchestral parts) for the works performed in the first four seasons makes it impossible to assess the working practices of Haydn as a music director in this period, the relationship between the Eszterháza repertory and that evident in Vienna is an interesting one. The vast majority of the new works performed at Eszterháza, over three-quarters of them, had previously been performed in Vienna in the 1760s and 1770s. However, it would be misleading to state that the Esterházy court was politely copying Habsburg taste. In fact the opposite was true. Comic Italian opera had been regularly performed at the court theatre in Vienna through to 1776 when Joseph II decided not to renew the contract of the Italian company in order to give preference to developing opera in the German language, which dominated the repertoire until 1783. At a time when Vienna was being force-fed a diet of German opera, Eszterháza continued to offer Italian opera, including many works that had previously been successfully performed in Vienna. Joseph II's strategically managed development of opera in the German language was never to be replicated in Eszterháza, where the German language continued to be associated with the unambitious offerings of the marionette theatre. This divergent policy ensured that Mozart's *Die Entführung aus dem Serail*, the composer's most frequently performed opera in his lifetime, was never performed at Eszterháza, however much Haydn may have admired the work.

Between 1777 and 1781 Haydn composed three operas of his own, *Il mondo della luna* (first performed in August 1777), *La vera costanza* (April 1779) and *La fedeltà premiata* (February 1781), all of which reflect the prevailing, wider characteristics of the repertoire at Eszterháza. They are all *dramma giocoso* works based on pre-existing librettos, fitting in perfectly with similar operas by Anfossi, Paisiello, Piccinni and others. Haydn's library contained several volumes from a complete printed edition of Goldoni's comedies and for the third and last time in his career Haydn turned to that author for the text of a *dramma giocoso*, *Il mondo della luna*. Although it had been previously set by four composers, Avandano, Astarita, Galuppi and Paisiello, none of these had been performed in Vienna and one senses that Haydn was shrewdly attempting to carve out a separate identity for himself and for Eszterháza. If so, it didn't work. It was never revived.

The choice of text for the next opera, *La vera costanza*, was more problematic since a setting by Anfossi, first performed in Rome in 1776, had been performed in Vienna in January 1777, inviting comparison of a kind that Haydn otherwise tried to avoid for his own operas. There is also an inexplicable mystery about the origins of the work. Dies claimed that the opera was commissioned by the Viennese court but that a squabble about the allocation of roles led Haydn to withdraw the work; it was then given its first performance at Eszterháza. Given that the Viennese court did not have an Italian opera company after the spring of 1777 the commission, if true, must have taken place earlier and may have reflected the *succès d'estime* that Haydn had achieved with his oratorio *Il ritorno di Tobia* in Vienna in 1775. A murky story is further complicated by the fact that the surviving music for Haydn's *La vera costanza* dates from 1785, rewritten because the original music had been lost in the 1779 fire. This surviving version includes music from the Anfossi setting, almost certainly a convenience in 1785 that Haydn would not have risked in the original version.

Haydn's third *dramma giocoso*, *La fedeltà premiata*, returns to the principle of choosing a libretto that was unknown in Vienna. It was taken from a recent opera by Cimarosa called *L'infedeltà fedele*, first performed in Naples in 1779. Just turned thirty Cimarosa (1749–1801) was a new composer for Haydn and almost certainly the score was acquired with a view to presenting it at Eszterháza. Perhaps captured by its attractive presentation of *dramma giocoso* characters in a pastoral rather the normal contemporary setting, Haydn decided to set the libretto himself, changing the title to *La fedeltà premiata* to avoid confusion with his own earlier opera *L'infedeltà delusa*.

La fedeltà premiata opened the 1781 season in the newly rebuilt theatre; in that season sixty-nine performances were given of ten operas, six of them premieres. As part of this new energy an Italian named

Nunziato Porta arrived at the court in the summer. He was to have a marked influence on the development of opera at Eszterháza for the next nine years, until the disbandment of the company in 1790.

Very little of Porta's life before Eszterháza is known, not even his place and date of birth. Surviving copies of opera librettos on which he is named as the author suggest an active career in Italy, especially Venice, but he had worked north of the Alps too, in particular Prague. It was in that city in 1776 that he wrote a libretto on the Don Giovanni story set by Righini, *Il convitato di pietra ossia Il dissoluto*, and it was this work that inaugurated Porta's association with Eszterháza in July 1781. His annual stipend of 150 gulden, plus some firewood and candles, was considerably less than most of the singers and instrumentalists whose professional lives he virtually governed. One has the sense that Porta's career as a librettist was not a particularly flourishing one and that he grasped the opportunity of sustained employment at Eszterháza.

Unlike Haydn, however, Porta had a broad experience of the operatic world and was someone who could give an assured direction to the development of opera at the court. Under his guidance the number of operas given in a particular year rose to seventeen in 1786 and was never fewer than ten, more active than many public opera houses of the time. The mix between first performances and revivals varied; in the early 1780s there were more first performances but as the available repertoire expanded once more after the fire, the number of revivals increased towards the end of the 1790s. Typically, the total number of performances per season averaged around 100; if one takes the longest season to be ten months (from February to November) that equates to one performance every three days. The most active, on occasion probably frenetic year was 1786, when 125 performances of 17 different works took place, 8 premieres and 9 revivals.

As well as the number of performances Porta had an impact on the repertoire. It became considerably less dependent on works that had previously been performed in Vienna. For instance in 1786 of the eight premieres only one, Righini's *L'incontro inaspettato* (on a libretto by Porta himself) had previously been performed in Vienna; instead that particular year the repertoire drew heavily on operas recently performed in Milan, works by Cimarosa (*La ballerina amante, Chi dell'alturi si veste presto si spoglia* and *I due baroni di Rocca Azzura*), Sarti (*Idalide*) and Zingarelli (*Alsinda*). Other Italian cities from which Porta drew the repertoire included Florence, Genoa and Venice. The ad hoc policy of reflecting the development of opera in northern Italy and decreasing the dependence on Vienna explains why Mozart's Italian operas are notably absent from the Eszterháza repertoire. It was not until 1790 that plans were made to perform a Mozart opera, *Le nozze di Figaro*, at Eszterháza, following its successful revival the previous year in Vienna; but Prince Nicolaus's death in September and the closure of the opera house caused these plans to be abandoned. But Mozart was not alone. A number of operas from the Viennese repertoire of the 1780s, some extremely popular, were never performed at Eszterháza, including Salieri's *La grotta di Trofonio* and Soler's *Una cosa rara*.

This divergence in repertoire between Eszterháza and Vienna reflected distinctly differing tastes. While in Vienna in the 1780s the Burgtheater continued to offer comic Italian opera, overwhelmingly of the *dramma giocoso* type, under Porta's guidance (and, naturally, with the prince's approval) the repertoire at Eszterháza became more varied, with performances of serious operas too. Beginning in 1783 with Sarti's *Giulio Sabino*, Porta regularly included such operas in the repertoire; in 1786, for instance, three of the eight new operas performed were serious works, Traetta's *Ifigenia in Tauride*, Sarti's *Idalide* and Zingarelli's *Alsinda*. None of these works was performed in Vienna in the 1780s.

Not surprisingly, Haydn's operatic output responded to the changes initiated by Porta. The year 1782 saw the first performance of *Orlando Paladino*, a *dramma giocoso* whose libretto was fashioned by Porta using an earlier version he had prepared of a setting by Guglielmi, performed in Prague in 1775. Haydn's next opera was not another *dramma giocoso*, but a serious opera ('dramma eroico') entitled *Armida*, a tale of conflicting loyalties, duty and love, set at the time of the Crusades

6. March from Act I of *Armida*, mainly in the hand of a copyist but the dynamics and the names of the instruments are in Haydn's hand (1784).

(see Figure 6). Porta took his text from Tozzi's opera *Rinaldo* given in Venice in 1775, amending it a little. Haydn, encouraged by Porta, knew that he was writing something that reflected wider operatic tastes, ones not evident in the Viennese repertoire of the time. On I March 1784 he wrote excitedly to his publisher, Artaria, in Vienna: 'Yesterday my *Armida* was performed for the 2nd time. I'm told that it's my best work to date.'[1] Although *Armida* continued to be performed at Eszterháza Haydn was never to follow up his 'best work to date' with another serious opera for the court, or, indeed, any kind of opera. From the middle of the 1780s Haydn was always conscious and responsive to his fame as a composer of instrumental music and he found it difficult to find the time to devote himself to a new opera, increasingly unnecessary as the repertoire relied more and more on revivals.

If Haydn played an insignificant role in the fashioning of the repertoire in the 1780s his contribution to the development of the company itself, that is the troupe of singers, was crucial. Maintaining the standard of the court singers had always been part of his duties. With the setting up of the permanent company in 1776 and the continually expanding repertoire, this responsibility became a major part of Haydn's working life. It also affected his personal life.

At first the opera company consisted mainly of local, German singers, Haydn's colleagues like Maria Elisabeth Prandtner, Leopold and Barbara Dichtler, Catarina Poschwa and Vito Ungricht who now, *ipso facto*, constituted the opera company. Over the following years there was a deliberate campaign to recruit singers from Italy and reduce the number of German singers. Already by 1779 twelve of the sixteen singers used were from Italy. The longest local survivor was the tenor Leopold Dichtler; only when he stopped singing in 1788 and was given a pension did the company became an entirely Italian one.

The personnel was constantly changing: some singers stayed for one season only, occasionally only part of a season, before moving elsewhere, while others stayed several years. Although the total number of available singers averaged about twelve or thirteen in the 1780s, Haydn and Porta always tried to ensure a core complement of five sopranos, four tenors and one or two basses. For a *dramma giocoso* this was enough to cover the typical disposition of a pair of *parti serie* lovers (soprano and tenor), their equivalent in the buffo camp (soprano and bass) and minor comic roles (sopranos and basses); often some of the more adaptable tenors were required to undertake bass roles. As well as the voice type the capability and dramatic aptitude of the singers were important. There were usually two female and two male singers who could undertake the lead roles in opera seria and the serious roles in *dramma giocoso*; at the other end of the dramatic spectrum there was a need for singers who were comfortable in the comic antics of the *parti buffe*. While there was some migration between groups this basic division was well understood at Eszterháza, as elsewhere. The longest serving 'serious' soprano was Metilde Bologna, wife of Nunziato Porta, who arrived with her husband in 1781 and remained until 1790.

Singers from Italy were paid more than their German equivalents, and certainly more than the orchestral players, but the prince could always save money by employing couples for less money than if they had been engaged as single people. Metilde Bologna arrived with her sister, Maria, on a joint salary and married couples included Maria and Guglielmo Jermoli (soprano and tenor), who worked at the court for a brief period in 1777 and then for a longer one in 1779–81, and Maria and Antonio Specioli (soprano and tenor), who were resident for three years from 1782 to 1785.

With the constant arrival and departure of singers, and the mixing of new productions with the revivals of old ones, making sure that the singers were comfortable with their roles was a major part of Haydn's routine. Occasionally performances had to be postponed or cancelled because of the illness of a singer and the lack of available cover. The performance history of two of Haydn's own operas suggest that he felt that certain works could be performed only by the singers who had first sung them at Eszterháza. The soprano Barbara Ripamonti came to Eszterháza in April 1778, one of the first Italian singers to be engaged. She came with her husband, a violinist, Francesco, and they were given a three-year joint contract worth 1,100 gulden per annum. In the event they stayed only two years but during that time Haydn wrote two leading serious roles for her, Costanza in *L'isola disabitata* and the central, commanding role of Rosina in the *dramma giocoso La vera costanza*. She and her husband left the court in April 1780, shortly after the birth of twins. She returned, without her husband, in 1784 and stayed a further two years. It was during this period that *La vera costanza* was revived; it was never performed when she was not at court. Her other opera, *L'isola disabitata* was never to be revived.

The Italian singer who stayed the longest at Eszterháza was a much more indifferent performer, Luigia Polzelli, who arrived in March 1779 and stayed until the company was disbanded in September 1790. In the late 1770s singers of secondary comic roles at Eszterháza, such as Maria Elisabeth Trever and Anna Zannini, did not tend to stay for long and the details of Polzelli's initial engagement suggest that she, too, was viewed as a short-term appointment. She arrived with her husband, Antonio, a violinist, at the beginning of a season and they were engaged on a joint salary of 465 gulden 40 kreuzer, the lowest in the entire singing establishment. Born in Naples in 1750, the only detail of her career before Eszterháza that is known is her participation in a production of Paisiello's La frascatana in Correggio in 1778. In the first two seasons at Eszterháza she undertook minor roles in comic opera such as the innocent young girl, the loyal servant or the scheming, quick-witted maid. By Christmas 1780 the prince had evidently decided that her time at Eszterháza was up and dismissed her and her husband. Almost immediately the order was rescinded and both were now allowed to stay until further notice. Though details of the dismissals and change of mind are not known it is assumed that Haydn had intervened, as he had occasionally done in the past for favoured colleagues. This time the motive was more personal than musical. Luigia had probably been his mistress for over a year; she was twenty-nine, he was forty-seven.

No portrait of Luigia Polzelli has survived but details of her physical appearance are known from her Italian passport, transcribed by Pohl in the middle of the nineteenth century. She was of average height with a dainty figure, a slender long face, olive skin, dark lively eyes and chestnut-coloured hair. She and her husband already had a son, Pietro, born in Bologna in 1777. A second child, possibly a girl, was born in Eszterháza in 1780 but did not survive; perhaps Haydn was her father. On 22 April 1782 Polzelli's second son was born and it was an open secret that Haydn was the natural father. Almost in comic defiance of the open secret, the son was named after Polzelli's husband, Antonio. Two further sons were born in the 1780s, Luigi Filippo (in 1787) and Gaetano Domenico (1788), both fathered by the husband. Every birth of a child was followed by a period of absence from the stage, something that no doubt irritated the prince but which Haydn willingly accommodated.

Haydn was not the first person to fall for a pretty, vivacious woman, nearly twenty years younger, from a different culture and who shared the concerns and intrigue of his daily life. His own comment, 'My wife was unable to bear children, and I was therefore less indifferent to the charms of other women'[2] seems cruel and illogical but related to the particular circumstances of the affair with Polzelli they have some meaning. The comment has the glib, unserious witticism of an elderly lawyer or a doctor in a *dramma giocoso*, appropriate to the world that Polzelli and Haydn shared from day to day. More particularly, the reference to children is a revealing one. Haydn was fond of the two eldest boys, Pietro even more than Antonio, helped their youthful instruction as musicians and took an interest in their adult careers even when, in the 1790s, the affair with Luigia had become a thing of the past. In the 1780s the Polzelli family provided a companionship that was otherwise entirely missing in Haydn's adult life. Frequently a marriage witness and a godfather, this loving relationship allowed him to experience the emotional charge of family life. For this he was prepared to accommodate Polzelli's limitations as a singer, even when that involved a considerable amount of work.

Haydn's direct contact with a particular new opera began as soon as the manuscript score arrived at Eszterháza, whether from Vienna or north Italy. A quick perusal would reveal whether it was capable of being performed at the court and, occasionally, a work was put to one aside, never to be performed. The next stage was to go through the opera more systematically, adapting it for the circumstances at court, decisions that were motivated by the practical as much as by the aesthetic. Haydn decided who the appropriate singers should be, adding their names to the score. His instincts were to shorten rather than to expand the opera, to omit rather than to add, adding comments like 'can be left out' or simply putting a line through the music. If the opera had a large cast, one or two of the minor roles were omitted, likewise any small-scale ensembles in which they took part. Since Eszterháza did not employ clarinets, trumpets and timpani, these parts had to be redistributed. The few choral numbers that occurred in Italian opera of the time could only be included if they were sung as ensembles. He was impatient with repetitive music, cutting whole paragraphs and changing the tempo from slow to fast; an extreme instance of the latter occurred in Salieri's *La fiera di Venezia*, given in 1782, when the tempo of an aria for a comic character Belfusto (bass) was changed from Andante maestoso to Allegro vivace. More subtly Haydn often added dynamic nuances to the score, mirroring his practice in symphonies where the distinction between *piano* and *pianissimo*, *forte* and *fortissimo* are real ones and extra bite is imparted by *sforzando* accents.

A number of Italian opera composers in the 1770s and 1780s continued to write the occasional aria that was accompanied by strings alone; Haydn always added oboes and horns. Overtures that were in the increasingly dated three-movement format of fast–slow–fast were cut to the more progressive one-movement format and he often simplified excessive vocal coloratura.

Much of this editorial work was done very quickly by annotating the score, though Haydn occasionally had to resort to supplementary musical notation on separate sheets of manuscript paper. The edited musical score was then passed to Johann Schellinger, a resident copyist who, when he was not busy providing the performance material, worked as a stage prompter. He had been engaged on a casual basis as early as 1777, when it became clear that the regular court copyist who worked for Haydn, Joseph Elssler, could not cope with the increasing demands being made by the opera house. Schellinger became a key figure, someone who ensured that the operas, as composed or edited by Haydn, were neatly copied as individual parts for the singers and instrumentalists so that they could be learnt, rehearsed and performed with the minimum of difficulty. The two must have sat side by side or in adjacent rooms in the musicians' house at Eszterháza for days on end, every year, carefully realizing each opera in turn, and sometimes being forced to adjust plans according to changing circumstances. But Schellinger could not always cope with the volume of work and other people were occasionally pressed into service as emergency copyists, including Joseph Elssler, the director Nunziato Porta, the singer Leopold Dichtler, even Haydn himself. Like all professional music copyists of the time Schellinger was paid per unit of paper used, a *Bogen*, which allowed up to eight sides of musical handwriting. At the end of 1786, the busiest year in the history of opera in Eszterháza, Schellinger submitted a detailed bill for his work on twelve named operas; orchestral parts were charged at 5 Kreutzer per *Bogen* and numbered 1,817 *Bogen*; because the Italian text as well as the musical lines (voice and bass) had to be copied the vocal parts were more expensive, 7 Kreutzer per *Bogen* and numbered 1,749. With a total of 3,266 *Bogen* this was equivalent to 26,128 sides which, even allowing for the fact that not all sides were used and that Schellinger subcontracted some of the work, is a staggering figure.

While Schellinger got on with copying the parts from the master score, Haydn occasionally had to devote additional time to the composition of new arias, replacing ones found in the purchased score. Sixteen so-called insertion arias survive by him, composed between 1779 and 1790. Usually the existing text was used, sometimes one was taken from another opera altogether, probably suggested by Porta. In the wider operatic world the usual reason for composing insertion arias was to satisfy a particular singer who felt uncomfortable with the existing aria, either because it was too difficult or not difficult enough. Given his impatience with vapid display it is not surprising that, for Haydn, the latter was never a reason for composing a new aria. A handful of arias exists for tenors and basses, including the composer's long-term colleague, Leopold Dichtler, but most had to be composed for the limited talents of his mistress, Luigia Polzelli, at least five, perhaps as many as ten. She was most comfortable with syllabic settings that avoided decoration, shortish phrases that did not demand sophisticated breathing, a vocal range that did not stray much either side of the stave and with an accompaniment that doubled the voice rather than allowed it to compete with the orchestra. This may have been how Haydn managed to keep Polzelli on stage without revealing her limitations but, conveniently, they were also techniques habitually associated with the musical characterization of the roles allotted to Polzelli, the maids and peasants of comic opera. Clearly musical discretion on stage facilitated private indiscretion off stage.

Between 1776 and 1790 there was hardly a day in Haydn's life that was not, at least in part, taken up with the business of opera. It took three to four months to set up a new production and he was constantly surrounded by manuscript scores, manuscript parts, a director, Porta, who was pushing the repertoire in a new direction, singers who could be difficult and an obliging mistress; works by many of the leading Italian composers of the day from Anfossi to Zingarelli were adapted or revived and, not least, he composed five operas of his own. Singers came and went, the opera house burnt down, performances were given in front of an audience that ranged from the meagre to the hundreds, in front of his fellow courtiers or in front of the cream of aristocratic, occasionally imperial society. It was a busy lifestyle, but it was also a claustrophobic one that occasionally wore the Kapellmeister down.

Despite the immense amount of scholarly work that has been accomplished in the field in the last fifty years, Haydn and the opera house remains stubbornly apart from the orthodox image of the composer in this period. Aggravated by the absence of Haydn's operas from the standard repertory, that image is still dominated by the symphonies, quartets and other instrumental works that he wrote. Documenting the prevalence of opera is a useful jolt; it certainly cannot be ignored.

Even more intriguing within the context of a biography is to ask what effect this period of sustained contact with Italian opera had on Haydn the man. In the narrowest perspective it gave a composer who never had the chance to go to Italy to do the next best thing, immerse himself totally in the operatic fashions and conventions of the day. Eszterháza must have seemed like an Italian enclave at the time and no doubt this was the period during which the composer's knowledge of the language, written and spoken, improved immensely. The wider culture of Italian opera, comic and serious, must have played a formative part in Haydn's personal development too, part of the *Bildung* of the man. Religion never featured in Italian opera and there was nothing here that could alter Haydn's ingrained, traditional piety. Other aspects of contemporary life, however, were played out on stage and may well have led to an increasingly multi-grained personality. In serious opera there was a deference to nobility and an emphasis on virtue and duty, while *dramma giocoso*, on the other hand, showed an interaction of classes, the solution of a problem through guile and wit and the sympathetic celebration of the foibles of humanity. All these qualities must have enhanced Haydn's sensibility. Yet this was only a part of his life in the period.

Nunziano Porta

Luigia Polzelli

Italian opera influencing Haydn's musical personal sensibilities

4 'My misfortune is that I live in the country'

The first five months of 1781 were, as always, very busy ones for Haydn at Eszterháza. After the rebuilt opera house was opened in February with the premiere of *La fedeltà premiata*, there were first performances at the court of Anfossi's *Isabella e Rodrigo* and Paisiello's *L'avaro deluso*; also three operas were revived in this period, Gazzaniga's *La vendemmia*, Salieri's *La scuola de' gelosi* and Sarti's *Le gelosie villane*. In total Haydn directed thirty-three performances before the end of May. At the same time he was amusing himself with a totally different musical challenge, the writing of twelve German songs that were to be published in Vienna by the firm of Artaria. On 27 May Haydn wrote to his publisher: he was worried that he had not responded appropriately to the chosen texts, wanted to make sure that he was properly paid, had a suggestion for the dedication on the title page, Mademoiselle Elizabeth Clair (Prince Nicolaus's mistress) and hoped the collection would appear in readiness for her name day in November. The second half of the letter turns to more general matters.[1]

> Now something from Paris. Monsieur Le Gros, Directeur of the
> Concert Spirituel, wrote to me in the most flattering way about my
> Stabat mater, performed there four times with the greatest
> applause; the gentlemen asked permission to have it engraved. They
> made me an offer to engrave all my future works on the most
> favourable terms for myself, and were most surprised that I was so
> singularly successful in my vocal compositions; but I was not the

least bit surprised, for they have not heard anything yet. If they could only hear my small opera, *L'isola disabitata*, and my most recent, pre-Lenten opera, *La fedeltà premiata*: for I assure you that no such work has been heard in Paris up to now and even perhaps in Vienna; my misfortune is that I live in the country.

I enclose Herr Boccherini's letter; please present my compliments to him. No one here can tell me where this place Arenas is. It cannot be far from Madrid, however; please let me know about this so that I can write to Herr Boccherini myself.

I remain most respectfully,

Your most obedient servant Joseph Haydn

PS Lots of people like the portrait. Return the painting to me in the same case.

Here is a completely different Haydn, a businessman selling his compositions, someone who is in touch with the leading public concert organization in Paris who, moreover, were offering to arrange the publication of future compositions, a composer who had received compliments and greetings from Boccherini (who worked for the Spanish Infante, Don Luis, in Madrid) and a human being who was flattered by the engraved portrait that Artaria had prepared and that was soon to circulate in Vienna. As a man of commerce and a recognized artist with an international reputation these aspects of Haydn's personality contrasted strongly with the dutiful Kapellmeister who worked tirelessly in Eisenstadt and Eszterháza. They were also indicative of the tensions that were to characterize his life and deepen his personality in the 1780s. Already in this letter, written a mere five years after the autobiographical sketch in which Haydn had indicated his 'wish to live and die' in the service of Prince Esterházy, there is some frustration: 'my misfortune is that I live in the country'.

The circumstances that led to these indicative changes are easily traced to the late 1770s. The Esterházy administration was constantly updating its records to reflect not only the arrival of new musicians but also their changing conditions of service. On at least three occasions in the 1770s Haydn was given a new or an amended contract, in 1771,

1775 and 1779, largely confirming minor changes that had already been put into action. In 1771 Haydn was asked to produce his existing contract but could not do so, claiming that he had lost it. No amended contract from that year has survived, or from 1775. The one from 1779 does exist and may well reflect changes enshrined in previous contracts or, at the very least, recognition of some existing practices. In comparison with the fourteen wordy clauses of the contract that Haydn had signed when he first joined the court as Vice Kapellmeister in 1761, the 1779 contract has six short clauses followed by the statement that all previous 'resolutions, conventions and contracts' are to be regarded as null and void. The first two clauses cover similar ground to the second and third clauses of the 1761 contract, that is Haydn's general demeanour as Kapellmeister:[2] 'Herr Haydn is to conduct himself in a manner that is edifying, Christian and God-fearing' and 'Herr Capellmeister is to treat his subordinates at all times with great goodness and forbearance'. The third clause is equivalent to the previous fifth clause, a catch-all requirement to perform any music, at any time and any place, as required by the prince. The fourth clause represents a tightening of something that is implicit in the 1761 contract without being spelt out, that Haydn needed special permission to be absent from court. The fifth clause indicates that both parties may cancel the contract, apparently without notice; maybe the coming and going of opera singers had already persuaded the Esterházy authorities that requiring a period of notice was simply impracticable. The sixth clause confirms the long-standing arrangement that Haydn was to receive a new winter and summer uniform in alternate years; within ten years the Kapellmeister and his musicians successfully negotiated a cash substitute, having built up a small wardrobe of lightly worn uniforms. The remainder of the clause confirms Haydn's basic salary in cash as 782 gulden and 30 kreutzer and his victuals, the ones he had secured when he agreed to take over the post of organist in Eisenstadt in the winter months, plus the forage for the two horses he had been given as a gift in 1776 by Count Erdödy for teaching the promising young Ignaz Pleyel. Haydn signed the contract on 1 January 1779. Shortly afterwards someone in the Esterházy administration must have thought it a good idea to remind the Kapellmeister that if he could not play the organ in Eisenstadt during the winter it was his responsibility to find and pay a deputy; this additional, undated clause was also signed by Haydn.

The extensive nature of Haydn's musical and administrative duties and his proven sense of conscientiousness did not require the more detailed prescriptions of the 1761 contract; even the entirely new responsibilities associated with his work in the Italian opera house and the marionette theatre do not feature. However, the content of one clause in the 1761 contract, the fourth, is conspicuous by its absence. This was the clause that effectively gave artistic ownership of Haydn and his music to the prince, forbidding the composer to sell his music outside the court and requiring him to seek approval before accepting any outside commission. While Haydn had to be reminded of this following Werner's letter of complaint in 1765, a decade later the prince may have come to think that these were unnecessary constraints on his Kapellmeister and, as regards the selling of music, something that was virtually impossible to supervise. Austrian aristocratic and monastic libraries were full of symphonies and items of church music by Haydn, some supplied by the composer, most circulating in illicit copies; music publishers in Amsterdam, Berlin, London and Paris had acquired some of these copies and published unauthorized editions of symphonies, quartets, trios and other instrumental works by him. In recognizing the rapidly changing status of Haydn in the world outside Eszterháza the prince knew that he still had first call on the services of his Kapellmeister, subtly ensured in that apparently innocuous clause that required him to ask for special permission to be absent. Such permission was given from time to time but it was also occasionally refused, to the increasing annoyance of Haydn in the 1780s.

One particular commercial development in Vienna may have influenced the tone of the 1779 contract, the founding of the first successful music publishing firm in that city, Artaria. In comparison with Amsterdam, Berlin, London and Paris music publishing arrived late in Vienna, a reflection of the conservative commercial life of the city in general. Music of all kinds was usually distributed in manuscript copies, a fundamental and pervasive part of musical life; there were as many as 100 or more music copyists in Vienna who sometimes worked in collaboration with a composer or an institution, such as the court opera, sometimes independently. At its most responsible it was a highly professional business but it was also prone to racketeering. Illicit secondary copies, that is copies of copies, were in circulation, ones that invariably deteriorated in their musical reliability, sometimes to the point of being unusable, and while the music-copying industry sustained and promoted all musical life from the salon to the opera house, the dance hall to the church, it also denied income to a composer and could damage his musical reputation. Booksellers and printers in Vienna had occasionally issued printed music and Haydn himself in 1774 had arranged for a set of six keyboard sonatas (Hob. XVI:21–6) to be issued by the firm of Joseph Kurzböck, duly dedicated to Prince Nicolaus Esterházy, but this was a rare, for Haydn unique, event before the setting up of the Artaria firm.

The Artaria family came from the small town of Blevio on Lake Como in northern Italy, arrived in Mainz in 1765, where they established a business selling engravings and maps. Two cousins, Carlo and Francesco, left Mainz for Vienna in 1766, where they soon established a similar business in the Kohlmarkt, around the corner from the Michaelerhaus, where Haydn had once lived. Ten years on they began importing music editions from Paris, a successful venture that led them to expand their expertise and experience from maps and drawings to music. The first music publications appeared in 1778, a set of string trios by one Paola Bonaga. For the first few years music publishing was a sideline as Artaria tested the traditional dominance of music copyists, but gradually the number of publications grew; by the mid-1780s Artaria was a major presence in the musical life of Vienna, aided by the award of an imperial privilege, 'cum Privilegio Sacrae Cesareae Majestatis', usually engraved on title pages as 'C.P.S.C.M'. Haydn's music was a major part of this success, over sixty publications up to 1790, as Artaria's preferences as a music publisher pushed the composer's career in new directions.

Commercial caution meant that Artaria aimed its music publications predominantly at the domestic market, typically keyboard music for the cultivated amateur (especially young women) or string trios and quartets for the more skilled practitioner. Haydn responded readily to this market. His first publication with the firm was of six keyboard sonatas (Hob.XVI:35–9, 20) issued in April 1780 as op. 30, followed by piano trios, more sonatas, sets of variations, and arrangements for keyboard of movements from symphonies and of *The Seven Last Words*; while this allowed Haydn to publish some music that he had actually composed much earlier in his career, a good deal was new and certainly the 1780s were to see the greatest concentration on keyboard music in Haydn's career. His renewed interest in the string quartet in the 1780s also fitted well into Artaria's sense of the market and, even if the initiative came from the composer, it was one that he knew was certain to succeed. Haydn's op. 33 quartets, his first for nine years, were published in December 1781, followed by op. 50 in 1787, opp. 54 and 55 in 1789–90, and the quartet arrangements of *The Seven Last Words* in 1787 and of three of the 'Paris' symphonies in 1788. Haydn's first songs, the subject of the letter quoted above, were also published by Artaria, two sets of twelve each published in 1781 and 1785, all part of the notably expanding market for German lieder in Vienna in the 1780s that featured works by Hofmann, Mozart, Stadler, Vanhal and others.

In general Artaria avoided publishing symphonies, for two simple economic reasons: the engraving of, say, twelve orchestral parts (one flute, two oboes, two bassoons, two horns, first violin, second violin, viola, cello and bass) was considerably more expensive than engraving four parts for a string quartet and, secondly, the number of potential sales was fewer; the firm preferred to leave such music to the manuscript copying trade. Only two symphonies by Mozart, for instance, were published by Artaria (K319 and K385). In Haydn's case, however, Artaria made an exception, eventually publishing thirty-four symphonies. The first six of these, 'Sei Sinfonie a Grand Orchestra', are not part of the familiar tally of 104; issued in 1782 they consisted of six overtures, five to operas (*L'isola disabitata, L'incontro improvviso, Lo speziale, La vera costanza* and *L'infedeltà delusa*) and one to the oratorio *Il ritorno di Tobia*. With this publication Artaria and Haydn were able to test the market because, as the composer indicated, the works were shorter than his normal symphonies and that 'will make the engraving very cheap'.[3]

As this comment suggests Haydn was an adroit advocate of his music, mixing genuine self-esteem with blatant self-interest. Thus the German lieder were described to Artaria as surpassing 'all my previous ones in variety, naturalness and ease of vocal execution'[4] (there were no 'previous ones') and the Fantasia in C for piano was promoted as a work 'whose tastefulness, singularity and special construction cannot fail to win applause from connoisseurs and amateurs alike'.[5] Self-esteem and self-interest occasionally provoked anger from Haydn when faced with something he did not approve of. When the composer learnt in January 1782 that Artaria's publication of the op. 33 quartets was imminent he fired off a letter pointing out that this undermined the pre-publication manuscript copies that he was offering to selected individuals:[6] 'I wish you had shown sufficient consideration for me to delay the announcement till I had left Vienna; it is a most usurious step on your part . . . this action must cause the cessation of all further transactions between us.' If this outburst seems at odds with the gentle diplomacy with which Haydn carried out his duties as Kapellmeister, 'the mildness and leniency' of the first contract, then the tone of his next letter could be interpreted either as more typical of Haydn's normal disposition or a cleverly calculated climb down:[7] 'I must apologize for having written my last letter to you in the heat of anger, and I hope that nevertheless we shall remain good friends . . . Well, it happened that way; next time both of us will be more cautious.'

Haydn drove a hard financial bargain too, especially as the relationship became an established one. He charged 30 ducats (equivalent to 135 gulden) for the first set of twelve lieder, 300 gulden for six piano sonatas and 100 ducats (450 gulden) for six quartets; particularly lucrative was the single-movement Fantasia in C for which he demanded and received, despite Artaria's protestation, 24 ducats (110 gulden). Measured as a proportion of his annual income at the Esterházy court of 782 gulden 30 kreutzer these fees were substantial ones, in the case of a set of six quartets over half his annual salary. It seems uncomfortable to suggest, but part of the motivation for the composition of the remarkable series of quartets in the 1780s – op. 33, op. 50, op. 54/55 and op. 64 – may have been a financial one. Certainly, there is plenty of evidence to suggest that Haydn had a mercenary streak to his personality, an insistence that verged on the obsessive and teetered occasionally into the unscrupulous.

When he was paid for the overtures in 1782 he requested that the coins should be 'full weight' (Austrian currency represented the metallic value of its coins, not its indicative value), placed in a small box, sealed, wrapped in waxed linen and addressed simply to 'Mons. Haydn', 'for I don't want anyone in my house here to know of my transactions',[8] a set of instructions designed to keep the money away from his wife. Just over a year later, in October 1783, the young Swedish composer Joseph Martin Kraus visited Haydn in Eszterháza. In a letter to his parents he wrote as follows.[9]

In Haydn I got to know a jolly good soul, except for one thing – money. He could not understand why I had not brought a pile of music with me on my journey to sell as the opportunity arose . . . Sterkel [the German composer whose opera Il Farnace had been performed in Naples in 1782] had written to him to ask for some arias for his sister in exchange for an equivalent number from his Naples opera. Haydn shook his head, no ringing coins there. It's a curious thing with most artists. The closer one examines them, the more they lose the halo that the amateurs and critics have bestowed on them.

Carlo and Francesco Artaria might well have agreed with Kraus. In 1788, in anticipation of a substantial fee for the composition of three piano trios (Hob.XV:11–13), Haydn ordered a new piano from Schantz and asked Artaria to pay the maker directly, commenting breezily 'Please excuse the liberty: it is bestowed on a man who is grateful.'[10]

While such behaviour probably irritated Artaria, the firm also actively promoted a public image of the composer beyond that which might be sensed from his music alone, an early instance in Haydn's career of an outside image that could be juxtaposed with the realities of daily life as a Kapellmeister. The portrait referred to in the postscript to the letter of 27 May 1781 was an engraving of the composer that Artaria, reflecting the long-standing experience of the firm in graphic presentation, had prepared for sale. It was executed by Johann Ernst Mansfeld (1739–96), one of the most skilled portrait engravers of the day (see Figure 7). In the background of the montage, in front of an oak tree, stands one of the nine muses of Greek mythology, Euterpe, the muse of lyric poetry who is holding two flutes (the instrument habitually ascribed to her). Haydn's head and upper body, with its neat wig and smart but lived-in clothing, are contained within a hanging medallion headed Josephus Haydn, the Latin form of his name that he often used in his correspondence but rarely in his music. In the foreground a laurel wreath loosely binds three instruments together, a lyre, a flute and a trumpet, suggesting a range of musical expression; the instruments rest on open pages of music, realistic in the sense that they are in the oblong format associated with domestic music making and that the single lines with a treble clef suggest something played on a flute, unrealistic in that there are only four staves per page and the notation is meaningless. The instruments and music rest on a keyboard which is, in turn, supported by a plinth with an inscription from Horace: 'Blandus auritas fidibus canoris ducere quercus' (Blandish the listening oaks with your singing strings, *Odes*, I.xii).

Haydn's Latin was certainly up to understanding the quotation and he approved the entire presentation, regularly ordering copies of the engraving so that he could distribute them to friends and acquaintances. At his death in 1809 he owned a collection of over fifty engravings; perhaps Mansfeld's image of the composer began this interest.

7. Engraving of Haydn by J. E. Mansfeld (1781).

Fewer than a handful of Artaria's publications of music by Haydn contained a dedication to a patron, but they do reveal the kind of person who might have been given the engraving of the composer as a gift in addition to the printed music, and offer a glimpse of the social surroundings in which the composer occasionally moved in the 1780s. Haydn thought better of the idea of dedicating the German songs to

Prince Esterházy's mistress and instead opted for Franziska Liebe Edle von Kreutzner, daughter of a retired member of the imperial army, who proceeded to receive a special copy of the songs bound in red taffeta; presumably she was a capable amateur singer and pianist. The earlier six sonatas (Hob.XVI:35–9, 29) were dedicated to two sisters, Maria Katherina and Franziska Auenbrugger, daughters of a well-known physician in Vienna and later known to the Mozart family, too, as players of skill and refinement. Prince Nicolaus's niece, Countess Marianne Grassalkovics, whose summer palace was not far from Eszterháza and whose family were frequent guests of the prince, received the dedication of three piano trios (Hob.XV:6–8).

With the opera season at Eszterháza regularly running from February to November, Haydn's visits to Vienna were usually restricted to a few weeks in December and January, sometimes extended, sometimes curtailed, supplemented by the occasional fleeting visit at other times of the year. Visitors to Eszterháza no doubt brought news of the latest events in Vienna, musical and otherwise, but Haydn was largely dependent on the *Wiener Zeitung* for more regular news. It was an official newspaper that appeared twice a week, giving priority to events at court, accounts of state visits and summary accounts of events abroad; the later pages contained advertisements, including ones by Artaria and some of the music copyists in the city. Reviews of musical performances were entirely absent, making it very difficult for Haydn to form a picture of public response in Vienna to performances of operas at the Burgtheater or the few public concerts such as those featuring Mozart; by definition private concerts were private and it was even more difficult to acquire a consistent sense of that milieu.

Even from the remoteness of Eszterháza Haydn would have noticed that the 1780s was a period of considerable social and political change in Vienna, to the extent that it became a very different city from that which the composer had lived in during the 1740s and 1750s. Under Maria Theresia the period of turbulence that had marked the first two decades of her reign was followed by consolidation and quiet reform. Her son, Joseph, who was co-regent from 1765, succeeded to the throne in 1780 and accelerated the process of reform, producing a more centralized Habsburg state and a liberal social environment that was founded on Enlightenment principles; when various political crises threatened the viability of the Austrian Monarchy at the end of the 1780s the former did its job robustly while the latter began to wither.

For Joseph II, Enlightenment was something that could be applied and controlled from above, by decree and by bureaucracy, and its central purpose was to produce loyal subjects who served the state. Basic education at primary and secondary level was improved and university education for the gifted promoted; remembering his own patchy education Haydn would have welcomed the former in particular. A more unified and humane justice system was imposed with the death penalty abolished except for crimes against the state. Censorship was relaxed, unleashing, for a while, a degree of political debate and dissension that was invigorating, even if it was also often scurrilous rather than intellectually engaging. Egalitarianism resulted in the private parks of the Augarten (in the Leopoldstadt) and the Prater being opened to the public and, in a powerful sign of the new spirit of enquiry and self-confidence, the city gates were left permanently open.

The German language was promoted, both as a centrally unifying force within the linguistically diverse Habsburg dominions, and as the cultural equal of French and Italian. A national theatre for spoken drama was founded in 1776 followed by the National Singspiel for opera in the German language. Although the German company was disbanded in 1783 and the old preference for an Italian company reinstated in the Burgtheater, German opera, not least through Mozart's extremely popular *Die Entführung aus dem Serail*, had established a permanent, ambitious presence in Vienna that allowed it to continue without the support of the court. Even Haydn's operas benefited a little from this process. Apart from a concert performance of *L'isola disabitata* in the Burgtheater in March none of his Italian operas was performed in a public theatre in Vienna in their original language; however, a German translation of La fedeltà premiata (Die belohnte Treue) was given in the Kärntnertortheater in 1784 and of La vera costanza (Der flatterhafte Liebhaber) in the Landstrasse Theatre in 1790. Thirty-three miles to the east lay Pressburg (Bratislava), then capital of Hungary. Count Johann Nepomuk Erdödy opened a small opera house for the local nobility and military and presented four operas by Haydn in German translation during the decade: La vera costanza, La fedeltà premiata, Orlando Paladino (Ritter Roland) and Armida. Since Joseph II was pursuing a deeply unpopular policy of requiring the Hungarian territories to use German rather than their native language, Haydn's operas, presented to an influential audience, would have played an unassuming part in this cultural imperialism.

It was in religious life that Joseph II's reforms had the most noticeable and widespread effect. Without wishing to deny the right of every Austrian citizen to celebrate the Catholic rite Joseph aimed to curtail the wider influence of the Catholic church in society, making it less dependent on Rome and more on Vienna, focused on serving the community through medical care and education, and stripping its ritual of extravagance and superstition. Across the Austrian territories over 250 monasteries and convents were dissolved in ten years, approximately half the total number, with over 5,000 clergy being given the choice of transferring to another order, becoming socially active parish priests or leading a secular life helped by a small state pension; the Barmherzige Brüder remained unscathed because of their widely practised role of administering health care. Within the inner city of Vienna three of the thirteen monasteries and six of the seven convents were dissolved, with the buildings put to secular use or sold; Haydn's sister-in-law, Therese Keller, his first love, was a nun in the Franciscan convent of St Nicolaus and decided to pursue a secular life, with an annual pension of 200 gulden. Private chapels in aristocratic houses were forbidden too and the one in the Esterházy palace in the Wallnerstrasse was put to alternative use, as was the Theresienkapelle in the Bohemian Court Exchequer in the Wipplingerstrasse, where Haydn had played the organ in the 1750s. The fondness for religious public processions that had caught the eye of Charles Burney was uncompromisingly challenged and they were reduced in number to two a year plus the customary ones in *Bittwoche* (two weeks before Whit Sunday) and on Corpus Christi; the often extravagantly colourful wooden carvings and statues that had featured in them were also banned. The selling of relics and other idolatrous items was forbidden and no pilgrimage that entailed an absence of more than one day was allowed, ending, at a stroke, the long tradition of pilgrimages from Vienna to Mariazell that Haydn had experienced thirty years earlier. In 1782 Haydn was commissioned to write a mass by Anton Liebe von Kreutzner (Franziska's father) to be performed in Vienna either prior to, or on return from, a pilgrimage to Mariazell; this must have been one of the last pilgrimages before they were forbidden. Religious brotherhoods, such as the one that supported the Mariazell pilgrimages, were disbanded also.

Joseph II had strong views about the place of music in worship. In a series of reforms he encouraged greater use of the German language in church services, reduced the number of services that featured instrumental music and the number and kind of churches that were allowed to perform such music. Haydn's own church music had circulated widely in the Austrian territories, both original works and contrafacta, and for many Austrians up to the 1780s he was more associated with church music than instrumental music or opera. The great tradition of Austrian church music that had dominated Haydn's early musical experience was now being systematically pared down. Church music had always provided the mainstay of employment for performing musicians in Vienna itself and dozens upon dozens lost their livelihood in the mid-1780s; had Haydn pursued the likely career of singer, violinist, organist, composer in Viennese churches that had beckoned in the 1750s he, almost certainly, would have been out of work in the 1780s. All these changes to the religious life of the city took place over a period of ten years but Haydn would have noticed major differences every time he visited the city. In England in the summer of 1794 he paid a visit to the ruins of Waverley Abbey, dissolved by Henry VIII two centuries earlier, jotting down in his notebook, 'my heart was oppressed at the thought that all this once belonged to my religion'.[11] Similar sentiments of sadness and irrevocable change might well have occurred to him during his visits to Vienna in the 1780s.

Music was a consuming hobby for Joseph II and he systematically allotted one hour per day to its cultivation, either as a performer (keyboard, cello or voice) or in debate with court musicians. He also attended the opera regularly and played a meddling part in determining its repertoire and its singers. But he was not keen on Haydn's music. The symphony had never been a central part of musical entertainment at the court; as for quartets there was a preference for the dated works of Gassmann (1729–74), with their worthy fugal movements; church music, understandably, gave precedence to the music of the court composer, Giuseppe Bonno (1711–88) and was much more likely to feature older music by previous court composers such as Fux (1660–1741) and Haydn's teacher Reutter (1708–72) than new music by composers not employed by the court; as for Italian opera, Joseph wholeheartedly accepted the guiding influence of Salieri, founded on the natural law that Italian opera was best provided by Italian composers. The particulars of the story of *La vera costanza* and the Habsburg court may never be known, yet it is clear that there was, at best, an indifference to Haydn's music in imperial circles.

Haydn's relationship with the Tonkünstler-Societät also was a difficult one, one that failed, lamentably, to build on the success of the performances of *Il ritorno di Tobia* in 1775. The society existed for the benefit of musicians in the city of Vienna and, since Haydn spent most of his time in Eszterháza, key members of the society did not regard him a natural member of their organization. Nevertheless, when Haydn petitioned the society to join in 1778, they accepted and charged him a fee, which he duly paid; in confirming his membership they indicated that he would be required to compose new music specifically for the society and, if he did not, his membership would be rescinded. Haydn, very reasonably, protested: the stipulation had been added after he had paid, he was wholly at the mercy of the society as to what music was required and he probably would not be able to oblige anyway because of his extensive duties at the Esterházy court. More tetchily, he sensed the manoeuvrings of a Viennese establishment that resented him: 'Perhaps because I am a foreigner. In my case, foreign means only that my person is of no use to the natives ... Now, my good friend! I am a man of too much sensitivity to permit me to live constantly in the fear of being quashed. The fine arts and such a wonderful science as that of composition allow no fetters on their handicraft. The heart and soul must be free if they are to serve the widows and collect profits.' He then demanded reimbursement of the admission fee and ended the letter firmly ensconced on the moral high ground: 'For my part, however, despite such a crude and threatening treatment, I shall, if time and circumstances so permit, compose various new pieces for the widows at no cost.'[12] He never did.

Even though Haydn was not a member of the society, the biannual charity concerts of the Tonkünstler-Societät often featured a symphony by him in its concerts in the 1780s, probably purchased from Traeg (the main music dealer in the city) or from Artaria. In 1781, three years after the row, the society approached the composer with the request that Il ritorno di Tobia be performed at its two Christmas concerts. For revising the score and directing the two performances Haydn wanted complimentary tickets or an honorarium, but the society refused and Hasse's unseasonal oratorio Santa Elena al Calvario was given instead. Three years later, an accommodation was reached and a new, revised version of the oratorio was given in Lent, on 28 March and 30 March. Haydn directed from the harpsichord but on this occasion the singers were not from the Esterházy court (as they had been in 1775) but consisted of leading figures from the Italian opera company in Vienna, Valentin Adamberger, Caterina Cavalieri, Stefano Mandini, Nancy Storace and Therese Teyber, a rare instance of Haydn the 'foreigner' working with the 'natives'. Ironically, Adamberger became ill and had to be replaced for at least one of the performances by Carl Friberth, Haydn's old colleague at the Esterházy court who had sung in the first performances and was now living and working in Vienna as a church musician.

Outside the music establishment in Vienna Haydn was a welcome occasional guest and, though there is no regular testimony, there is an increasing sense in the 1780s that he valued the company of the salon society that flourished in that decade. The impulse for writing the two sets of German songs came from Haydn's visits to the household of Franz Sales von Greiner (1732–98), a Habsburg civil servant whose house in the Neuer Markt (Mehlgrube) in the centre of Vienna became a favoured venue for literary and musical salons. Haydn sought his advice on the choice of texts, wanting variety and showing concern about the tastefulness of some of the subject matter. When the first set was about to be published Haydn warned Artaria not to distribute copies before he had had the chance to sing some of the songs himself in 'educated society' ('in den critischen Häusern').[13] Something of the ambience of such society may be deduced from the songs.

In a predominantly, but not exclusively, male environment Haydn would have sat at the keyboard to accompany himself, an intimacy of composer and amateur performer emphasized by the fact that the right hand of the pianist offers considerable help to the singer and that all the songs have a simple strophic structure. Only two songs respond to some of the greatest names of contemporary German literature, one that sets a text by Herder ('Das strickende Mädchen') and another by Lessing ('Lob der Faulheit'), though lesser names such as Bürger and Gleim figure too; a significant number of the texts are by unknown poets, quite likely figures from Greiner's circle of acquaintances. A typical contrast of mood occurs between the fourth and fifth songs of the second set, 'Gegenliebe' and 'Geistliches Lied', the first a straightforward celebration of the joy of 'mutual love' in an idiom that anticipates Schubert at his most uncomplicated (Beethoven was to set the same text with an equally direct tune but one that was later transformed into the theme of the finale of the Ninth Symphony); 'Geistliches Lied' is a more powerful response to the simple drama of a two-verse poem about the inadequacy of man when faced by God's majesty and Christ's sacrifice, a text that Joseph II might have regarded as overly sentimental but whose characteristics lay deeply embedded in the Austrian psyche. *Pietas Austriaca* was never puritanical and Haydn's songs contain two that can only be described as saucy, though he was momentarily worried that they were not suited to polite society; the fact that they were eventually published says something about that society. 'Eine sehr gewöhnliche Geschichte' (The usual story) in an unsubtle tale about Philint being refused admission through Babett's front door, at least until the fourth verse; in 'Die zu späte Ankunft der Mutter' (Mother arrives too late), two young lovers are seated under flowering trees on the bank of a stream, the mother is worried but arrives only to be greeted by the daughter's exclamation 'It's happened. You can go now.' More individual, to the extent that it worked best when the composer himself presented the song, is 'Lob der Faulheit' (In praise of sloth) in which the composer-cum-singer arduously tries to sing a line above slow-moving chords in A minor, finding much needed respite in the concluding A major chord.

Another career civil servant who supported Haydn's career in Vienna was Franz Bernhard von Kees (1720–95). As he marched up the ladder in the justice department of the Lower Austrian regional government Kees began organizing private concerts and he may have known Haydn as early as the 1760s. Certainly by 1777 he was able to act on his behalf, signing a receipt for the payment of a fee for a set of dances for the Redoutensaal. In the middle of the 1780s Kees organized private concerts twice a week in which Haydn symphonies were regularly played alongside music by Dittersdorf, Gyrowetz, Hoffmeister and Mozart. Haydn would have been able to attend very few of these concerts but his presence is documented on one occasion, probably in the winter of 1788–9, when some new symphonies by the Viennese composer Johann Baptist Schenk (1753–1836) were given in the presence of Baron van Swieten; Haydn congratulated Schenk and offered some encouraging words. Kees's collection of Haydn's symphonies was so extensive that he eventually prepared a special catalogue of them, probably in 1792.

It is not known when Haydn first met Mozart but by the end of the 1780s their friendship, based on mutual affection and regard, was a profound one, probably the closest between two major composers in the entire history of Western music, even though the opportunities to nurture that relationship were rare. Haydn was twenty-four years older than Mozart and that generation gap, plus the fact that he spent most of his time at Eszterháza, meant that he probably did not have extensive knowledge of the younger composer's music until the 1780s; Mozart, on the other hand, would have been very aware of Haydn's music and his reputation, from the works that reached Salzburg, were available in manuscript copies in Vienna and published in Paris. Mozart's library contained manuscript copies of Haydn's op. 17 quartets, acquired in the early 1770s. About 1780 he studied three of them in detail, no. 2 in F, no. 4 in C and no. 6 in D, adding many dynamic markings; shortly afterwards he embarked on a quartet in E major, subsequently abandoned, that is clearly modelled on Haydn's op. 17 no. 1, also in E major.

Probably the nearest the two composers came to meeting before the 1780s was in March 1768; Mozart spent virtually the whole of that year in Vienna and he could have attended the performance of Haydn's Stabat mater that was directed by the composer in the church of the Barmherzige Brüder in the Leopoldstadt on the afternoon of Friday 25 March. After Mozart moved to Vienna in 1781 the biannual concerts of the Tonkünstler-Societät, especially the Christmas ones, might have occasioned the first meeting. In 1784 Michael Kelly, a tenor at the Italian company in the Burgtheater, attended a private concert and party hosted by the composer Stephen Storace, sister of Nancy, whose comic opera Gli sposi malcontenti was premiered in Vienna the following year. Other guests from the opera world included Paisiello and the poet Giambattista Casti. There was a string quartet ensemble. 'The players were tolerable, not one of them excelled on the instrument he played,' wrote Kelly in his memoirs 'but there was a little science among them, which I dare say will be acknowledged when I name them: the First Violin, Haydn; the Second Violin, Baron Dittersdorf; the Violoncello, Vanhal; the Tenor [viola], Mozart . . . after the musical feast was over, we sat down to an excellent supper and became joyous and lively in the extreme.'[14] Kelly's memoirs were not written down until the 1820s and while it gives a vivid picture of this event, the details are not convincing. Mozart playing the viola certainly rings true but Vanhal is not otherwise known to have played the cello and Dittersdorf, a much better violinist than Haydn, is more likely to have played first violin.

By the time of this oft-quoted social event Mozart had embarked on a set of six quartets prompted by the publication of Haydn's op. 33; it is possible that Storace's party included performances of some of them in 1784. Early in the following year Haydn heard all six at two private concerts, one on 15 January, the other a month later, on 12 February. Mozart's father was present at the second event and wrote proudly to his daughter Nannerl, recounting Haydn's considered view of his son:[15] 'Before God and as an honest man I tell you that your son is the greatest composer known to me either in person or by name. He has taste and, what is more, the most profound knowledge of composition.' When the quartets were published by Artaria the following autumn they were dedicated to Haydn: 'Composti e Dedicati al Signor Giuseppe Haydn . . . Dal Suo Amico W. A. Mozart'. As well as the formal dedication Mozart persuaded Artaria to include a lengthy letter, written in Italian rather than German and using the familiar personal pronoun 'tu', in which the six 'sons' are entrusted to their musical guardian, Haydn:[16] 'From this moment I resign to you all my rights in them, begging you however to look indulgently upon the defects which the partiality of a Father's eye may have concealed from me and in spite of them to continue in your generous Friendship for him who so greatly values it.'

In the same year Haydn had become a Freemason, almost certainly encouraged by Mozart for whom it was a new enthusiasm. Mozart was initiated on 14 December 1784 and just over a fortnight later, on 29 December, Haydn applied for membership of the 'True Concord' (Zur wahren Eintracht) lodge. Following a successful ballot the initiation was set for 28 January but Haydn had already returned to Eszterháza and the ceremony had to be postponed until 11 February. One of his three sponsors was Count Georg von Apponyi, Hungarian Chamberlain to the imperial court who had a palace in Pressburg.

Mozart was unable to attend because the first of his 1785 subscription concerts was being held the same evening; the Master of the Lodge, Ignaz von Born, was absent too. Haydn was addressed by the acting orator, Joseph von Holzmeister, Chief Clark of the Imperial War Ministry. It is easy to dismiss the extended metaphor of his speech, the parallel between the harmony of music and the harmony of the brotherhood, as obvious and laboured, but in a society that was only just beginning to articulate and debate a musical aesthetic its sentiments may well have seemed stimulating as well as sincere.[17]

> You, newly elected Brother Apprentice, know especially well the designs of this heavenly gift, harmony; you know its all-embracing power is one of the most beautiful fields of human endeavour; to you this enchanting goddess has granted part of her bewitching power, through which she calms the stormy breast, puts to sleep pain and sorrow, brightens melancholic and cloudy thoughts and turns the heart of humans to joyful speculation.

After this ceremony Haydn is not known to have attended a single further meeting. For over two years Masonic records dutifully list him as an 'absent brother'; thereafter not even his name appears. Unlike Mozart, who responded readily to its tenets, Haydn's brief association had no lasting effect. He had joined at a time when it was particularly fashionable to do so amongst the Viennese aristocracy, bourgeoisie and mercantile classes, an admixture of society that Haydn had already encountered in the emerging salon culture of the decade, and he would have viewed it as a natural extension of that milieu. In the same way that his duties at Eszterháza prevented him from being a regular member of Viennese society in general, it prevented him from attending Masonic meetings in particular. Meanwhile, motivated by his usual desire to control what was going on in society at large Joseph II had embarked on a series of reforms that ensured that Freemasonry gradually lost its allure for fashionable society. Count Apponyi, for one, ceased to be a member and Haydn put aside the little interest he ever had.

At the same time as Haydn's career and outlook were beginning to be marked by the musical and social practices of Vienna, the composer was reaching out from Eszterháza to an even wider world, to England, France, Germany (that is those parts of the Holy Roman Empire that lay outside the Austrian Monarchy), Italy and Spain, intensifying a reputation that had been developing over two decades. Before Artaria had issued the op. 33 quartets Haydn had written letters to several potential subscribers abroad, offering pre-publication manuscript copies, including to Joseph Caspar Lavater, the well-known writer and physiognomist living in Zürich, Prince Kraft Ernst Oettingen-Wallerstein in Bavaria, Abbot Robert Schlecht of Salmannsweiler (near Linzgau in present day Baden-Württemberg) and, possibly, Archduke Ferdinand in Milan. Of these individuals Haydn had met only the last-named, but he clearly knew that all would be receptive to such a letter. The firm of Artaria itself had an international network of distribution; a family member still ran the original shop in Mainz and the publishing firms of Longman and Broderip in London and Sieber (later Le Duc) in Paris both imported Artaria's music publications on a regular basis in the 1780s.

The court of Oettingen-Wallerstein was one of the most musically active in Germany. Like members of the Esterházy family Prince Kraft Ernst was a capable amateur musician, had received a university education (Göttingen and Strasbourg) and travelled widely. His political allegiances were firmly directed towards the Habsburgs, nurtured by attending the Savoyan Ritterakademie in Vienna that had been founded by Maria Theresia in 1746 for the training of loyal aristocrats. Consequently his musical tastes, too, lay in that direction rather than being informed by practices of musical courts closer to home such as Mannheim or Stuttgart. Haydn's music was systematically acquired by the court with the symphony collection eventually numbering over eighty. The prince willingly accepted Haydn's offer of pre-subscription copies of the op. 33 quartets; fourteen months later he was to complain about the delay in delivering them.

A similar relationship existed with a network of courts in the Spanish capital, Madrid. Music was a favoured pastime of the heir to the Spanish throne, the Prince of the Asturias (the future Carlos IV), and the repertory of his orchestra included symphonies by Haydn, some acquired directly from the composer. Haydn also forwarded a manuscript score of *L'isola disabitata* to the court – a serious opera was a more appropriate gift than a comic one – and received a snuffbox in return, delivered to Eszterháza by a member of the Spanish legation in Vienna. For much of the 1780s Haydn also regularly sent music to Countess Osuna y Benavente in Madrid and to the Duke of Alba; the fondness of the latter for Haydn's music is evident from Goya's portrait of c.1795 in which the duke is clearly seen holding a manuscript of 'Cuatro canciones con Aconpañamiento de Fortpiano del Sr. Haydn'. Churches and monasteries throughout the country had copies of Haydn's Stabat mater, its popularity leading to the direct commission from Cadiz Cathedral in 1786 for an orchestral setting of Christ's final utterances on Calvary, *The Seven Last Words from the Cross*. At a time when Joseph II's reforms were systematically limiting the role of music in Catholic worship Haydn was able to demonstrate the evocative power of his art in eight successive slow movements and a concluding Il *Terremoto* (Earthquake). With Artaria's cooperation something of the expressive reach of the music could be experienced in Austrian drawing rooms in the arrangements that were issued for string quartet and for piano, though they are a poor substitute for the orchestral version.

Haydn's direct contacts with Italy in the 1780s were less extensive. Ferdinand IV, King of Naples was married to one of the daughters of Maria Theresia, Maria Carolina, and through her influence musical life at court featured Austrian and German instrumental music, including many symphonies by Haydn, alongside the more expected fare of Italian opera. The eccentric king liked to project a common touch and learnt to play the lira organizzata, a modified hurdy-gurdy that emitted four types of sound, a melody from a set of wooden pipes, a melody from stopped strings, a drone string bass and a haze of sound produced, as in Nicolaus Esterházy's baryton, by a set of sympathetic strings. Between 1786 and 1790 Haydn composed six concertos and nine notturni for an ensemble that included two of these instruments. Given that Haydn had composed his last baryton trio in 1778 it seems strange that when he had freedom to decline he should devote so much time a decade later to composing music for another idiosyncratic instrument. No details of the commission are known; probably 'ringing coins' were a factor.

'Ringing coins', of the most sought-after kind, were certainly a feature of a commission from Paris for six new symphonies, though Haydn would have recognized too that such a commission, from one of Europe's most fashionable and progressive musical cities, was an incontrovertible indication of his status and reputation. There was already the sense that musical history was being made on behalf of the composer in that city; without his active participation – he was never to visit Paris – Haydn's symphonies had found a new home, key works in concerts in front of an audience of several hundred played by an orchestra of several dozen and the subject of debate in the musical press. Central to musical life in Paris was the Concert Spirituel, a concert series founded in 1725 and which, by the 1780s, gave two dozen or more concerts per year. Haydn's symphonies had featured occasionally in its repertoire from the early 1770s but a decade later there is a dramatic increase in the number of symphonies performed, amounting to a craze; by the late 1780s at least eight out of every ten performances of a symphony was of a work by Haydn: a key composer to go with a key genre. It was against this background that another, rather more exclusive organization, the Concert de la Société Olympique commissioned six brand new symphonies from Haydn, nos. 82–7 (the 'Paris' symphonies). 'Olympique' referred to a particular Masonic lodge in the city, the Loge Olympique de la Parfaite Estime, that sponsored twelve annual concerts for its members and those of an affiliated women's lodge, a potential audience of over 500 people. Three-quarters of the members were aristocrats, including the Vicomte de Noailles, the Duc d'Orléans, Count d'Ogny and the

Princesse de Lamballe; the last named was a long-standing companion of Marie Antoinette and they often attended the concerts together; as a result Marie Antoinette became a devotee of Haydn's music in a way that her brother, Joseph II, never did.

Almost certainly the initial approaches to Haydn were made through Masonic circles in Vienna and, since other composers who wrote new works for the organization, such as Cambini and Philidor, were made honorary members if they were not already Freemasons, establishing Haydn's Masonic status was probably a prime concern. They were determined to get their man, offering the composer a fee of 25 louis d'or per symphony plus a further 5 louis d'or for the publication rights. During his visit to the French capital in 1778 Mozart had reported that the standard fee for a symphony was 5 louis d'or; Haydn was being paid five times the going rate, yielding a total for six symphonies of 180 louis d'or. This was equivalent to over 1,300 gulden, far in excess of any fee that Artaria paid the composer and nearly 70 per cent more than his annual income from Prince Esterházy.

Haydn responded imaginatively to the commission with six works of unprecedented charm, eloquence, energy and drama. Although precise information has not survived, they were probably first performed in the 1787 season in the usual venue, the Salle des Gardes on the first floor of the Palace of the Tuileries, with an orchestra in excess of sixty in number. One of the second violinists was Jean-Jérôme Imbault, who had just started a supplementary career as a music publisher. He was given the publication rights and the six symphonies were duly made available in the following year 'engraved after the original scores owned by the Olympic Lodge'. At the head of the first violin part of no. 85 Imbault inscribed the words 'La Reine de France', an indication that Marie Antoinette had heard this symphony and had responded enthusiastically; 'La Reine' remains in use as a nickname for the work. Another member of the orchestra, the cellist Count d'Ogny, was anxious to continue the link between Paris and Haydn and commissioned three further symphonies from him, nos. 90–2, presumably on equally favourable terms, though no details have survived.

By this time, 1788–9, another musical capital had surpassed even Paris in its enthusiasm for Haydn: London, a city that was to usurp the role of the French capital in the history of the symphony at the end of the century. For over twenty years public musical life in London outside the opera house had closely followed the practices of Paris. Under the leadership of Johann Christian Bach and Carl Friedrich Abel, who presented a series of weekly subscription concerts that, at their most popular, ran from January to May, fashionable new genres such as the symphony and the symphonie concertante had captured the imagination of the public. Music publishing too reflected and promoted this vitality. Unlike France, however, the local dominance of two composers, Bach and Abel, led to a repertoire that was less eclectic than that in Paris. One of the first symphonies by Haydn to make an impact in London was no. 53 in D, played in the Bach–Abel concerts in 1781 and published later that year; it soon acquired the nickname 'Festino' after the Festino Rooms in Hanover Square where the concerts were held.

On New Year's Day 1782 J.C. Bach died. Under the direction of Abel the concerts limped on for one season before the Earl of Abingdon took over the venue and the evening (Wednesday) for a new series entitled the Hanover Square Grand Concert. The earl wished to retain the idea of a resident composer who presided at a concert and whose music was featured throughout the series, and the newspapers were full of reports that Haydn was to be engaged, the beginning of seven years of regular speculation. An influential figure behind the scenes was Charles Burney who, since his abortive attempt to see the composer in person in Vienna in 1772, had come to regard him as the greatest living composer and regularly stoked English enthusiasm for his music. He persuaded Sir John Gallini that he should recruit Haydn as the resident composer for the King's Theatre, Haymarket, the home of Italian opera in London and where the late Johann Christian Bach had held the same post. Opera-house politics in London were as complex and as devious as any in Europe. These were now joined by the rival machinations of concert organizers as almost annual plans were mooted for Haydn's appearance in London at one or the other, or both. For his part Haydn regularly

wanted to work in London

discussed the financial details of the proposed visits, forwarded some music, but, ultimately, was unable to accept because of his commitments at Eszterháza, since the London concert season ran from January to May, covering the first months of the opera season at the court. He almost certainly asked the prince for permission to travel but he was indispensable and permission was refused.

Meanwhile Haydn's music came to dominate concert life in London where he was, effectively, resident composer *in absentia*. For instance in 1785 the Wednesday evening concerts were run by an organization called the Hanover Square Grand Professional Concert run by the 'professors', that is the performers themselves. There were twelve concerts; only three did not contain a symphony by Haydn. One of the 'professors' was the oboist Johann Christian Fischer who at his benefit concert after the final subscription concert was able to present the first performance in London of Haydn's 'Farewell' symphony:[18] 'The Concert will end with a Sinfony of Haydn, (never performed here), in which the Performers one after another retreat, and leave only two Violins to conclude.'

In the composer's continued absence musical society in London began to build up an image of Haydn the man that mixed the truth with the fanciful and the inaccurate. Amongst the copious notes that Burney kept for his music history was the following record of a conversation with Clementi, who had visited Haydn at Eszterháza in 1781:[19] 'Clementi, who saw him in Hungary at Prince Esterhausi's [*sic*], says he is a little, brown complexioned Man, turned of 50 – wears a wig – and when he hears any of his own Pieces performed that are capricious he laughs like a fool.' In its issue of October 1784 the widely read society journal, the *European Magazine, and London Review*, included a biography of Haydn together with 'an excellent Engraved Likeness of him', the engraving first issued by Artaria. The biography concludes with four aphoristic statements, at least two of which were open to scrutiny.[20]

> As a man, he is friendly, artless, and undesigning;
> As a husband, affectionate, tender, and exemplary;

As a performer, neat, elegant, and expressive;
As a composer, chaste, masterly, and original.

When it became clear that Haydn was not able to be present at the 1785 concert season the *Gazetteer & New Daily Advertiser* expressed its disappointment by contrasting British values of liberty and culture, tinged with a bit of routine anti-Catholicism, with the wholly oppressive and backward environment that Haydn found himself in. Clearly he would be better off in Great Britain and should be kidnapped.[21]

There is something very distressing to a liberal mind in the history of Haydn. This wonderful man, who is the Shakespeare of music, and the triumph of the age in which we live, is doomed to reside in the court of a miserable German Prince, who is at once incapable of rewarding him, and unworthy of the honour. Haydn, the simplest as well as the greatest of men, is resigned to his condition, and in devoting his life to the rites and ceremonies of the Roman Catholic Church, which he carries even to superstition, is content to live immured in a place little better than a dungeon, subject to the domineering spirit of a petty Lord, and the clamorous temper of a scolding wife. Would it not be an achievement equal to a pilgrimage, for some aspiring youths to rescue him from his fortune and transplant him to Great Britain, the country for which his music seems to be made?

This skein of admiration, rumour and gossip was about to become even more tangled, as a result of Haydn's opportunistic approach to the publication of his music. In 1781 William Forster, a violin maker in London who was branching out into music publishing, approached Haydn via the British Embassy in Vienna, enquiring whether he could supply music that could be sold in London. The composer was delighted and within a matter of months began delivering music on a regular basis to Forster, symphonies, piano trios, the op. 50 quartets and *The Seven Last Words*. Amongst the piano trios was a set of three (Hob.xv:3–5), in C, F and G. Pushed by time and anxious to receive the due fee from Forster, Haydn actually composed only one of them, the G major trio, making up the set with two trios by his former pupil, Pleyel; the true composer, who was in Italy at the time, was unlikely to find out about the Forster publication, while Forster was even more unlikely to trace their true author. Or so Haydn must have thought. He then compounded the deceit by selling the works to Artaria too, once again taking the gamble that neither Pleyel nor Forster would find out. However, he seems to have been unaware of Artaria's business relationship with another London publisher, Longman and Broderip, one that effectively meant that music published in Vienna by Artaria could be made available in London. Both Forster and Longman and Broderip claimed the right to sell the three 'Haydn' piano trios in London, and at first tried to settle the dispute amicably. Early in 1788, however, Forster started legal proceedings against Longman and Broderip, a case that lasted six years during the course of which it emerged that Pleyel was the actual composer of two of the trios.

A similar incident was recorded in *The Times* in the same month as the legal case started, this time involving no fewer than four sets of sources for the 'Paris' symphonies. Haydn had sold the publication rights for the symphonies to Imbault (Paris), but he also sold them to Forster in London and to Artaria in Vienna, two further fees; in addition he had promised to send manuscript parts of the same symphonies to the Professional Concert for their 1788 season, yet another fee. With gentle admiration rather than censure *The Times* headed its report 'A Specimen of Foreign Ingenuity'.[22]

> Haydn, the celebrated German composer, sold a *Set of Symphonies* to Forster. He sold the same set to a music seller in Paris [Imbault]. The Gentlemen of the *Professional Concert* sent to him some time since, for a new set, for their Concert at Hanover Square, which arrived by express from Vienna, on Monday last, at Mr. Cramer's house. Several of the musical amateurs attended at the opening of the Budget; but when the Budget *was* opened, Oh! grief to tell! it produced not a new set of symphonies, but the *identical* set which the ingenious composer had sold twice before [to Imbault and to

Forster]; and which Messrs. Longman and Broderip had also purchased [from Artaria], and dedicated to his Royal Highness, the Prince of Wales.

It was to take another fifty years for music copyright laws to have effective jurisdiction across national boundaries and Haydn had ruthlessly exploited this fact, as, later, did his pupil Beethoven. Moreover, Haydn, after the initial shock, emerged with his integrity intact in the eyes of the London public, with protracted newspaper coverage over the next few months gradually giving the impression that he had been the innocent victim rather than the perpetrator.

Regular correspondence with publishers, impresarios and individuals anxious to obtain music from Haydn was becoming increasingly time-consuming and often fraught as the composer played one off against the other. He was not the only one creating mischief. The leader of the second violins at Eszterháza was Johann Tost, who began to supplement his work as a player with part-time copying and music distribution. He left the court in March 1788 to pursue these new commercial ambitions. Haydn encouraged them and gave him the authority to sell his most recent symphonies, nos. 88 and 89, and the six quartets of op. 54 and op. 55. Tost went straight to the publishing capital of Europe, Paris, secured Sieber as a publisher for these works, boosted his status as a go-between by falsely promising further symphonies and then, in order to prove his self-assumed status, passed off a symphony by the Bohemian composer Gyrowetz as a work of Haydn. In a comic turn of events Gyrowetz attended a concert in Paris expecting to hear a symphony in G by Haydn, only to be greeted by his own composition.

The 1788 opera season at Eszterháza was a particularly long one, from early February to late December with a brief lull in May when Haydn may have taken the opportunity to visit Vienna, but he had to wait until January and February of the following year for his next lengthy stay. One of the minor mysteries of Haydn's life in the 1780s is where he stayed on these occasional visits to Vienna. The Esterházy palace in the Wallnerstrasse was probably available to this long-serving

Kapellmeister; alternatively he may have lodged with some old friends such as Carl Friberth or Johann Michael Spangler, both struggling to earn a living as church musicians in Vienna. There is no record of Haydn travelling with his wife and none of his letters refers to her. After the house in Eisenstadt had been sold in 1778 Maria Anna Haydn's existence must have been a miserable one, moving between the musicians' quarters in Eisenstadt and Eszterháza, and constantly aggravated in the 1780s by her husband's relationship with Luigia Polzelli. A casual note in a mason's bill in 1784 that Maria Anna's kitchen in the musicians' quarters at Eszterháza was being used by somebody else and that her utensils had been placed in the corridor may suggest a move, perhaps to Vienna, where she could have stayed with her sister, Theresa, now leading a secular life. By the end of the decade – certainly no later than 1791 – she lived in rented accommodation on the Wasserkunstbastei; it is possible that Haydn stayed there too.

Haydn's stay in Vienna in the winter of 1788–9 was shorter than usual, no more five or six weeks, and he was given little notice of the imminent return to Eszterháza. He was clearly disaffected: no sooner had he begun mixing with new and old friends during the sociable Carnival season than he had to leave. Over the next two years disaffection mixed with stoicism seems to have been Haydn's predominant mood, but it sometimes descended into mild depression and was marked by a new propensity to complain about irritating minor medical conditions, a nasal polyp, catarrh and sore eyes (probably eye strain). In a letter to the promising young composer Joseph Eybler (1765–1846) he apologizes for not being able to attend a private concert in Vienna in which a symphony of his was to be played, also for the hurried nature of the letter (one of ten letters that he has had to write) and asks that his warm greetings be forwarded to Albrechtsberger and Mozart. All this was perfectly genuine, but there was another reason for writing. Haydn had promised a friend some dance minuets, had no time to deal with the request, could Eybler forward some and not tell anybody, 'Sed hoc inter nos' ('mum's the word' would be an idiomatic translation). It's not known whether Eybler obliged.

Haydn had become a particularly welcome guest in the Genzinger household in Vienna. Peter Leopold von Genzinger was a physician to Prince Nicolaus Esterházy, happily married to Maria Anna, with five children. She was a capable amateur pianist whose curiosity about music extended to making piano reductions of symphonies to gain insight into the compositional process. In June 1789 she sent an arrangement of a slow movement from a symphony by Haydn to Eszterháza for the composer's approval. Haydn replied, laying on the charm. Her handwriting was 'lovely' (in fact it was very poorly formed), the arrangement was fit for publication, had been carefully prepared particularly if she had scored the music up from the orchestral parts rather than relying on a score, and he looked forward to being of further service. Over the next eighteen months she became more and more a confidante for Haydn in a way that his wife had never been and his mistress Luigia Polzelli could not be. Even though Genzinger and Polzelli were the same age, thirty-nine to Haydn's fifty-seven, their place in the composer's life was quite different. As a musician she was talented but not a professional, she shared Haydn's unquestioning Catholic belief (indicated by the placing of three rudimentary crosses at the head of her letters) and was an educated woman of society. Even if she had not been married, a close relationship between her and a musician would have been unlikely. Destined to be platonic it nevertheless often showed a studied determination to remain so. Both parties were careful to forward and reciprocate compliments from and to Peter von Genzinger and the children and, on one occasion in May 1790 in response to some gossip-mongering, Haydn felt obliged to reassure Maria Anna that his intentions were entirely honourable. The situation was not unlike that which was to figure several times in Beethoven's life: an idealized friendship with a woman who was not available, *die ferne Geliebte*. One of Haydn's works performed in the Genzinger household was the cantata for voice and piano, 'Arianna a Naxos', performed by the sixteen-year-old daughter, Josepha. Even though the thwarted love of Ariadne for Theseus was one of the most familiar operatic stories of the period, performances of Haydn's cantata at the

Genzinger household must have provoked a frisson of recognition between mother and composer. He certainly asked Maria Anna to remind Josepha to pay particular attention to the articulation of three words, 'chi tanto amai' ('who loved so much').[23]

In 1789 Haydn spent late winter, spring, summer, autumn and early winter at Eszterháza where he directed six new operas and nine revivals; the last performance was on 6 December, *L'arbore di Diana* by Martín y Soler. In early November the Kapellmeister received an unexpected visitor, an Englishman named John Bland, someone who was to influence the direction of Haydn's career for the next six years. He had been a music publisher in London since the mid-1770s but in the late 1780s embarked on a much more ambitious phase in his business life. In 1788 on a journey to Vienna he established a commercial relationship with the publisher Hoffmeister that allowed him to sell music by that firm in London, including several works by Mozart and the few by Haydn that were issued by the firm. The following year he made a return journey to Vienna to negotiate directly with Haydn, Mozart, Kozeluch, Vanhal and others, with a view to publishing new music by them in London, feeding the ever-expanding enthusiasm in that city for music from Vienna. Another Englishman, Forster, had been the first foreigner publisher to negotiate directly with Haydn; John Bland was the first to visit Haydn in person. He secured the rights to publish 'Arianna a Naxos', three piano trios (Hob.xv:15–17) and the op. 64 quartets. In addition to a fee, Bland also flattered Haydn by forwarding him some prime examples of British manufacture, a watch and some razors.

There was another element to the negotiations between Bland and Haydn. In the competitive world of musical commerce in London Bland had established an association with the violinist Salomon and his intermittently successful concert series at the Pantheon that was intended to rival the long-standing, very successful one between Longman and Broderip, the violinist Cramer and the Professional Concert. For Haydn the latter axis, extending to Artaria in Vienna, had become a rather fraught one characterized by evasiveness, suspicion, broken promises and legal action. The new axis offered a fresh beginning to Haydn's reputation in London. In addition to the agreed items of music to be published by Bland, Haydn offered Salomon, via Bland, a new cantata, a 'brand new and magnificent symphony' for his exclusive use and an orchestral version of 'Arianna a Naxos'.

Haydn left Eszterháza on 30 December 1789 for Vienna, where he stayed until 4 February. As well as the welcome company of the Genzinger household this short period in the city enabled Haydn to deepen his friendship with Mozart, who invited him to rehearsals of his latest opera, Così fan tutte, an invitation garnished with the promise of some opera-house gossip. There were also performances of a new version of Le nozze di Figaro. Almost certainly Haydn would have told Mozart of the plans to present Le nozze di Figaro at Eszterháza where, for the first time anywhere, it would have been performed alongside its dramatic companion, the first part of Figaro's story, Paisiello's Il barbiere di Siviglia.

Haydn was more despondent than ever when he returned to Eszterháza and after five days of frustrated inactivity wrote another confiding letter to Maria Anna von Genzinger, including a melancholy listing of all the fine Viennese food he was missing.[24]

I found everything at home in confusion, my pianoforte which I usually love so much was perverse and disobedient, it irritated rather than calmed me, I could sleep only very little, even my dreams persecuted me; and then, just when I was happily dreaming that I was listening to the opera Le nozze di Figaro, that horrible north wind woke me up and almost blew my nightcap off my head. I lost 20 pounds in weight in 3 days, for the good Viennese food I had in me disappeared on the journey; alas! alas! I thought to myself as I was eating in the refectory here, instead of that expensive beef, a piece of a 50-year-old cow, instead of ragout with little dumplings, mutton with yellowing carrots, instead of Bohemian pheasant, a leathery roasted joint, instead of those fine and delicate oranges, a Dschabl or horrible lettuce, instead of pastry, dry apple fritters and hazelnuts – that's what I have to eat. Yes, yes I thought to myself if I could only have a little bit of what I'd left on the plate in Vienna. Here in Eszterháza nobody asks me 'Would you like chocolate, with or without milk, do you take coffee, black or with cream? What can I offer you dear Haydn? Would you like a vanilla or strawberry ice?' If only I had a good piece of Parmesan cheese, especially in Lent, so that I could swallow those black dumplings more easily.

In his mid-seventies Prince Nicolaus was rapidly becoming an old man. His habitual preference for Eszterháza over Vienna was fuelled by increasing discomfort caused by Joseph II's chronically insensitive attitude to the status of Hungary. This nominal King of Hungary had declined to attend the traditional coronation ceremony in Pressburg, ordered the transfer of the Hungarian crown to Vienna, refused to summon the Diet, imposed changes unilaterally and demanded the use of German as the official language. Although the Esterházy family, including Nicolaus, had always been intensely loyal to the Habsburgs, these changes were unsettling and made relationships with fellow Hungarian magnates increasingly tense. Finding it difficult to steer a middle course, Nicolaus preferred to stay away from Vienna. On his deathbed in January 1790 and faced with imminent revolt, Joseph II rescinded many of his actions, including agreeing to the transfer of the Hungarian crown back to Pest. With the Hungarian policy of the Habsburgs suddenly at its most considerate Nicolaus was able to demonstrate his sympathies, allowing the palace at Kittsee to be used as a staging post for the procession carrying the Hungarian crown back to Pest, and travelling some distance with it while also dispensing alms to the poor. But Nicolaus was tired of manoeuvring and refused to assume his previous position as Sheriff of the county of Sopron, a task he bequeathed to his son, Anton.

Tiresome diplomacy was cruelly joined by personal grief. On 25 February, exactly a week after the overnight stay of the Hungarian crown at Kittsee, Nicolaus's wife, Princess Maria Elisabeth, died. Although she had never shared her husband's liking for Eszterháza, preferring to remain in Eisenstadt, the relationship was a close one and the prince was distraught. Haydn, the dutiful Kapellmeister, who also had a genuine affection and regard for the prince, reported to Genzinger that he first sought to console him by arranging evening concerts without any vocal music before, later, reviving a favourite opera, Gassmann's *L'amore artigiano*, last given ten years before. Haydn provided three new insertion arias for the revival and there were eight performances over the next few months.

With revivals of works by Cimarosa, Guglielmi, Martín y Soler and Sarti, and new productions of operas by Cimarosa, Paisiello and Salieri, some sense of equilibrium was established at Eszterháza by the summer. At the same time Haydn was becoming ever more indiscreet about his trying circumstances, informing Genzinger that he had unsuccessfully asked for leave of absence several times. On 27 June he was exasperated:[25] 'It really is sad always to be a slave, but Providence wills it so. I'm a poor creature! Always plagued by hard work, very few hours of recreation, and friends?' Still, life as a Kapellmeister went on, Haydn spending some of his time preparing the music of Mozart's *Le nozze di Figaro* and Salieri's *Axur, re d'Ormus* for performance in the autumn. Late in August the prince became ill and it was decided that he should be taken to the palace in Vienna in order to receive the best possible medical care. It was to be in vain and on 28 September Nicolaus died, aged seventy-five, and after twenty-eight years as the reigning prince. Opera performances had been abandoned at Eszterháza and Haydn was already in Vienna, where he would have heard the bells of the Michaelkirche toll for three days in memory of a faithful servant of the Habsburg dynasty whom he, in turn, had served so faithfully.

As the assumption of the post of Sheriff of Sopron suggests, Nicolaus would have discussed the future of the Esterházy estate with his son, Anton. It had not always been an amicable relationship. Well into middle age – he was fifty-two when he succeeded his father – Anton was something of spendthrift, causing his father considerable worry about the future solvency of the family. An agreement had been reached that an independent financial curator should look after the financial affairs of the estate after Nicolaus's death until Anton's own financial situation was completely under control. Anton did not share his father's consuming interest in music, preferring the more esoteric pastime of mineral and fossil gathering. It was as much this lack of interest as a desire to demonstrate where a good deal of Esterházy expenditure had always been incurred that informed Anton's decision to dismantle the musical life of the court. Only the small ensemble for church music in Eisenstadt was retained, including Haydn's brother Johann; later, a wind band was established for ceremonial duties and the hunt. The remaining musicians were paid for the last time at the end of September, subsequently receiving six weeks' severance pay. One singer, Filippo Martinelli, had been at the court for barely five weeks, others such as Mathilde Bologna, Vito Ungricht and, of course, Luigia Polzelli, had many years of faithful service behind them as had the director Nunziato Porta; a few of the instrumentalists, such as Franz Pauer (horn), Joseph Oliva (horn and violin) and Carl Schiringer (double bass and bassoon), had even longer periods of service, going back to the 1760s. All were dismissed. Only two of the most senior members of the musical court were retained, Haydn as titular Kapellmeister and Luigi Tomasini as violinist, on a reduced salary of 400 gulden each, enough to ensure that their services as providers of music and musicians for special, one-off occasions could be called upon if necessary. These two were also beneficiaries of Nicolaus's will, Haydn receiving a pension of 1,000 gulden, Tomasini one of 400 gulden.

With a total annual income of 1,400 gulden Haydn was comfortably off, much more so than Mozart, and at the age of fifty-eight could have looked forward to several years of semi-retirement as Esterházy Kapellmeister, supplemented by income from commission fees, publication and some teaching. He had toiled, as he latterly would have described it, as a Kapellmeister for over thirty years (if the Morzin period is added to the Esterházy period) and much of October was spent at Eszterháza bureaucratically ratifying the demolition of a way of life; by November he was back in Vienna, a wholly free agent. Yet the habitual energy that had characterized that way of life remained and within a few weeks he had made an audacious decision on his future.

Rather briskly he turned down two offers of employment. Prince Nicolaus's daughter, Maria Anna, was married to Prince Anton Grassalkovics whose principal palace was in Pressburg. Haydn was offered the post of Kapellmeister but he rejected it, probably thinking that it was too similar to the Esterházy post, even though it did not have the treadmill of the opera season. There was also a standing invitation from Ferdinand, King of Naples for the composer to visit Naples and the king, who was in Vienna from September 1790 through to March 1791, no doubt reminded Haydn of this possibility. Living in Vienna certainly had its attractions for Haydn, the salon culture as represented by the Genzinger family, proximity to Artaria and the company of Mozart and other musicians. But he had never been part of the musical establishment and was still viewed as an outsider. Despite his extensive, in some ways unrivalled, experience as a director of Italian opera, he himself had not composed one for six years and, as Mozart would have reminded him, it was always going to be difficult to challenge the presence of the Italians in the city; moreover, following the death of Joseph II and the accession of Leopold II the whole direction of the company seemed to be changing, still Italianate but with new personnel and a new emphasis on serious opera. In the autumn of 1790 it was an uncertain time in Vienna too.

In London, Prince Nicolaus's death had been reported in the newspapers, also the rumour that Haydn was going to travel to the court of the King of Naples. Since the previous autumn Bland's association with Salomon had gained a third individual, Sir John Gallini, now manager of the newly rebuilt, but not yet reopened, King's Theatre in the Haymarket. Earlier in the decade Gallini had often been at the forefront of plans to bring Haydn to London as a composer of opera and as a resident composer in the Professional Concert. That plan was revived once more, this time with Salomon, the newly installed leader of the orchestra at the opera house, as the concert organizer. In the autumn of 1790 they divided their responsibilities,

Gallini was in Italy looking for singers, Salomon was in Germany looking for instrumentalists; at the same time both could point any inquisitive composer towards Bland as a London publisher. Salomon was in Cologne on his way back to London when he learnt that Haydn was no longer tied to the Esterházy court.

Suddenly and decisively Salomon changed his plans. He travelled to Vienna to persuade Haydn, in person, that this was the opportunity to fulfil the promise of several years and travel to London where he would be the resident composer at the new opera house and a new concert series. As a fellow German speaker Salomon was no doubt persuasive but Haydn was initially reluctant. Even Mozart, a seasoned traveller, urged caution. When he told Haydn that he spoke too few languages (not entirely fair, he did speak Italian and understood French) the composer replied 'my language is understood all over the world',[26] a confident assertion of the international popularity of his music. The British ambassador in Vienna, General Jerningham, was called in to persuade Haydn, Prince Anton agreed to release him and lent him 450 gulden for travelling expenses, a contract was agreed on 8 December, Salomon and Haydn departed some time after 16 December and an anticipatory report appeared in the *Morning Chronicle* in London on 27 December.

It is possible to view Haydn's decision to travel to England as a bold solution to local circumstances that were not entirely congenial. He did not wish to serve as Kapellmeister to another aristocratic family, musical Vienna had few openings for a man of his considerable experience, he did not want to travel to Naples and, not least, living with his wife was not especially appealing. At the same time London was not a leap into the unknown. For nearly ten years, through correspondence and then personal contact, he had acquired an understanding of the musical scene in the city and of his popularity there. He was now to experience it at first hand, the central figure in a narrative that had already been set in motion.

Images of Haydn: 1790

Charles Burney, *A General History of Music, From the Earliest Ages to the Present Period* (1789), ed. Frank Mercer (New York, 1957), vol. 2, pp. 958–60.

I am now happily arrived at that part of my narrative where it is necessary to speak of HAYDN! the admirable and matchless HAYDN! from whose productions I have received more pleasure late in my life, when tired of most other Music, that I ever received in the most ignorant and rapturous part of my youth, when every thing was new, and the disposition to be pleased undiminished by criticism or satiety . . .

JOSEPH HAYDN, maestro di capella to his serene prince Ester-házy, was born at Rohrau, in Lower Austria, in 1733. His father, a wheelwright by trade, played upon the harp with the least knowledge of Music, which, however, excited the attention of his son, and first gave the birth to his passion for Music. In his early childhood he used to sing to his father's harp the simple tunes which he was able to play, and being sent to a small school in the neighbourhood, he there began to learn Music regularly; after which he was placed under Reutter, maestro di capella of a cathedral at Vienna; and, having a voice of great compass, was received into the choir, where he was well taught, not only to sing, but to play on the harpsichord and violin. At the age of eighteen, on the breaking of his voice, he was dismissed from the cathedral. After this, he supported himself during eight years as well as he could by his talents, and began to study more seriously than ever. He read the works of Mattheson, Heinichen, and others, on the theory of Music; and for the practice, studied with particular attention the pieces of Emanuel Bach. At length he met with Porpora, who was at this time in Vienna, and, during five months, was so happy as to receive his counsel and instructions in singing and the composition of vocal Music. In 1759, he was received into the service of Count Morzin as director of his Music, whence, in 1761, he passed to the palace of prince Esterházy, to whose service he has been constantly attached ever since.

The first time I meet with his name in the German catalogues of Music, is in that of Breitkopf of Leipzig, 1763, to a *Divertimento a Cembalo* [Hob.XVI:5], 3 *Concerti à Cembalo* [actually two, Hob.XVI: 1 and 5], 6 *Trios* [actually 1766], 8 *Quadros* or *Quartets* [1765] and 6 *Symphonies in four and eight parts* [1766]. The chief of his early Music was for the chamber. He is said at Vienna to have composed before 1782, a hundred and twenty-four pieces for the baryton, for the use of his prince, who is partial to that instrument, and a great performer upon it. Besides his numerous pieces for instruments, he has composed many operas for the Esterházy theatre, and church Music that has established his reputation as a deep contrapuntist. His Stabat Mater has been performed and printed in England, but his oratorio of *Il ritorno di Tobia*, composed in 1775 for the benefit of the widows of musicians, has been annually performed at Vienna ever since, and is as high in favour there, as Handel's *Messiah* in England. His instrumental *Passione* [*The Seven Last Words*], in parts, is among his latest and most exquisite of productions. It entirely consists of slow movements, on the subject of the last seven sentences of our Saviour, as recorded in the Evangelists. These strains are so truly impassioned and full of heart-felt grief and dignified sorrow, that though the movements are all slow, the subjects, keys, and effects are so new and so different, that a real lover of Music will feel no lassitude, or wish for lighter strains to stimulate attention.

His innumerable symphonies, quartets, and other instrumental pieces, which are so original and so difficult, have the advantage of being rehearsed and performed at Eszterháza under his own direction, by a band of his own forming, who have apartments in the palace and practise from morning to night, in the same room, according to Fisher's account, like the students in the conservatorios of Naples. Ideas so new and so varied were not at first so universally admired in Germany as at present. The critics in the northern parts of the empire were up in arms. And a friend at Hamburg wrote me word in 1772, that 'the genius, fine ideas, and fancy of Haydn, Ditters, and Filtz, were praised, but their mixture of serious and comic was disliked, particularly as there is more of the latter than the former in their works; and as for rules, they knew but little of them.' This is a censure which the admirable Haydn has long since silenced: for he is now as much respected by professors for his science as invention. Indeed, his compositions are in general so new to the player and hearer that they are equally unable, at first, to keep pace with his inspiration. But it may be laid down as an axiom in Music, that 'whatever is *easy* is *old*, and what the hand, eye, and ear are accustomed to; and on the contrary, what is *new* is of course *difficult*, and not only scholars but professors have it to learn.' The first exclamation of an embarrassed performer and bewildered hearer is, that the Music is very *odd*, or very *comical*, but the queerness and comicality cease, when, by frequent repetition, the performer and hearer are at their ease. There is a general cheerfulness and good humour in Haydn's allegros, which exhilarate every hearer. But his adagios are often so sublime in ideas and the harmony in which they are clad, that though played by inarticulate instruments, they have a more pathetic effect on my feelings, than the finest opera air united with most exquisite poetry. He has likewise movements that are sportive, *folatres*, and even grotesque, for the sake of variety; but they are only *entre-mets*, or rather *intermezzi*, between the serious business of his other movements.

Charles Burney (1726–1814) had been working on his mammoth project, a complete history of music from Egyptian times to the end of the eighteenth century, for over a quarter of a century. As a product of the English Enlightenment, Burney's history is not only wide-ranging in its coverage but in its sympathies too, curious about music in all periods and in all countries, and wishing always to inform and direct contemporary public taste. During the 1780s he had been an influential figure behind the scenes in trying to lure Haydn to London and the opening sentences of the section on the composer proclaim an enthusiasm that was both personal and typical of a wider cultured society.

Although the fourth and final part ('Book') of the history was published in 1789 the section on Haydn was written a few years earlier in 1786–7, as is suggested by the description of *The Seven Last Words* as a recent work. In addition to being familiar with the many publications of the composer's music that were available in London, Burney sought to gain some understanding of when Haydn's music began to circulate widely by looking at the sales catalogues of the Leipzig firm of Breitkopf. Frustrated that he had not been able to meet the composer when he was in Vienna in 1772, Burney avidly collected information and anecdotes from others. Two individuals are identified in the account, the British ambassador in Vienna, Sir Robert Murray Keith, who as early as 1778 provided Burney with some information on Haydn's career to date, and John Abraham Fisher, a violinist who had travelled with Nancy Storace to Vienna, where they got married, played a violin concerto in the interval of one of the performances of Il ritorno di Tobia in 1784 and visited the composer in Eszterháza.

Despite these scholarly attempts to broaden his understanding of Haydn's career Burney reflects, very faithfully, the English view of the composer. Opera and church music are pushed to one side in favour of instrumental music, especially symphonies and quartets, whose aesthetic credentials are stoutly defended, particularly the mixing of the comic and the serious. Even at the end of the 1780s this was a provocative view of the rival merits of vocal and instrumental music, but it was also a progressive one that, more generally, promoted a new parity of Italian and German musical traditions. Burney, the enthusiastic historian, anticipated the evaluation of Haydn as the founding father of modern instrumental music. The composer was about to play his role to the full.

5   London – Vienna – London

Salomon and Haydn took about ten days to travel from Vienna to London, the longest journey the composer had made since the period as Kapellmeister to the Morzin family at Lukavec in Bohemia in the 1750s. As well as giving the two of them the opportunity to discuss, in more detail, plans for the forthcoming months, the journey also afforded the composer some indication of the esteem in which he was held. The travellers paused in Munich, where they met the Konzertmeister of the Bavarian court (formerly in Mannheim), the violinist and composer Christian Cannabich (1731–98) and then journeyed through the Swabian countryside to Wallerstein, home of Prince Krafft Ernst von Oettingen-Wallerstein, who had been in regular contact with the composer for nearly ten years. The electoral court in Bonn was a particularly rewarding stop. It was Salomon's birthplace, his father had been a musician at the court, he himself had joined the retinue at the age of only thirteen and he still had family there. From 1784 the reigning elector was Maximilian Franz, the Austrian archduke who had visited Eszterháza with members of his family on two occasions in the 1770s and, as elector, had strengthened the political allegiance between the electorate and Vienna, a relationship that affected its musical life too. The young Beethoven had already been to Vienna to study with Mozart, a visit that had to be curtailed a few weeks after his arrival because of the death of his mother. Music featured prominently in the life of the court with a retinue of over fifty musicians, one of the largest in Europe, serving the three traditional areas of opera, church and chamber. Haydn's masses, symphonies, quartets and trios were all well represented in the court library. That a favoured son, Salomon, should be bringing a favoured composer, Haydn, to Bonn was an event that was savoured by all.

Salomon and Haydn arrived on Saturday 25 December. Already that evening Haydn was a guest at the Lesegesellschaft,[1] a reading and debating circle that was open to all members of the town regardless of status and which had recently commissioned the commemorative Cantata on the Death of Joseph II from Beethoven. The following morning, St Stephen's Day, Salomon and Haydn attended mass in the court chapel, during which the musical forces of the elector performed an unidentified mass by Haydn. After the service the elector himself introduced the composer to the assembled musicians (including Beethoven) and paid for a subsequent celebratory meal.

It is not known when Salomon and Haydn left Bonn but by the last day of the year they were in Calais. After attending early mass on 1 January the two boarded ship at 7.30 in the morning, had to wait several hours for the wind to rise, finally reaching Dover by late afternoon by which time the tide had ebbed, preventing the ship from docking; willing passengers (including Haydn) were transferred to smaller boats. All this was vividly described by the composer in a letter to Maria Anna von Genzinger.[2]

> Some of the passengers were afraid to board the little boats and stayed on board, but I followed the example of the greater number. I had remained on deck during the whole passage, so as to gaze my fill at that mighty monster, the ocean. So long as it was calm, I wasn't at all afraid, but towards the end, when the wind grew stronger and stronger, and I saw the monstrous high waves rushing in at us, I became a little frightened, and a little indisposed too.

The following evening, Sunday 2 January, Salomon and Haydn arrived in London.

London, the capital of Great Britain, was a very different city from Vienna, capital of the Austrian Monarchy and of the Holy Roman Empire. Approaching a million in population it was nearly ten times the size of the Austrian capital, physically expressed in the rapid expansion of the city westwards towards Hyde Park and northwards towards Hampstead; Haydn himself picked up the random statistic that 38,000 homes had been built in the previous thirty years. It was a confident, entrepreneurial city reaping the early wealth of the Industrial Revolution, and one that had capitalized on its long seafaring tradition to become a major centre of international trade. Over the decades, parliamentary democracy had curbed the powers of the monarchy without affecting its standing and from the 1780s onwards William Pitt the younger nurtured a national self-confidence that enabled it to contain any radical or republican dissent that emerged during the years of the French Revolution. It was an informed democracy too in which freedom of speech was more likely to result in sensational libel cases than in authoritarian censorship. London, as Haydn soon noted, had several daily newspapers that freely reported on national and international events, including the *Morning Chronicle*, *Public Advertiser*, *The Times* and *The World*.

This open-mindedness was evident in its musical life too, commercially progressive and, now that Haydn was a temporary resident, one that could justifiably claim to be the best in Europe. As Haydn's own popularity in London had already demonstrated, musical taste was both cosmopolitan and contemporary, but this was not the complete picture. As well as 'modern' music England cultivated 'ancient' music, by which it understood music from Purcell's time onwards, a distinctive national tradition that embraced wholeheartedly the music of Handel, particularly his oratorios and anthems. While there was some dispute about the respective merits of the 'ancient' and the 'modern' it was one of Burney's abiding principles to seek the good in both, a discriminating pluralism that was an appropriate parallel to the cosmopolitanism. Rival national affiliations in music were, nevertheless, apparent: the Italians were associated with the King's Theatre, home of Italian opera, the English were more associated with church music, ancient music and the many catch and glee clubs, while a distinct, smaller community of German musicians, like Salomon himself, were associated with the newest fashions in instrumental music. Plenty of individuals crossed these loyalties. As a German, Haydn found a natural constituency in London for his instrumental music but he was to engage enthusiastically with the Italian tradition and, a wholly new experience, the English one too.

Two particular aspects of musical life, the active public concert life and the competitive publishing scene, had become familiar to Haydn over the previous decade and Salomon, no doubt, would have filled his head with the politics of musical life in London, but nothing could have quite prepared the composer, a comparative recluse, for the hustle and bustle of musical life and his central role in it. His popularity and celebrity were such that he had little control over his own image and he had become public property in a way that was unthinkable at that time in Vienna and wholly impossible in Eszterháza.

Haydn's first encounter with his status occurred on his second evening in London. He had stayed the first night at the home of John Bland in High Holborn, while Salomon prepared his permanent lodgings in Great Pulteney Street. On the evening of Monday 3 January Haydn attended a performance of Stephen Storace's English opera, *The Siege of Belgrade*, almost certainly intrigued by the topicality of the subject matter, the twenty months it took the Austrian army to capture Belgrade from the Turks in the recent war (1788–90). The correspondent of the *Morning Post and Daily Advertiser*, however, was more interested in Haydn's presence than Storace's opera.[3]

> Haydn was at Drury-Lane Theatre on Monday Evening. On his entrance the Band arose through a general impulse of curiosity. Mr. Haydn stooped forward and made his bow; Mr Shaw returned it by a bow, and the Gentlemen of the Orchestra all bowed. The Audience did not seem to understand the farce, or the Gentleman of the Bow [the police] might have had a reprimand for this unprecedented complaisance.

Within days Haydn was regularly receiving visitors, dining out every night and was fêted in concerts such as those given by the Academy of Ancient Music and the Anacreontic Society; within weeks he had been introduced to the Prince of Wales and to the Duke of York: 'Everyone wants to know me,' he wrote to Genzinger.[4] Valiantly he tried to keep mornings free from social commitments so that he could begin work on composing music for London.

Although Salomon's discussions had allowed little time for detailed planning, within a week the two key elements of the visit were in place, the opera for Sir John Gallini and the concerts for Salomon. The Gallini project was particularly exciting since Haydn's opera was to form part of the first season of the newly rebuilt King's Theatre in the Haymarket, the traditional home of Italian opera in London, which had been destroyed by fire – some newspapers alleged arson – in June 1789. An experienced librettist was engaged, Francesco Badini, and the subject matter was to be the story of Orpheus and Euridice. Gluck's celebrated treatment was as well known in London as anywhere in Europe and the choice of the same subject for Haydn was clearly an indication of ambition. Certainly Haydn, who seems not to have been consulted about the choice, thought about the inevitable comparison with Gluck, consoling himself with the fact that Badini's treatment was different, beginning the action before Orfeo and Euridice are married and eschewing the formal happy ending in favour of the death of the lovers. Working even more quickly than he had done at Eszterháza, he had essentially completed the work by the end of March, anticipating a performance in May. But Gallini's enterprise was in serious trouble. He had forgotten to secure a licence for the new theatre and, in order to recoup some of his financial outlay, instead presented some concert performances, an opera by Paisiello and miscellaneous programmes of instrumental, vocal and ballet. Haydn participated in many of these concerts and wrote a concert aria ('Cara deh torna in pace') for the tenor, Giacome Davide, who was supposed to be singing the role of Orfeo, and an Italian catch. Both these works have disappeared. Haydn's opera, *L'anima del filosofo*, did survive, but it was never given in

London or, indeed, anywhere else in the composer's lifetime. This was an inglorious end to the long-standing plans to present Haydn as an opera composer in London. He consoled himself with the knowledge that he had been paid (the amount is not clear) and that the money was in a bank in Vienna. The other aspect of his work for London, instrumental music for a new subscription series organized by Salomon, was more than fulfilling expectations. It seemed that in order for Haydn to become a successful composer of symphonies he had first to fail as an opera composer.

Salomon had given details of his subscription series in a newspaper advertisement on 15 January.[5] Addressed, as was customary in such announcements, to the 'Nobility and Gentry' it offered twelve weekly concerts beginning on Friday 11 February in the favoured venue of the Hanover Square Rooms. Advanced subscriptions, at 5 guineas each, were available from Lockharts the bankers in Pall Mall and, again reflecting local custom, the tickets were colour-coded to ensure equal distribution between the sexes, green tickets for the ladies, black for the gentlemen, with the instruction that they could not be given to the opposite sex; 'Mr. Haydn will compose for every Night a New Piece of Music, and direct the execution of it at the Harpsichord.' Although this first series never sold out, sufficient subscriptions came in to enable Salomon to firm up his plans. However, six weeks in January and February proved insufficient to gather an orchestra and the necessary vocal and instrumental soloists together, and the opening concert was first postponed until 25 February and then to 11 March. Salomon would have lost little credibility for these postponements; they were a recurring feature of concert life in London and may even have heightened expectation. It did, however, allow a rival series, the established Professional Concert with their superior performers, to begin their season of twelve concerts on 7 February. The newspapers tried to engineer more friction between the two organizations than actually existed. Haydn was given free entry to the Professional Concert, in the form of an ivory disc on a blue ribbon, and attended at least two of their concerts. Following the practice of the previous decade each Professional Concert included at least one work by Haydn, but the organizers could not, of course, claim that they were brand new ones.

Haydn's contract with Salomon required him to compose six symphonies for which he was to receive £300, plus a further £200 if the copyright was transferred to Salomon. Haydn could not possibly fulfil this commitment during the 1791 season given that he was also composing an opera; yet he did, unbelievably, complete two new symphonies, nos. 95 and 96, performed in the latter stages of the season. With some imaginative planning Salomon and Haydn were, however, still able to fulfil their promise of 'a New Piece of Music' in every concert. They were of four kinds. Symphonies nos. 90, 91 and 92, which had been composed for Count d'Ogny in Paris, were not yet known in London; Haydn brought the first and last of these with him and they were given in the 1791 season, but he had forgotten to pack no. 91 and wrote several urgent letters to Genzinger in Vienna asking her to forward the music which, to his increasing irritation, did not arrive until the middle of the following season. The second, more unexpected source for new music in a public concert lay in the genre of the quartet. Public as well as private concerts in London regularly featured music for small ensembles, including quartets. Haydn's latest quartets, op. 64, had been finished only a few months earlier, in the autumn of 1790; the composer had brought them with him to consolidate the promise that Bland could publish them in London; they could now be pressed into service as new concert pieces and three were duly given during the season. Haydn had also brought some of the music for two lire organizzata and ensemble that he had written for the King of Naples, again music that was otherwise unknown; he adapted two of these for the more conventional instrumental ensemble of flute, oboe, two horns and strings, providing attractive concertante music that contrasted with his quartets and symphonies. Finally, a 'new' concert aria was announced to be performed by Nancy Storace, specially engaged for the season by Salomon; almost certainly this was 'Miseri noi, misera patria' written in the 1780s and, again, an unfamiliar item that was featuring in the continuing negotiations with Bland, though in the event it was never published by the firm.

Haydn's music was the constant strand in the programmes, emphasized by his presence on stage, where he helped to direct the performances from the keyboard. But other composers featured too. In general the composers of vocal items and concerto-like items were not identified but the centrality given to the symphony, especially the German symphony, is emphasized by performances of works by Gyrowetz (also resident in London), Hoffmeister, Kozeluch, Pichl, Pleyel and Rosetti.

April and May in the concert life of London saw a surge in the number of public concerts as the leading figures from the Italian opera as well as the various concert series were granted benefit concerts to boost their income. Haydn's benefit was slotted in between the ninth and tenth of Salomon's concerts, on Monday 16 May, in the Hanover Square Rooms and it was then that the cantata for Davide, 'Cara deh torna in pace', was given its first performance. Haydn made £350 and, ever the diplomat, placed a notice of thanks in the *Morning Chronicle*. It was obviously prepared by a fluent and elegant English speaker, but its multi-clause structure and verbal tenses hint at a German original.[6]

> Mr. Haydn, extremely flattered with his reception in a Country where he has long been ambitious of visiting, and penetrated with the patronage with which he has been honoured by its animated and generous Inhabitants, should think himself guilty of the greatest ingratitude, if he did not take the earliest opportunity of making his most grateful Acknowledgments to the English Public in general, as well as to his particular Friends, for the zeal which they have manifested at his concert, which has been supported by such distinguished marks of favour and approbation, as will be remembered by him with infinite delight as long as he lives.

Haydn continued to explore the full range of musical life in London, as a participant in other people's concerts or as a member of the audience. In the last week of May he attended the Handel Commemoration Festival, a series of four concerts in Westminster Abbey given by forces numbering up to 1,000 or more. The programmes included 'Zadok the Priest', *Israel in Egypt, Messiah* and extracts from other oratorios. Musically overwhelming, it must also have impressed Haydn as a confident display of national identity such as he had not witnessed since his days as a choirboy in imperial-royal Vienna: the royal family, who attended in numbers, happily took on the mantle of Englishness in a venue, Westminster Abbey, that covered everything with a Protestant identity.

The following week on 9 June Haydn was in St Paul's for a charity service given under the aegis of the Society for Promoting Christian Knowledge, designed to foster an awareness of the charitable role of the Church of England in educating children of the poor. Haydn heard 4,000 children sing an Anglican chant by John Jones, and was again moved to tears. He was to tell Griesinger, 'No music ever moved me so deeply in my whole life.'[7]

Haydn's visits to Westminster Abbey and St Paul's invite the question whether he was able to practise his own, Catholic faith in London. While there is no direct evidence that he did so, it was, in fact, perfectly possible and, for that reason, very likely. Chapels associated with foreign embassies that represented Catholic countries offered public access to worshippers and three in particular, those attached to the Bavarian, Portuguese and Sardinian embassies, had strong musical traditions. When the Bavarian embassy vacated its premises in Golden Square in 1788 a new Catholic chapel was built on the same site, Our Lady of the Assumption and St Gregory, and maintained a strong link with the embassy. This chapel was a mere two minutes' walk from Haydn's lodgings in Great Pulteney Street and the hypothesis that he carried on his Catholic devotion here is a persuasive one.

Charles Burney was the likely instigator of the decision by Oxford University to make Haydn an honorary Doctor of Music, an award that was rarely given. The ceremony took place in the Sheldonian Theatre on 8 July, Haydn breaking the formality of the occasion a little by uttering, in his newly acquired but still heavily accented English, 'I thank you.' A three-day 'Grand Music Festival' accompanied the event and at a concert in the Sheldonian Theatre on 7 July Haydn directed a performance of Symphony no. 92, prompting the nickname 'Oxford'. As a token of his gratitude Haydn gave the university a concise display of his learned musicianship, 'Thy voice o Harmony is divine'; this is a three-part puzzle canon that has to be read forwards, backwards, upside down and in four different clefs before it can be fully experienced.

Haydn had begun jotting down his impressions of life in England in notebooks roughly equivalent to the modern A6 in size and designed to be carried in his pocket. Eventually four were to be used; during the first visit two were used interchangeably. Written in ink, occasionally in pencil, entries were often prompted by facts and figures. For the Oxford ceremonies Haydn noted his expenditure: 6 guineas for the trip, 1½ guineas to have the bells rung and half a guinea for the robes. Although the university had made him pay for the privilege Haydn was immensely proud of the honour, something that no Austrian university could bestow since they did not have music as a discipline, and a title, Dr Haydn, that he proceeded to use for the remainder of his life.

From London Haydn corresponded regularly with the three women in his life, Maria Anna von Genzinger, Luigia Polzelli and his wife, Maria Anna, though the content of the letters to and from the last-named can only be inferred from references in the correspondence with the first two. Haydn sent his wife some money and some English sewing needles; she bothered Haydn with some tittle-tattle, including that Mozart had badmouthed him, and, more seriously, that she had seen a house in the rapidly developing southern suburb of Gumpendorf that she wanted to purchase. After the disbandment of the opera company at Eszterháza Luigia Polzelli had moved with her ailing husband and sons to Vienna and then to Italy; she and Haydn remained in touch and, for a long time, he genuinely missed her. Her vocally more gifted sister, Theresa Negri, was now in London and had sung in some of Salomon's concerts. As Haydn forwarded money to Luigia, he included some news about Theresa, asked solicitously about Pietro (though, oddly, never about Antonio) and offered moral support as she nursed her husband. Following his death Haydn wrote a lengthy letter to Luigia in which appropriate sentiments of condolence take a wholly callous turn as he contemplates the death of his wife and life with Luigia.[8]

> As far as your husband is concerned, I tell you that Providence has done well to liberate you from this heavy yoke, and for him, too, it is better to be in another world than to remain useless in this one. The poor man has suffered enough. Dear Polzelli, perhaps, perhaps the time will come, which we both so often dreamt of, when four eyes shall be closed, Two are closed, but the other two – enough of all this, it shall be as God wills.

Three women had, in fact, recently become four as Haydn began a friendship with an English widow, Rebecca Schroeter (1751–1826), already the subject of lingering notoriety in polite society because of the circumstances surrounding her marriage to Johann Samuel Schroeter (c.1751–88). Born Rebecca Scott she was the daughter of a wealthy businessman who owned a handsome house on the edge of Greenwich Park in Blackheath, south of London. Johann Schroeter, a pianist, composer and teacher, was engaged to teach Rebecca and visited the family home several times a week. The two fell in love and, recognizing that neither her family nor society in general would have regarded marriage between a 'foreigner' who, moreover, was a jobbing musician and a 'young lady of fashion' as appropriate, decided to wed in secret. The family tried to pay off Schroeter with the considerable sum of £500 and then to prevent Rebecca receiving the vastly more considerable sum of £15,000 due to her from her father's will. The two eventually married and lived a happy life in musical circles in London until Johann's untimely death in 1788. They knew Salomon and he, very likely, introduced Rebecca to Haydn during the 1791 concert season. She was forty, Haydn was fifty-nine and for the time being the relationship was a formal one.

Salomon and Haydn had already agreed that there should be a second season of concerts in the following year and on 20 July 1791 the composer wrote to Prince Anton, requesting an extension to his leave of absence. On 12 August the prince replied, stating firmly that the Kapellmeister had already stayed longer in London than anticipated and that he should indicate the date of his return immediately. Haydn was in an impossible position and in the end decided to stay in London and to bear the consequences back home. Much of August and September was spent in the country house of a banker, Nathaniel Brassey, Roxford in Hertingfordbury (near Hertford) from where on 17 September he wrote to Maria Anna von Genzinger. Not only does he explain his troubling dilemma but hints, for the first time, at the wider ambivalences of his continuing to stay in England.[9]

> I am all right, thank the good Lord! except for my usual
> rheumatism; I work hard, and in the early mornings I walk in the
> woods, alone, with my English grammar, I think of my Creator, my
> family, all the friends I have left behind – and of these you are the
> one I most value. Of course I had hoped to have the pleasure of
> seeing you sooner, but my circumstances – in short, fate – will have it
> that I remain in London another 8 to 10 months. Oh, my dear
> gracious lady! how sweet this bit of freedom really is! I had a kind
> prince, but sometimes I was forced to be dependent on base souls. I
> often sighed for release, and now I have it in some measure. I
> appreciate the good sides of all this, too, though my mind is
> burdened with far more work. The realization that I am no
> bond-servant makes ample amend for all my toils. But, dear though
> this liberty is to me, I should like to enter Prince Esterházy's service
> again when I return, if only for the sake of my family. I doubt
> whether this will be possible, however, for in his letter my prince
> strongly objects to my staying away for so long.

Haydn spent most of the autumn in London, relieved by visits to Cambridge and a two-day stay at Oatlands, the country residence of the Duke of York, where Haydn made music with the duke (and others) until two o'clock in the morning. Although no public announcement of Salomon's plans for the 1792 season had yet been made the later stories that Mozart, too, was to be engaged are given some credence in a further letter from Haydn to Genzinger, in which he asks her to inform Mozart that if he has queries about Haydn's remuneration in London he should ask his banker (Fries) and Prince Esterházy. Any such plans, however tentative, had to be abandoned for ever following Mozart's death on 5 December. Rumours of the death reached London by 20 December; on the following day *The World* became the first English newspaper to confirm the news, adding the simple statement 'By his death the Musical World will sustain an irreparable loss'.

Haydn was able to discuss this loss with a former pupil, Ignaz Pleyel (1757–1831) who arrived in London on 23 December. They had not seen each other for nearly ten years; after working for Count Ladislaus Erdödy he had moved to Italy and then to Strasbourg. His op. 1, a set of quartets, was published in Vienna in 1783 and dedicated to the count, and marked the beginning of a rapidly burgeoning career as a composer of instrumental music, especially quartets and symphonies, that reflected the increasing status of those genres; his op. 2 was another set of quartets, dedicated this time to Haydn. In London, as in Paris, Pleyel's music flourished in the wake of Haydn's music, even if someone like Charles Burney complained that it was too reminiscent of the master. Pleyel had been engaged by the Professional Concert as their resident composer for the 1792 season, an obvious opportunity for the newspapers to ratchet up tension between the two organizations, now headed by a teacher and his former pupil, particularly as it was common knowledge that the Professional Concert had tried to tempt Haydn to join them before settling for Pleyel. Both Haydn and Pleyel rose above the situation and enjoyed a cordial few months in each other's company; the Professional Concert in the Hanover Square Rooms on Mondays featured Haydn's music as well as that of Pleyel, and Salomon's concerts on Fridays in the same venue included some Pleyel alongside Haydn; indeed the very first item in Salomon's 1792 series, directed by Haydn, was a symphony by Pleyel. In the end, supposed competition and rivalry served only to boost interest in both series.

Salomon began his weekly series on 17 February intending, like the Professional Concert, to include twelve concerts, but the enthusiasm of the audience led to an additional, thirteenth concert, right at the tail end of the social season, on 6 June. The basic pattern of a mixed programme of songs, arias, chamber works and orchestral works was maintained, with symphonies forming the cornerstones at the beginning and/or end of each half. Haydn now had four brand new symphonies ready (or nearly so) for performance, nos. 93, 94, 97 and 98, and these first performances were supplemented by repeat performances of works that had been particularly well received. In friendly recognition of the popularity that Pleyel achieved with some of his symphonies concertantes (works for multiple soloists and orchestra) Haydn wrote one of his own, for oboe, bassoon, violin and cello with orchestra; if Burney thought that Pleyel's music was too similar to Haydn's, then this is a work that showed that Haydn could ape Pleyel if necessary. A further novelty, again repeated later in the series, was Haydn's first vocal work in the English language (apart from the puzzle canon for Oxford University), a setting of a text by John Wolcot (1738–1819) that exploits the fashionable subject of a storm, its unsettling horror juxtaposed with an unreal, eventually comforting, calm. This was not the first time that Haydn had composed a musical storm but it did mark his introduction to the English strain of pastoral imagery that was to figure in *The Creation* and *The Seasons*. Haydn's benefit concert was on 3 May where he, once more, cleverly tapped into the English fascination with the pictorial, by concluding the concert with 'the Earthquake', that is the last movement of *The Seven Last Words*; the concert also included a repeat performance of his symphonie concertante and the likely first performance of Symphony no. 95 in C major (see Figure 8).

Rebecca Schroeter was a regular attender of these concerts. No fewer than sixteen letters were written by her to Haydn between March and June, demonstrating increasing affection and devotion, to the point of infatuation. No sooner had Haydn been a welcome dinner guest than he was being invited to the next dinner, often with the request that he should arrive a few hours early; she is solicitous about his health, hopes that he has slept well and that he is not

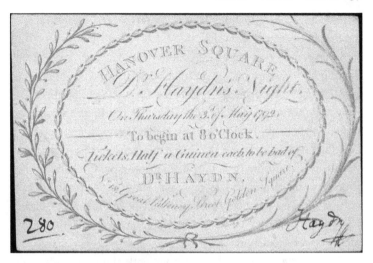

8. Ticket for Haydn's benefit concert, May 1792.

overworking; she willingly undertakes some music copying for him, encourages his curiosity about English poetry and writes ecstatically about her love of his music. Haydn, rather laboriously, copied these letters into one of his notebooks and later indicated to Griesinger that if circumstances had been different he would have married the 'English widow', as he called her; he also managed to give a different gloss to the relationship by stating that she was sixty years old (that is the same as Haydn) when, in fact, she was nearly twenty years younger. She had already, scandalously, married Johann Schroeter; she was now, very persistently, in pursuit of the leading figure in London's musical life, Joseph Haydn. More than once her letters suggest that this relationship was no longer a platonic one. In one she writes, 'I thought you seemed out of Spirits this morning, I wish I coul'd always remove every trouble from your mind. Be assure D: I partake with most perfect Sympathy in ALL YOUR SENSATIONS, and my regard for you is STRONGER EVERY DAY.'[10] In another Haydn crossed out a few words with such effectiveness that not even modern technology has been able to deduce what originally lay underneath; presumably they were so personal or shocking that they later embarrassed him, even though he had first copied them faithfully.

Haydn continued to remain in contact with Genzinger and Polzelli, assuring both that he was returning to Vienna in the summer. More formally, but with a palpable sense of anticipation, on 4 April 1792 he wrote to Prince Anton that his services would soon be at his complete disposal once more. It was later agreed that Haydn should return via Frankfurt in time to attend the coronation services there associated with the election of Franz II as Holy Roman Emperor; like his father before him the prince was to represent the Bohemian nobility but, whereas Nicolaus had not taken any musicians in 1764, Anton clearly felt that having Haydn in Frankfurt would add considerably to his lustre.

While Haydn, increasingly tired from work and from social obligations, looked forward to returning to Vienna, he was prepared to commit himself, at least in principle, to returning for the 1793 season. He could have left London immediately after the last Salomon concert but decided to delay the journey so that he could arrive in Frankfurt in mid-July. June was more relaxed. He went to Windsor Castle ('The view from the terrace is divine'), the races at Ascot ('The riders are very lightly clad in silk, and each one has a different colour . . . they are as lean as a greyhound') and to Slough to one of the great attractions of the day, Herschel's telescope ('It is 40 feet long and 5 feet in diameter. The machinery is very big, but so ingenious that a single man can put it in motion with the greatest ease').[11]

In a letter to his brother-on-law[12] Salomon indicated that he wished to accompany 'beloved Papa Haydn' (den lieben Papa Haydn) to Bonn but, in the event, was unable to because of pressing business in London. It is possible that Salomon and Haydn had already hatched the idea of bringing the young Beethoven to London as a pianist-composer and that the intended visit by both was meant to pursue this idea. It was left to Haydn to set up the plan that Beethoven should first journey to Vienna in the autumn and then accompany him on the return visit to London.

Haydn was, finally, back in Vienna by 24 July. By the end of the month he had resumed his bureaucratic duties at the Esterházy court. As Kapellmeister he was now listed at the head of the 'Chor Musique' that still provided the music for church services in Eisenstadt though this was largely a sinecure. Circumstantial evidence suggests that he may have spent a few weeks in the late summer of 1792 reclaiming personal belongings he had left in Eszterháza nearly two years earlier. In Vienna he lived with his wife in the house on the Wasserkunstbastei and soon acquired an unlikely lodger, Pietro Polzelli, now an eager pupil; according to Haydn his wife was happy with the arrangement but, in general, their relationship was as distant as it had always been; within a year he was reporting to Luigia Polzelli that she 'is always in a foul mood, but I don't really care any more'.[13] Haydn, however, was very taken by the house she had seen in the semi-rural suburb of Gumpendorf. He liked its tranquillity, a quality that it maintains today, even though it is now in a thoroughly built-up area; purchasing the house must have appealed also to his sense of vanity, the son of a wheelwright from Rohrau who had become a Kapellmeister, a Doctor of Music, someone who was fêted by English society and who was now in a position to own a house in Vienna. It cost him 1,370 gulden (equivalent to c. £150 at the contemporary exchange rate of 9 gulden to the pound), easily affordable by someone who had saved the proceeds of the sale of the house in Eisenstadt and added to it considerably with the money he had earned in London; he even had enough money to build an extra floor to the house, changes that took three years to bring about.

Apart from some dances (twelve German dances and twelve minuets) for the annual masked ball of the Gesellschaft der bildenden Künstler in November, Haydn composed very little music in Vienna in 1792. After London he seemed content to disappear into anonymity, an impression that is confirmed by an entry in Ignaz de Luca's latest publication, a directory for the city of Vienna, listing everything from monasteries and parishes to death rates and postal charges. There is a small section on musicians in Vienna largely, as elsewhere in the volume, a list with the occasional comment. For Haydn, de Luca reminds his readers that he had provided a 'true and interesting' biography in his earlier volume, *Das gelehrte Oesterreich*, and informs them that the composer has visited England where his talent met with due attention; 'he now lives as a pensioned person in Vienna, treasured by connoisseurs'.[14] This incipient sense of a musical elder statesman lay behind a rather more eccentric decision by the reigning Count Harrach, Karl Leonhard, to erect a small statue in honour of Haydn as part of the reshaping of the gardens in the palace in Rohrau. Following the English practice of moulding a natural landscape, a river was re-routed, an island created and a monument to Rohrau's most distinguished son placed on a bank, greeting walkers when they might have expected a figure from Classical mythology.

Beethoven had arrived in Vienna in mid-November and began lessons with Haydn almost immediately, the master taking the gifted composer back to basics by making him work through species counterpoint using Fux's *Gradus ad Parnassum*. By now it was clear to Haydn that he was not going to visit London in 1793, though he seems not to have finally told Salomon until January. He did not have a collection of new music, particularly symphonies, that could be presented to the voracious English public and he was increasingly troubled by an old complaint, a nasal polyp, that required an operation. At the very last minute Salomon was forced to organize a series of twelve subscription concerts without the presence of the composer but with his music as a continuing thread. Luckily for him the Professional Concert, too, had lost the services of its resident composer, Pleyel.

Meanwhile Haydn had summoned up the energy to do something very unusual in the musical life of Vienna, present a public concert of his own music. Unlike London, public concert life in Vienna was wholly undeveloped; the last subscription series had been the one organized by Mozart in 1788 (if, indeed, it took place) and single public concerts tended to be for the benefit of a performer rather than a composer. Haydn booked an unusual venue too, the Kleiner Redoutensaal, for his concert on 15 March and made the bold and unprecedented decision of presenting three symphonies (selected from nos. 93, 96, 97 and 98), leavened by some Italian arias. In London at least two or three newspapers would have advertised the concert and subsequently reported its success in lengthy reviews. In Vienna there was nothing; the only known references are incidental ones, in a diary and in a letter. One person who was not at the concert was Maria Anna von Genzinger who had died on 20 January, aged only forty-three.

From May onwards Haydn, and Beethoven too, spent most of his time in Eisenstadt, initially saddened by another death, that of Eleonora Jäger at the age of seventy-two; she had entered the service of the Esterházy family in 1753 and with great persistence and humour had managed to persuade reigning princes of the value of the Chor Musique, a natural ally for the Kapellmeister. Apart from signing receipts and perhaps playing the organ in services in the palace, there was little for Haydn to do in Eisenstadt in 1793. It was then that he seems to have decided that he would prepare for a second visit to London, writing six quartets (opp. 71 and 74), the whole of Symphony no. 99 and portions of two more, nos. 100 and 101.

Beethoven's stipend from Bonn was still being paid in anticipation of his eventual return to the court. In November Haydn forwarded a report to Elector Maximilian about his progress. He enclosed a number of compositions by Beethoven that had been written in the last few months, also an emolliently worded plea, of the kind that had always worked with Prince Nicolaus, that the young musician's stipend should be continued and that some accumulated debts paid. The elector was not impressed. Most of the music, he claimed, had already been written in Bonn, he could not see why Beethoven was short of money and wondered whether he might as well return home immediately. None of the correspondence mentions the trip to London that had been part of the original understanding; whether that plan had already been put to one side or was forgotten as a consequence of Maximilian's displeasure is not known. In the end the stipend was maintained, Beethoven stayed in Vienna and his instruction was passed on to Albrechtsberger.

Haydn left Vienna on 19 January, not on the regular stagecoach but in a travelling coach lent to him by Gottfried van Swieten. He was accompanied on this occasion by Johann Elssler (1769–1843), a copyist in his early twenties, who had worked intermittently for the composer for some six years; his role soon became that of a valuable general assistant. Travelling along the road to Linz and then Passau it took them a week to get to Wiesbaden where, at the 'Zum Einhorn' inn, the two were surprised to hear a Prussian officer in an adjacent room playing the slow movement of the 'Surprise' symphony on a piano. From Wiesbaden the journey probably took them along the Rhine (though avoiding Bonn), through the Austrian Netherlands to Calais. Haydn and Elssler arrived in London on Tuesday 4 February 1794. For the duration of the second visit to the English capital they lived in the very fashionable area of St James's, in Bury Street; ten minutes' walk to the north-west took them to the Hanover Square Rooms; ten minutes' walk to the south-west took Haydn to Rebecca Schroeter's house in Buckingham Gate.

The London press had already created a sense of anticipation for the person they now routinely called Dr Haydn: Salomon himself had first announced that the series of twelve subscription concerts would begin on 3 February before postponing the first concert to 10 February while one newspaper, *The Oracle*, reported that 'The Doctor has been writing with all his original fancy and fertile combination; and the present winter will perhaps give us works, which shall advance even higher the celebrity of Haydn'.[15] Haydn was now accustomed to the feverish nature of musical life in London, had already prepared some symphonies for the concerts and had an assistant, Elssler, to help with the practicalities. He would have been relieved to learn that the rather trying enmity of Salomon and the Professional Concert that was whipped up by the press was no longer a feature of musical life. In 1793 the Professional Concert season had not been a successful one and, after first trying to negotiate collaboration between themselves and Salomon, the organization mooted the possibility of a concert series jointly promoted with the King's Theatre. Throughout these discussions everyone realized that Salomon was the leading figure, held the trump card in Haydn and could effectively dictate the pattern of concert life in London. Not only did he have exclusive call on any new works by Haydn, but he also owned the performance material for the six 'London' symphonies to date and was able to control subsequent performances; the Professional Concert had to rely on older symphonies by Haydn, less compelling in their musical argument and without the sense of them being 'London' symphonies. The Professional Concert disbanded and Salomon promptly moved his concerts from the Friday to the Monday; they were now, beyond any doubt, the highlight of the musical season.

Haydn seems to have persuaded Salomon that not every single concert needed a new work by him and during the course of the season only six premieres were given, three quartets from op. 71 and op. 74 and three symphonies, nos. 99, 100 and 101. Alongside the music of Dr Haydn there were two other strands to the concerts. First there were arias and duets from Italian opera sung by the popular, if temperamental soprano, Gertrud Elisabeth Mara, and, a new singer in London, the bass Ludwig Fischer. He was well known in Vienna as the singer who had created the role of Osmin in Mozart's *Die Entführung aus dem Serail* and, according to one newspaper report, it was Haydn who recommended him to Salomon. Determined to avoid the excessive pressure of earlier seasons Haydn did not rush to compose works for these two singers; indeed no vocal work by the composer seems to have been given during the 1794 season. The second appealing strand in the concerts were two instrumental soloists, Giovanni Battista Viotti (1755–1824), violin, and Jan Ladislav Dussek (1760–1812), piano; it is less surprising that Haydn did not write any concertos for the violin or the piano since music of this kind was still much more likely to be composed by the performer than by a commissioned composer.

During this, his third season, Haydn remained endlessly fascinated by life in London but he was no longer overwhelmed by it and, as his spoken and written English continued to improve, he was less the startled outsider than someone who increasingly felt part of the social and cultural scene. Dr Haydn or the Shakespeare of music, as he was often dubbed, grew ever more responsive to England.

During his first visit he had begun amassing a collection of newspaper cuttings, as a reminder of his success. While much of the newspaper coverage celebrated Haydn's musical mastery in very broad terms, some of the particular comments on his music proclaimed a musical aesthetic for the composer that he, in turn, absorbed, exploited and extended. In 1794 the first performance of Symphony no. 99 prompted the following response from the *Morning Chronicle*:[16]

> It is one of the grandest efforts of art that we ever witnessed. It abounds with ideas, as new in music as they are grand and impressive; it rouses and affects every emotion of the soul. – It was received with rapturous applause.

Ambition, novelty, variety and the ability to excite were all qualities that characterized the reception of a Haydn symphony and prompted the audience to unfettered, rather than merely polite, applause. These qualities automatically translated themselves into admiration for their creator, seated at the piano in the middle of the stage. When Symphony no. 101 was given its first performance on 3 March the same commentator described the composer as 'the inexhaustible, the wonderful, the sublime Haydn!' Warming to his theme of undiminished inspiration he continues, 'Every new Overture [symphony] he writes, we fear, till it is heard, he can only repeat himself; and we are every time mistaken.'[17] Occasionally a critic would latch on to a particular element of compositional technique, a sense of discrimination that is passed on to the reader. The following comments on Haydn's thematic economy in Symphony no. 101 ('Clock') get to the heart of the composer's methods.[18]

> Nothing can be more original than the subject of the first movement; and having found a happy subject, no man knows like Haydn how to produce incessant variety, without once departing from it. The management of the accompaniments of the andante, though perfectly simple, was masterly.

The popular success of the 1794 season was Symphony no. 100 in which Haydn boldly expanded the aesthetic of his symphonies once more by capturing the latest horrors of the French Revolution and its consequences. The Reign of Terror was at its height in Paris, savage in its brutality and unpredictable as it turned on former revolutionaries such as Marat the painter and Robespierre himself. For a year Austria, Britain, Holland and Prussia had been at war with France. The course of the atrocities in France and the various military campaigns were regularly reported in the English newspapers and refugees from Paris were a common sight on the streets of London, some of whom attended Haydn's concerts. Haydn's symphony begins in the manner that London audience had come to expect, a slow introduction leading to an allegro. The slow movement, like those in no. 94 and no. 101, is suspiciously light, a dainty march. A sudden switch to the minor key unleashes a barrage of percussion instruments, wholly unprecedented in Haydn's symphonies (or, indeed, anybody else's) and which proceed to cast a dark shadow over the rest of the movement; at a later point a solo fanfare on trumpet leads to another outburst. For Haydn's audience this symphony captured the mood of the day perfectly. At the first performance on 31 March the slow movement had to be repeated, the symphony was given its second performance at the next subscription concert on 7 April and four further performances, at Haydn's benefit concert on 2 May, the last of the subscription concerts on 12 May, Salomon's benefit on 28 May and, 'for the last time this season', at Ludwig Fischer's benefit on 2 June. After the performance in Haydn's benefit concert the critic of the *Morning Chronicle* once more tried to articulate the effect of the slow movement, in particular the use of percussion instruments.[19]

> The reason of the great effect they produce in the military movement is that they mark and tell the story: they inform us that the army is marching to battle, and, calling up all the ideas of the terror of such a scene, give it reality. Discordant sounds are then sublime; for what can be more horribly discordant to the heart than thousands of men meeting to murder each other?

Topicality was a new characteristic in Haydn's music, first learnt in London but which, prompted by the continuing European wars, was to feature in later music by the composer. From topicality it was one short step towards patriotism: there is a sense in this symphony that Haydn's music, however incipiently, was promoting national resolve. Earlier in the century Handel, over a longer of period of time, had become identified as an English composer. There were signs that this was slowly happening to Haydn too during the course of his second visit.

On 3 June, a day after the sixth performance of the 'Military' symphony, on 3 June, London newspapers announced the publication of six 'original canzonettas' by Haydn which could be purchased either directly from the composer in Bury Street or from the new publishing firm of Corri, Dussek & Co. This was a clear attempt by Haydn to capitalize on his popularity amongst the nobility and gentry who attended his concerts and to spread it into the drawing room; he was confident in its likely success to the extent that he underwrote the costs of engraving and printing himself, which then allowed him to keep any profits. Artistically, he was encouraged by Anne Hunter, the author of the six poems that were set. She and her husband, the distinguished surgeon John Hunter, had met Haydn in 1792; John Hunter died in October 1793 and Haydn's songs are dedicated to 'Mrs John Hunter'. She must have helped Haydn with the accentuation, prosody and sentiment of her poetry, which are perfectly realized. At about this time Haydn made an arrangement of the national anthem, 'God save the King', probably for domestic music making rather than for a public occasion; it was never published and no manuscript has survived.

Haydn dealt regularly with the many music publishers in London. Having played a full part in encouraging the composer to visit London John Bland, by 1794, had lost interest in music publishing and sold his business the following year. For William Napier, Haydn made simple settings of 150 Scottish folksongs between 1792 and 1795, initially for nothing to help keep his business solvent. Corri, Dussek & Co. was established by Haydn's colleague in the 1794 concerts, Jan Ladislav Dussek, and his father-in-law, the violinist and impresario Domenico

Corri. As well as selling the first set of canzonettas they were the publishers of a second set and of the opp. 71 and 74 quartets. Longman and Broderip, meanwhile, were entrusted with the publication of two sets of piano trios, the second (Hob.xv: 24–6) dedicated to Rebecca Schroeter. A further four piano trios (a single work and a set of three) were published by the firm of Preston. Of these various firms Longman and Broderip (and its successors) was the most enduring, remaining in contact with the composer for the rest of his working life.

Unlike the first visit there is no extant correspondence between Haydn and friends in Vienna that sheds light on the composer's inner thoughts and feelings in 1794–5. His greatest confidante, Genzinger, had died and while he probably wrote to his wife and almost certainly to Polzelli in Italy, nothing has survived. Haydn, however, had received shocking news concerning Prince Anton Esterházy almost as soon as he had arrived in January 1794. The prince, who had been reluctant to allow his Kapellmeister to travel to London for a second time, died three days after the composer left Vienna, an unexpected death at the age of fifty-five. He was succeeded by his son, Nicolaus II, who was thirty-three. Within a matter of weeks the new prince, the fourth whom Haydn had known, decided that he wished to retain the services of his Kapellmeister together with those of the small musical establishment in Eisenstadt that attended the liturgy, the Chor Musique. Over time Nicolaus II was to expand the musical provision of the court but for the moment another interest, art, was the priority as he embarked on a lengthy tour of Italy, eventually returning with works by Correggio, Lorrain, Raphael and others.

With no immediate pressure to return to the Esterházy court, Haydn was able to fall in line with Salomon's plans to mount a fourth season of concerts. The period from June through to December 1794 was a comparatively relaxed one. He knew that he needed to provide three new symphonies for the next season and Symphony no. 102 was written over the next few months with, very likely, some preliminary work on no. 103 and no. 104 too. Reflecting the jingoistic mood of the time Haydn embarked on the composition of a patriotic ode entitled

Invocation of Neptune on a text that had been given to him by the Earl of Abingdon. It dated back to the seventeenth century and had already been used for a similar work by the composer Friedrich Hartmann Graf (1727–95), given in the Hanover Square Concert in 1784, a concert series sponsored by the earl; in it Neptune urges Britannia to assume her natural role as ruler of the waves. Like Abingdon and everyone else Haydn turned a blind eye to the bombastic, sometimes recondite text, and composed two movements out of a projected five or six, an aria and a chorus, probably intending to finish the work once he knew that a performance was likely. That opportunity never arose.

Fashionable jingoism even determined a short visit that Haydn made to Portsmouth in July. He had been invited to the Isle of Wight by its governor, Thomas Orde, and he took the opportunity to visit the naval dockyards at Portsmouth only a few days after George III and other members of the royal family had attended the celebrations following the sensational defeat of the French fleet at Cape La Hogue, the famous 'Glorious First of June'. Haydn was fascinated and wrote all kinds of detail in his notebook: 'some 3,500 Frenchmen are quartered in barracks', 'I went aboard the French ship-of-the-line called le just; it has 80 cannon . . . The ship is terribly shot to pieces. The great mast, which is 10 feet 5 inches in circumference, was cut off at the very bottom and lay stretched on the ground. A single cannon ball, which passed through the captain's room, killed 14 sailors. The dockyard [in the absence of a familiar German word Haydn writes 'die Dockyard'], or the place where ships are built, is of enormous size, and has a great many splendid buildings. But I couldn't go there, because I was a foreigner' and 'Low tide and high tide every 7 hours. In spring the tide recedes 14 feet, other times only 7 feet.'[20]

A month later Haydn undertook another short visit, this time to Bath and Bristol (or 'Pristol' as he wrote in his notebook). The visit was probably initiated by Andrew Ashe, the flute player in Salomon's orchestra, who also regularly participated in the active musical life of Bath. For some years the highlight of the winter season was a subscription series of concerts organized by Venanzio Rauzzini

(1746–1810), the castrato for whom Mozart had written 'Exsultate, jubilate' in Milan in 1773 and who now pursued a career as a teacher, composer and impresario. Theresa Negri (Polzelli's sister) had appeared in Rauzzini's concert the previous winter and she was only one of many mutual acquaintances who might have figured in the animated Italian conversation. 'Bath is one of the most beautiful cities in Europe,' wrote Haydn in his notebook; he then proceeded to note details about the local stone, the fact that the location of the city on a hillside meant that there were more sedan chairs than carriages, the commanding sweep of the Royal Crescent ('more magnificent than any I had seen in London') and that 'a most splendid room' was being built for those taking the cure, the famous Pump Room completed two years later.[21] Rauzzini had a town house in Queen Square and a villa in Perrymead where he entertained lavishly. In the garden of the villa there was a small monument in memory of a much loved dog, 'Turk'. Haydn copied the inscription and set the text as a round, 'Turk was a faithful dog and not a man'; Rauzzini, in turn, had the music added to the memorial stone.

As summer gave way to autumn Haydn would have been aware of increasing tension at home and abroad. In Vienna the imperial authorities had clamped down ruthlessly on Jacobin sympathizers, dissidents from the army were hanged, civilians were given jail sentences of up to sixty years and strict censorship and surveillance were imposed; it certainly had the desired effect but it also ensured that Vienna and Austria remained a repressive city and country for decades to come. London too was edgy. There was a bizarre attempt at regicide in September, as Haydn recorded in one of his note-books. The unlikely plan involved instigating a brawl under the king's box in the theatre and using the resulting tumult as cover for shooting a poisoned arrow from a blowpipe. The perpetrators were caught but the incident was not followed by censorship or any other form of repression. London was very different from Vienna.

Continuing strife on the European mainland began to affect Salomon's plans for the 1795 season. He is unlikely to have been able to travel abroad to seek new singers and instrumentalists. By December the previous idea of combining forces with the King's Theatre to present a series of concerts that united all the musical talent resident in London had been resurrected. There were two further factors that would have encouraged Salomon to be accommodating. Any collaborative effort could no longer be presented as a union with the Professional Concert since they had been absent from the scene for over eighteen months; more positively, there was a new purpose-built concert room in the King's Theatre that could be used for the proposed series. The concert room had been part of the original plans when the theatre was rebuilt in 1790 and, had it been completed then, would have been the venue for Salomon's concerts in 1791 as part of the ill-fated agreement with Gallini. But it proved too expensive and was not completed until 1794. It was larger than Hanover Square Room, seating 800 as opposed to 500, and it had access to other areas of the theatre such as the popular Coffee Room. On 12 January 1795 Salomon issued a notice in several London newspapers stating that he had agreed to participate in the new series at the theatre, as had Dr Haydn and Mr Viotti. In a magnanimous gesture he recognized that this concert could 'take up and further the plan of a National School of Music becoming the taste and grandeur of this kingdom',[22] a rather oblique reference to the need for a musical body that had a similar status to the Royal Academy of Art. Such a body was some years away and the Opera Concert of 1795, in the event, did nothing to advance that particular cause.

Very deliberately, the organizers attempted to present a unified front of musical talent. Haydn was, in fact, one of four named composers, joined by Bianchi (c.1752–1810), Martín y Soler (1754–1806) and Clementi (1752–1832). The first two were resident composers in the theatre that season and provided the vocal music for the concerts while Haydn and Clementi, by implication, provided the instrumental music. The solo performers included, from Salomon's side, Dussek and Viotti, but the leader of the orchestra was Wilhelm Cramer, the former leader of the Professional Concert. Haydn sat at the harpsichord but the overall director was Viotti, who would also occasionally supply new music. It was an unwieldy as well as an uneasy union of musical life, reflected in an erratic schedule that struggled to accommodate the availability of the participants. At first there were weekly concerts, from Monday 2 February to Monday 16 March. A break of three weeks followed after which the concerts were held every fortnight (13 April, 27 April and 11 May); the eighth and final subscription concert was held on 18 May, followed by two additional concerts, on 21 May and 1 June. In the course of this series only two new works by Haydn were given, Symphonies nos. 102 and 103, supplemented by performances of familiar works including the 'Military' symphony; this must have made an even more spectacular impact than in the previous year because the orchestra now numbered some sixty players, twenty or so more than Salomon had used in 1794, and with the wind parts doubled. No other works by Haydn were given. For vocal music by the composer, audiences had to wait until the benefit concert, 'Dr. Haydn's Night', on 4 May. Two symphonies provided the cornerstones of the concert, the first performance of no. 104 and, inevitably, the 'Military'. Alongside numbers from operas performed that season at the King's Theatre, there were two duets by Haydn and an entirely new concert aria ('New Scene') for the remarkable singer Brigida Banti; despite being unable to read either text or music she had dominated the Italian stage in London for eight years as a dramatic soprano, learning everything by rote. Haydn's aria 'Berenice che fai' was the last item of Italian operatic music that he was to compose and it made stirring demands on Banti's technique. The composer, however, was not particularly impressed, or perhaps Haydn the storyteller wanted to remember a lame English rhyme for later: 'Mad. Banti (She sang very scanty).' (Haydn may well have picked up the word 'scanty' fairly recently from a text given to him by Anne Hunter, the sixth of the second set of Canzonettas, 'Ah me, how scanty is my store'.) With real pride Haydn concluded the entry in the notebook: 'The whole company was thoroughly pleased and so was I. I made four thousand Gulden [c.£450] on this evening. Such a thing is possible only in England.'[23] In its report on 6 May, the *Morning Chronicle* struck a valedictory note, even if the chosen metaphor was a clumsy one: 'A Gentleman eminent for his musical knowledge, taste, and sound criticism, declared this to be his opinion, that, for fifty years to come Musical Composers would be little better than imitators of Haydn; and would do little more than pour water on his leaves.'[24]

Haydn was at the centre of English musical life, as a person and as a composer. Over five years he had managed to stand apart from the vicissitudes of musical rivalries and belonged to no faction. He had responded to a broad range of musical and commercial opportunities, from setting Scottish folksongs to beginning a patriotic ode, from piano music to symphonies. Throughout there was an eager recognition of an immediate public, much more extensive in number, character and variety than Haydn had ever experienced at the Esterházy court. From being a lonely Kapellmeister he had gradually assumed the mantle of distinguished national figure who, in the best tradition of the Enlightenment, educated as well as entertained his audience. He flourished on this interaction and the gradual expansion of technique and emotion evident in the twelve 'London' symphonies, in particular, demonstrated a three-way relationship between composer, performer and public that was well nigh perfect.

Haydn's personality too had changed. The endless curiosity about the novel, sometimes quirky aspects of English life that are evident in the four notebooks he compiled during the two visits suggests a continuing expansion of that liberality of outlook that had emerged in the 1780s, without ever losing those fundamental characteristics of modesty and simplicity, though the latter were now sometimes charmingly affected as the public projection of an expected persona. He had willingly agreed to have his portrait painted by Thomas Hardy (see Figure 9), to be hung in Bland's music shop in Holborn, and by John Hoppner, for the discriminating scrutiny of the Prince of Wales in Buckingham Palace. By the end of his second visit Haydn's knowledge of the English language was such that he was able to purchase, or receive as appropriate gifts, a ten-volume edition of the plays of Shakespeare, a book on Captain Cook's voyages, a guide to

9. Portrait of Haydn by Thomas Hardy (1791).

the Isle of Wight, as well as Burney's four-volume history of music. Haydn was now a connoisseur as well as an artist.

Haydn's last public appearance in London was at a benefit concert for his friend Andrew Ashe on 6 June in the concert room at the King's Theatre. As in earlier years Salomon would have tried to persuade him to stay a further year but he seems to have already decided to return to Vienna. During one of Haydn's private visits to Buckingham Palace George III and Queen Charlotte had urged the composer to settle in England, even offering him rooms in Windsor Castle during the summer. Haydn declined, saying that he felt a sense of obligation to the Esterházy family, a general homesickness and, rather disingenuously, that he needed to return to his wife. When the king offered to bring her over Haydn's response was, suddenly, very candid: 'She won't cross the Danube, let alone the sea'.[25]

Since Prince Nicolaus II had not indicated an immediate need for Haydn to assume his duties as Kapellmeister – he did not return from Italy until June 1795 – the composer was able to prepare for his return journey in a leisurely manner. Alone amongst the former allies, Britain and Austria remained at war with France, another factor that may have delayed Haydn's return. In order to avoid the usual journey across the Channel to Calais, inland through the former Austrian Netherlands, now ruled by France, and then through the borderlands of the Rhine, Haydn and Elssler decided to take a more northerly route via Hamburg, by sea from the port of London. On 15 August 1795 Haydn left the city for the last time.

6   Viennese composer, European composer

Haydn and Elssler stayed two or three nights in Hamburg. According to Dies, the composer had hoped to meet Carl Phillip Emanuel Bach only to be greeted by his daughter, Anna Caroline Philippine, who informed Haydn that her father had died in 1788. It seems unlikely that Haydn did not know that C.P.E. Bach had been dead for seven years; Charles Burney (London) and Swieten (Vienna) are only two who would surely have told him. Perhaps the courtesy visit to the daughter was just that, an act of homage to a composer whom Haydn had always held in high regard. The homeward journey continued southwards via Dresden and the pair arrived in Vienna towards the end of August.

Prince Nicolaus II had returned from Italy only in June and, although he had signalled his intention to reactivate musical life at the Esterházy court, not much of consequence had yet happened and for eight months or so Haydn was able to adjust to a quiet lifestyle in Vienna. The house in Gumpendorf was not yet ready and the composer took up residence in the inner city, in the Neuer Markt, a bustling square known for its butter, flower and grain traders. Sometime during the autumn and in the company of three members of the Harrach family, Haydn visited Rohrau, where the composer saw for the first time the monument that had been erected in the gardens of the palace 'to the immortal master of music'. Haydn also visited his old family home, where he kissed the threshold and reminisced about his childhood. This excursion reveals two intertwining aspects of Haydn's personality, the ambitious composer who had admired the statue erected in Handel's memory in Vauxhall Gardens, London and who now took great pride in his own permanent memorial, and the sentimental human being who drew continuing sustenance from his own background. In his will Haydn was to leave 75 gulden for the education of the two poorest orphans in Rohrau and a further 75 gulden for maintenance of the Harrach monument.

As he had done following the first London visit, Haydn organized a concert of his own music, presented in the Kleiner Redoutensaal on 18 December; the programme featured three symphonies (including the proven crowd-pleaser, no. 100) alongside a performance by Beethoven of his Second Piano Concerto and some Italian arias given by two singers from the Burgtheater, Irene Tomeoni and Domenico Mombelli. Following Haydn's concert other individuals featured the most recent symphonies of the composer in their benefit concerts, Maria Bolla (another singer at the Burgtheater), Joseph Suche (the music director at the Theater auf der Wieden) and Josepha Auernhammer (a gifted pianist); by the end of 1796 over a dozen public performances of Haydn's recent symphonies had taken place in Vienna, with the 'Surprise' rather than the 'Military' symphony emerging as a particular favourite. But this was a temporary phenomenon. Given that the city lacked the appropriate infrastructure to promote regular public performances of symphonies, particularly impresarios and concert organizations, Haydn would have known that this spate of performances could never lead to his symphonies acquiring the same public status as they had done in London and that the composition of some 'Vienna' symphonies to follow the 'London' symphonies was highly unlikely. Tellingly, in the following year, 1797, not a single symphony by the composer is known to have been played in public in Vienna.

The old tradition of the symphony being the mainstay of musical entertainment at aristocratic courts was fast dying out and Prince Nicolaus II never showed a desire to buck this trend. In 1796 the Chor Musique consisted of fifteen full-time employees: Haydn was assisted by a Klaviermeister, Johann Fuchs, a Konzertmeister, his old friend

Luigi Tomasini, and an organist, Johann Georg Fuchs; there were four named singers, six further string players and a bassoon player. Their function was the long-standing one of providing the music for services in the Esterházy palace in Eisenstadt and in the Bergkirche. There was an understanding that Haydn was not expected to participate regularly in these services and over time he began to transfer some of the routine administrative burdens also to his senior colleagues. However, unlike the first three princes whom Haydn had served, church music was especially valued by Nicolaus II and by 1802 the core personnel had increased to twenty-nine, supplemented as necessary by extra players and singers. In a period that witnessed only a limited recovery in the fortunes of church music following the reforms of Joseph II the flourishing of liturgical music at the Esterházy court was highly unusual. Haydn was gratified, and he benefited too. In October 1797 his salary of 400 gulden was increased to 700 gulden, which together with the continuing pension of 1,000 gulden from Nicolaus I brought his total income from the court to a comfortable 1,700 gulden; a uniform was also supplied. For the first time since the late 1760s and early 1770s Haydn was able devote himself to the composition of church music. Too much had happened in Haydn's life for him to have regarded this as a cosy exercise, a retreat into a comfort zone, and the six late masses (composed between 1796 and 1802) both embrace a long tradition and expand its expressive horizons by engaging with the world beyond the Esterházy court. Autumn, winter and spring were usually spent in Vienna where Haydn, by and large, was able to develop his career as an independent artist; the summer months were spent in Eisenstadt, participating in the occasional church service and preparing for a highlight in the Esterházy calendar, the celebrations surrounding the name day of Prince Nicolaus II's wife, Marie Hermenegild Esterházy.

She was a beautiful lady in her late twenties who had married the prince in 1783, when she was only fifteen. The marriage was not a happy one. Nicolaus was serially unfaithful and rampantly promiscuous, with one commentator suggesting that he had 200 mistresses and

10. Portrait of Princess Marie Hermenegild Esterházy by Elisabeth Vigée-Lebrun (1798).

100 children. The well-known portrait of her painted in oil by Elisabeth Vigée-Lebrun in 1798 shows her unmistakably as the lonely Ariadne deserted by Theseus (Figure 10). As if to compensate for the marital solitude Marie Hermenegild's name day in September of each year became the focal point of extended celebration in Eisenstadt, embracing the secular and the sacred. In 1796 a theatrical troupe under the direction of Johann Karl Stadler was engaged to give three performances per week in the castle, from 1 September to 15 October; its repertoire of nearly thirty plays and German operas included works by Dittersdorf (*Das rote Käppchen*), Müller (*Die Zauberzither*) and Mozart (*Die Zauberflöte*); the last named was given on 9 October, which may have

been the first time Haydn heard Mozart's opera. For the name day itself the court and the church had the choice of two dates: the fixed feast of the Nativity on 8 September or the moveable feast of the Most Holy Name of Mary on the following Sunday. In 1796 they chose the moveable feast, falling on 11 September, for a further reason. The previous year Pope Pius VI had beatified a seventeenth-century Capuchin monk, Bernard of Offida, for his miraculous work amongst the poor and the sick; 11 September was designated as his feast day. For this double celebration, the feast of Bernard of Offida and the name day of the princess, Haydn provided a new mass, the Missa Sancti Bernardi d'Offida.

By the time of the first performance Haydn had already begun a second mass, the Missa in tempore belli, first performed three months later, on 26 December in the Piaristenkirche in Vienna, as part of a service to commemorate the admission into the priesthood of Joseph Franz von Hoffmann. His father, who almost certainly commissioned the work, was Imperial-Royal Paymaster, a fact that probably encouraged the composer to write his 'war mass' (as one report described it). During the previous summer and autumn Austrian forces were under attack on two fronts: the Italian territories were being conquered by French troops under the inspired leadership of the young Napoleon, while on the western front French and Austrian troops were fighting for control of southern Germany. For the first time since the Turkish threat of 1683 Austria sensed an imminent invasion of its heartland. Haydn, remembering the many services he had participated in in his youth, as a singer, organist and violinist, to celebrate the defeat of the Turks, responded with a new work in the same bellicose tradition. His intuitive feel for the drama of Catholic worship in his homeland is most apparent in the Agnus Dei where the three traditional utterances of the text are undermined by ominous drumbeats and insistent fanfares. The following September the princess's name day featured a new mass by Haydn's colleague, Johann Fuchs; later in the month the Missa in tempore belli was given for the first time in Eisenstadt. By this time Haydn's mass would have been received with even more patriotic fervour, for in the intervening months the composer had become a national hero, perhaps the only national hero.

Austria had been at war with France since 1792, a war that was not always popular with its citizens, not so much because the country harboured revolutionary sentiments (these were crushed in 1794) but because they could not comprehend what the war had to do with them. That Vienna remained the capital of the Holy Roman Empire, the largest city in German-speaking Europe and the fourth largest city in the world was increasingly a matter of indifference as the country, controlled by censorship, became more and more inward looking and its population weary. Beethoven had neatly summed up the attitude of many Viennese when he wrote that 'so long as an Austrian can get his *brown ale* and his *little sausages*, he is not likely to revolt'.[1] By the middle of the decade Austrians were not particularly anxious to defend national sovereignty. One by one members of the international coalition that had been formed to contain the ambitions of the French had sued for peace, Belgium, Prussia, the Netherlands and Spain. By 1796 only Britain and Austria remained as France mounted its two-prong attack on Austria, from the south and from the west.

It was in these circumstances that Franz Joseph von Saurau, president of the administrative district of Lower Austria, conceived the idea of commissioning a national song (a 'Volkslied') that would stimulate national pride. As he later wrote, the idea was motivated by his admiration for the national anthem of Austria's coalition partner, 'God save the King'; almost certainly he would have encountered the existing, impromptu practice of singing that melody with German words, 'Heil Teutschlands Kaiser! Heil!/Heil unserem Kaiser! Heil!/ Heil Kaiser Franz!'[2]

> I have often regretted that unlike the English we had no national anthem fitted to display in front of the whole world the devoted attachment of the people to its wise and good fatherland, and to awaken in the hearts of all good Austrians that noble pride of nation which is indispensable if they are energetically to exercise each disciplinary measure considered necessary by the princes of the land.

Saurau asked Lorenz Leopold Haschka (1749–1827) to provide the text. In the 1780s Haschka had been one of those who responded enthusiastically to the liberalization of society under Joseph II, a Freemason who wrote verses attacking the pope, the church, spirituality in general and, ironically, the concept of sovereignty. By the mid-1790s he was a firm member of the political establishment, had been a police spy for a while, and was custodian of the university library in Vienna. Haschka responded with four eight-line verses that clearly take the 'God save great George our King' (the usual English text of the time) as a point of departure, while at the same time skilfully fashioning its own sense of propulsion: the first verse begins 'God save Franz the Kaiser / Our good Kaiser Franz / Long live Franz the Kaiser' ('Gott erhalte Franz den Kaiser / Unsern guten Kaiser Franz! / Lange lebe Franz der Kaiser') and all verses conclude with the exhortation 'God save Franz the Kaiser / Our good Kaiser Franz'.

Given that a national anthem was being manufactured at the heart of the Habsburg establishment it might have been thought that Saurau would have turned to a court composer for the music. Salieri was the first Kapellmeister, a respected and loyal servant, though someone whose knowledge of German, even after thirty years in Vienna was shaky, and whose international popularity was on the wane. Instead, and possibly guided by Gottfried van Swieten, Saurau turned to Haydn. His international reputation was continually expanding, he was particularly respected in Britain, had lived there for several years and remained in contact with the country. Saurau may well have been impressed too by the part that Haydn's symphonies, especially the 'Surprise' symphony, had played in several charity concerts that had taken place in Vienna in the autumn of 1796 to raise money for the Vienna Volunteer Corp that was to defend the city in the event of an invasion. In short Haydn personified the Austro-British sense of solidarity that Saurau was anxious to promote. For his part Haydn responded enthusiastically. He was a natural Anglophile, had witnessed at first hand the effect of 'God save the King', arranged the anthem and knowingly alluded to its opening notes in the main theme of the second movement of Symphony no. 98.

Haydn delivered the music towards the end of January 1797 and was rewarded with a substantial sum of money plus a snuffbox decorated with a portrait of the emperor. The sketches for the melody show that the sense of anticipation and resolution associated with the refrain 'Gott! erhalte' was achieved by a late decision to modulate firmly to the dominant key before the climactic top G. The result was unique: melodically fluent, carefully paced and, most subtly, beginning on the half-bar rather than on the full bar, to avoid over-accentuation; during the course of the nineteenth century successive arrangers shifted the musical phrasing on to the main beat to encourage brisk performances in the style of a military march, a distortion of Haydn's vision.

In a matter of days Saurau organized the distribution of Haschka's text and Haydn's music throughout the Habsburg Monarchy, Vienna, Graz, Brünn (Brno), Krakau (Kraków), Prague, Pest, Ofen and Trieste. Two different printers were engaged to provide the copies, a piano score of the first verse on the left page (Figure 11), the full four verses of

11. Piano score of 'Gott erhalte Franz den Kaiser' (1797)

the text on the facing side, and instructions given that it was to be sung for the first time on 12 February 1797, Franz's twenty-ninth birthday. In Vienna the emperor attended a performance in the Burgtheater of Dittersdorf's popular opera *Doktor und Apotheker* and the ballet *Alonso und Cora* (music by Joseph Weigl, one of Haydn's many godchildren) and responded with appropriate graciousness to the display of loyalty. As the repeated naming of the emperor in the text suggests, Saurau, Haschka and Haydn hoped for an impact that was immediate rather than one that was intended to survive through generations. As a musical rallying point, with Haydn alone increasingly receiving the credit rather than sharing it with Saurau and Haschka, it was to become the enduring emblem of Austrian identity right up to the First World War.

For Haydn, 1797 was the year that he became, finally, a Viennese composer. A decade earlier he had always felt something of an outsider; now he was, as the court newspaper the *Wiener Zeitung* put it when reporting on the first performances of the anthem, 'the most famous composer of our time'.[3] More than once Haydn was to say that he became appreciated in his native land only after he had achieved fame in England. The British inspiration for the Austrian anthem was the catalyst for this process, but it was not to be the last time that the composer engaged in these complementary loyalties.

In the same month as Haydn was completing the Volkslied he received further recognition of his new, central status in the musical life of Vienna, a letter from the Tonkünstler-Societät that granted him free tickets to all its concerts. The letter was signed by Salieri and the secretary of the organization, Paul Wranitzky. Wranitzky (1756–1808) was one of the most active musical figures in Vienna, a composer of symphonies and operas (including the popular *Oberon, König der Elfen*), a violinist and orchestral director in the court theatres, a frequent director of private concerts for Empress Marie Therese, an unofficial agent for the publishing firm of André (Offenbach) and, since 1794, a very energetic secretary of the Tonkünstler-Societät. He was a former pupil of Haydn and obviously knew the composer's side of the story about his strained relations with the Tonkünstler-Societät, alluding to them in the letter:[4] 'do not take this to be some small act of recompense, rather, for the best of reasons, an assurance of the eternal obligation that will always be owed to you'. This was a decisive move by Wranitzky, one that was to have a long-standing impact on the success of the organization and, with it, Haydn's reputation in the musical life of the city. For the next few years Haydn's music featured regularly in its biannual concerts, oratorios and the occasional symphony, usually directed by the composer himself. Long after the composer's death performances of The Creation were a regular and heart-warming part of the activities of the society, to the extent that when it was reorganized in 1862 the composer's surname was enshrined in the new name of the organization, 'Haydn', Witwen- und Waisen-Versorgungs-Verein der Tonkünstler in Wien ('Haydn', Charitable Society for the Widows and Orphans of Musicians in Vienna).

Alongside this increasingly powerful image of a benevolent and venerable public figure the final years of the eighteenth century in Vienna also saw a discriminating private image of the composer: Haydn as the absolute master of the string quartet. While posterity was to emphasize Haydn's fundamental contribution to the development of the symphony, that genre was an increasingly peripheral one in musical life in Vienna at the turn of the century with, instead, the string quartet emerging as the central instrumental genre of the time. From the mid-1780s onwards a number of composers had dedicated quartets to Haydn, including several former pupils: Pleyel (a pupil, op. 2, 1784), Mozart (the 'Haydn' quartets, 1785), Gyrowetz (op. 8), Grill (op. 3, 1790), Kospoth (op. 8, 1790), Eybler (op. 1, 1794), Jadin (op. 1, 1795), Brandl (op. 17, livre 1, 1799), Hänsel (a pupil, op. 5, 1799), Bachmann (op. 15, 1800), Bernhard Romberg (op. 1, livre 1, c.1800), Andreas Romberg (op. 2, 1802), Edmund Weber (a pupil, op. 8, 1804) and Wikmanson (op. 1, 1801). Andreas and Bernhard Romberg were two cousins whom Haydn had first met at the electoral court in Bonn, where they played the violin and the cello respectively. During a visit to Vienna, Andreas went with Haydn to a private musical evening. Haydn himself placed the parts of a quartet on the stands, the audience assumed it was work of his and showed their subsequent appreciation. ' "Did you really like it?" he asked at last. "That's very nice; because it is by that young man there – by our Andreas." '[5]

The patronage of Count Joseph Erdödy (1754–1824) was typical of many aristocrats. Whereas his father, Count Johann Nepomuk, had employed an orchestra of between seventeen and twenty players mainly for opera but also for some concerts, Joseph dismissed the retinue on inheriting the title 1789, as much an indication of changing fashion as for financial reasons. Instead he employed a string quartet that performed regularly in the family palaces in Vienna, Pressburg and Freystadl an der Waag in Slovenia (Galgócz, Hlohovec). In 1796 he commissioned a set of six quartets from Haydn for the substantial fee of 100 ducats (450 gulden). As was becoming increasingly common practice amongst musical patrons, this fee entitled Erdödy to exclusive ownership of the works for a period of time, after which Haydn was able to sell them, a practice that neatly nurtured the element of con- noisseurship associated with the genre. After the private release, as it were, of the six quartets in 1797, the public release occurred in 1799 when Haydn arranged for them to be published in Vienna by Artaria and in London by Longman, Clementi & Co. Etiquette demanded that the Artaria edition be dedicated to Count Joseph Erdödy, but the publisher went further. Instead of the customary plain title page, clouds and flowers surround the text, as if it were a memorial tablet, while a vignette of the composer taken from the painting by Thomas Hardy rests on top; the vignette, in turn, is about to be crowned with a laurel wreath. Artistically it was rather clumsy, but the symbolism was unmistakable.

By the time the op. 76 quartets were available in Artaria's shop in the Kohlmarkt many purchasers would either have already heard the works in private or heard about them. This set of six strongly individual works was the most challenging yet by the composer. Undoubtedly the most uncompromising first movement is that of op. 76 no. 2 in D minor, a ruthless essay in motivic unity; strikingly, this work reaches its resolution in a 'Hungarian' finale, appropriate for Erdödy since he held the office of Hungarian Court Chancellor. Tensions between Hungary and the central Habsburg authorities had subsided considerably in the 1790s and whether performers and listeners viewed Haydn's quartet as a musical expression of that accommodation must be a moot point. The political and social implications of the third quartet, in C major, were unmistakable however. The slow movement presents 'Gott erhalte Franz den Kaiser' whole, then in four variations led by each player (or loyal subject) in turn, first violin, second violin, cello and viola; as the fabric of the music becomes more complex so too does the harmony. Haydn's national anthem was as much at home in the discerning world of the salon as it was in the theatre.

In London, meanwhile, Haydn's quartets had enthused Charles Burney to such an extent that he had decided to translate the words of 'Gott erhalte' into English, neatly reciprocating the indebtedness of the Austrian anthem to the English one.[6]

> I had the great pleasure of hearing your new quartetti (opera 76) well performed before I went out of town, and never received more pleasure from instrumental music: they are full of Invention, fire, good taste, and new effects, and seem the production, not of a sublime genius who has written so much and so well already, but of one of highly-cultivated talents, who had expended none of his fire before. The Divine Hymn, written for your imperial master, in imitation of our loyal song, 'God save great George our King', and set so admirably to music by yourself, I have translated and adapted to your melody, which is simple, grave, applicating, and pleasing.

The composition of the op. 76 quartets and 'Gott erhalte' coincided with the beginning of work on *The Creation*, a project that consumed the composer for over a year. In a way that was wholly unprecedented in the history of music the work was written with the natural authority of an artist who was conscious of a European audience, rather than a local one. It origins go back to Haydn's second visit to London, where there were occasional rumours that the composer was working on an oratorio, a work that would have sealed his place in the Handelian tradition and demonstrated his unique ability to bring the ancient and modern traditions of English musical life together. Although overwhelmed by the grandeur of Handelian oratorio, especially the choruses, Haydn was too busy fulfilling his role as a modernist to give serious thought to writing an oratorio in London. Towards the end of the second visit he was given a libretto for an oratorio on the subject of the creation of the world. This text has not survived, allowing all kinds of rumour and speculation to circulate about its origins. Haydn thought the author was someone called 'Lidley' which seems a muddled conflation of three people he had known, Andreas Lidl (a baryton player at the Esterházy court who subsequently moved to London), Robert Lindley (a cellist in London) and Thomas Linley (whose work at the Drury Lane theatre in London including looking after the oratorio season). Other reports suggested that the violinist Barthélemon had played a role, opening the Bible at the first chapter of Genesis and saying 'There, take that, and begin at the beginning', while still another maintained that the text had originally been intended for Handel.

What is certain is that Haydn did not set a single word of the oratorio in London. Almost equally certain is that without the assistance of Gottfried van Swieten (1733–1803) in Vienna, he would never have composed the oratorio. A year younger than the composer, Swieten had served the imperial-royal family for over a quarter of a century, first as a diplomat in Brussels, Paris, London and Warsaw, then as president of the Commission on Education and Censorship under Joseph II and, from the same period to his death, Prefect of the Court Library (the forerunner of the Österreichische Nationalbibliothek). The last position came with a service flat alongside the gallery that overlooked the splendid hall in the library, and he also acquired a house in the Renngasse in the north-west of the inner city. As a diplomat he had been able to develop an interest in musical repertoire that was almost entirely unknown in Vienna, the music of

Bach, Graun, Handel and others. He acquired a large personal library of such material, regularly supplementing it with further acquisitions when he returned to Vienna. This was not mere antiquarianism but a genuine desire by a competent musician to understand the musical traditions of a different epoch. In Vienna he organized regular Sunday concerts in his apartment in the library to explore the repertoire and it was at these concerts that Mozart first became familiar with the music of Bach and Handel. To explore the larger choral works of Handel, in particular, Swieten gathered together an informal consortium of aristocrats who underwrote the performance costs, the Gesellschaft der associerten Kavaliere; at various times the interested aristocrats included Apponyi, Auersperg, Czernin, Erdödy, Esterházy, Fries, Harrach, Kinsky, Lichnowsky, Lobkowitz, Schwarzenberg, Sinzendorf and Trautmannsdorf. Handel's *Athalia*, *Judas Maccabaeus*, *The Choice of Hercules*, *Acis and Galatea*, *Alexander's Feast*, *Messiah* and *Ode to St Cecilia* were translated into German (by Swieten himself) and the orchestration modernized; for the last four works that task was undertaken by Mozart, who also participated in several performances.

Already in 1793 Swieten had tried to persuade Haydn to set a text by Johann Baptist von Alxinger, *Die Vergötterung des Herkules* (The deification of Hercules), in the manner of Handel. Haydn refused but offered some recompense by directing a German version of the chorus he had composed in London, *The Storm*. When two years later Haydn returned from London with a 'Handelian' libretto that he wished to set, Swieten viewed this as an irresistible opportunity to further his abiding interest in developing a Viennese Handelian tradition. The mutual ambition of composer and librettist-cum-animateur was bolstered by the success of two performances of the choral version of *The Seven Last Words*, with a text edited by Swieten, in the Schwarzenberg palace in March 1796. In order to facilitate cooperation Haydn lived for a while in the Krugerstrasse, a mere five minutes' walk from the court library.

As well as inviting speculation about its authorship, the loss of the original English libretto meant that Swieten's role in its editing and translating has always been uncertain: how much did he cut, add and modify when he translated it into German, and to what extent is the English in the first published edition Swieten's or that of the original, unknown author? Though this is frustrating it was not a deliberate act of obfuscation by Swieten (or Haydn); throughout the century oratorio texts were much more likely than opera texts to garner phrases and sentences from all manner of appropriate sources. To the three main sources that have always been recognized in *The Creation*, the first chapter of Genesis, passages from Milton's *Paradise Lost* and verses from the Psalms, it has recently been pointed out that Swieten's text also contains some material from Thomson's *The Seasons*, the principal source of Haydn's next oratorio.[7] In a letter that Swieten sent to the *Allgemeine musikalische Zeitung* at the end of December of 1798 Swieten corrected some misapprehensions about his role.[8]

> in order that our Fatherland might be the first to enjoy it, I resolved
> to clothe the English poem in German garb. In this way my
> translation came about. It is true that I followed the plan of the
> original faithfully as a whole, but I diverged from it in details as
> often as musical progress and expression, of which I already had an
> ideal conception in my mind, seemed to demand. Guided by these
> sentiments, I often judged it necessary that much should be
> shortened or even omitted, on the one hand, and on the other,
> that much should be made more prominent or brought into greater
> relief, and much placed more in the shade.

It is clear from this account that he had firm views about the musical realization of the text and the first surviving source for the work, Swieten's handwritten text in German, has many suggestions to this effect in the margin. Posterity has sometimes regarded this as a presumptuous exercise by Swieten but librettists who worked closely with composers in the eighteenth century often guided them and Haydn, for his part, had never been particularly keen to exercise independent judgement on the suitability of texts; as the composer would have recognized, Swieten was much more intimately acquainted with the conventions of Handelian librettos than he was. At the same time the marginal comments are more likely to reflect discussion and reflection than be a set of independent instructions; and this is what allowed Haydn to follow nearly all of them.

With this text as a guide to the shape of the whole as well as the content of individual numbers, Haydn set about composing the work in chronological order and with a fervour that was remarkable for a man in his mid-sixties. Inextricably mixed with the musical ambition of the work was a religious impulse, that unshakeable inner core of Haydn's personality that had always shaped his outlook and was now being projected into a genre that spoke more widely than any associated with the Catholic liturgy. Griesinger[9] wrote that

> His patriarchal, devout spirit is particularly expressed in *The Creation*, and he was bound to be more successful in this composition than a hundred masters. 'Only when I had reached the half-way mark in my composition did I perceive that I was succeeding, and I was never so devout as during the time that I was working on *The Creation*. Every day I fell to my knees and prayed to God to grant me the strength for a happy completion of this work.

Shortly after the composer's death Johann Elssler wrote an account of Haydn's daily routine. Although it does not mention a particular work or a particular period its details apply most appropriately to the time of *The Creation*, the second half of the 1790s, and can be fleshed out by other evidence. In the summer Haydn got up at 6.30, in the winter 7.00; after shaving he dressed, occasionally combining this with instruction to a pupil who, sometimes, lodged in the house in Gumpendorf. Breakfast was at 8.00 and then Haydn began work. Composing was habitually divided into two kinds of activity. The morning was devoted to the arduous task of conceiving the ideas, usually at the piano or clavichord, and sketching the general progress of a movement or a section of a work. He then took a break to receive visitors at 11.30, an increasingly common practice in the Viennese years, or to go for a lengthy walk, up to two hours. Lunch was from

2.00 to 3.00 after which Haydn either read a book for an hour or attended to some domestic task. Composition was resumed at 4.00, now devoted to the different and easier task of fully realizing the material that had been drafted in the morning. He went out at 8.00, returned at 9.00 and then either read a book or continued the second stage of the compositional process. With this strict, timetabled approach, one that demanded steady progress from sketch to finished score on a daily basis, Haydn gradually built up the composition. At 10.00 he had a light supper, typically bread and wine. Only when he was invited out to dinner did he break this habit. Haydn went to bed at 11.30.

When Haydn was composing *The Creation* he would happily play extracts from the work to visitors, though he concealed from everybody, including Swieten, the sublime *fortissimo* that announces the first light. One regular visitor in this period was a new acquaintance, Fredrik Samuel Silverstolpe (1769–1851), Swedish chargé d'affaires in Vienna from 1796 to 1803. As well as visiting him in the Krugerstrasse Silverstolpe regularly made the journey out to Gumpendorf, was not daunted when the composer happened not to be at home, and even went to Eisenstadt. Referring to him as 'Papa Haydn' or 'Vater Haydn' he was entranced by his descriptions of life in England, including the performances of Handel's music in Westminster Abbey and the award of the doctorate by Oxford University, and noted that Jako, the parrot purchased in England, occasionally shrieked 'Papa Haydn'. Silverstolpe was fascinated by his personality, perhaps a little perplexed too.[10]

> I discovered in Haydn two physiognomies, as it were. The one was penetrating and serious whenever he talked about anything that was sublime, and merely the term 'sublime' was enough to show him visibly moved. The next moment this sublime mood was driven away in a flash from his demeanour, and he became jovial to such an extent that it showed in his face and turned into the jocose. This was his usual physiognomy; the other one had to be induced.

On another occasion he drew attention to his self-effacing manner.

> Everything that he related bore the stamp of his goodness and his
> trust. Never did I hear him criticize anyone out of ill-will. About
> mediocrity he was silent; he melted with inner joy, however, if he had
> the possibility of displaying an emerging and capable talent. Morality
> always had a value in his thinking, and his comportment radiated
> nothing but modesty, honour and benevolence.

By mid-January 1798 the oratorio was finished, after some fourteen
months of intensive work. Johann Elssler and some assistants began
copying out the parts all of which were carefully checked by Haydn; for
instance a crucial *ff* was added to the first trombone part for the big C
major chord of instant light. The cost of preparing the parts was borne
by Swieten and his colleagues, the Gesellschaft der associerten Kavaliere, and the work was to be presented in a concert in front of an
invited audience on two successive nights in the Schwarzenberg palace
on the Neuer Markt. After a delay, to allow Princess Schwarzenberg to
recover from childbirth, the performance was set for 30 April. Meanwhile, on 1 and 2 April, the customary two concerts of the Tonkünstler-
Societät featured Haydn's *Seven Last Words* directed by the composer.
Silverstolpe attended the concert and noted that 'Haydn was applauded
several times, not only because of his music but also for his person'.[11]

After two rehearsals on 27 and 28 April the first performance duly
took place on Monday 30 April, beginning at 6.30 in the evening;
because of the expected crowd the customary market stalls had to be
cleared with Prince Schwarzenberg paying compensation to the
traders. The performers probably numbered between 140 and 160,
perhaps more; Antonio Salieri played the fortepiano and Haydn directed, 'giving the beat with two hands' according to an enthusiastic
letter from Princess Eleonore Liechtenstein to Countess Josephine
Harrach.[12] Two further semi-private performances were given at the
Schwarzenberg palace, on 7 and 10 May. To capitalize on its success a
formal first public performance was planned for Whit Sunday in the
Burgtheater. Special permission was needed to use the theatre on this

date and though Baron von Braun (who administered the court theatres) and Count Franz Joseph von Saurau were supportive, Emperor Franz was not inclined to make an exception, even for the composer of the national anthem. It proved impossible to find another date and since the social season was fast coming to a close the idea of a public performance was put off until the following year.

The Creation had consumed Haydn's energies for eighteen months, culminating in the direction of four performances in eleven days. Exhausted, as much by the adulation as by the industry, he was confined to his house in Gumpendorf for a month or so, the first instance in the ageing composer's life of declining physical energy. Recovering sufficiently well to travel to Eisenstadt he stayed at the Gasthof Engel at the top of the town and continued his recuperation by taking the sulphur baths in the village of Gschiess near Sopron. A new mass was expected for the name-day celebrations in September and Haydn embarked on its composition on 10 July, completing the work in just over six weeks, on 31 August. Haydn liked to have three clear months for the composition of a mass; this work was written in exactly half the time. The autograph score was headed simply 'Missa' but when Haydn entered the composition in the personal catalogue (the *Entwurf Katalog*) that he had kept since the mid-1760s he gave it a title, 'Missa in Angustiis', probably because it enabled the work to be more readily recognized in that increasingly untidy volume. 'In Angustiis' ('in straitened times' or 'in difficult circumstances') can be interpreted in two ways, ones that are not mutually exclusive. It may be a wry remark on the limited time he had to compose the work, an annotation in the same manner as 'sunt bona mixta malis' (the good mixed with the bad) that he wrote on the autograph of the abandoned *a cappella* mass of 1768, or it may refer to the tense political climate of the time. However, the case for the latter is not as compelling as might first be thought.

Having signed the Peace of Campo Formio with France the previous autumn Austria was no longer at war. Only Britain remained and the focus of the conflict had moved south, to Egypt and the Mediterranean, where Napoleon hoped to sever the link between Britain and India.

In an audacious naval manoeuvre Nelson routed the French fleet at the Battle of the Nile (1 August), ensuring that French forces were isolated in Egypt. Early in the nineteenth century Haydn's mass was to acquire the nickname 'Nelson' and, given the undoubted tension and drama of the music, it is easy to make a link between the work and Nelson's heroics. A more nuanced reading of the year 1798 in Austria suggests that such an association was not in the composer's mind. News of the stunning victory in the Battle of the Nile did not reach Austria until September, after Haydn had completed the mass. Rather, Austrian outlook in the summer of 1798 still reflected the relief that followed the signing of Campo Formio; the war was something that needed a watchful eye but could now, at long last, be viewed at a distance. Even Haydn, a committed Anglophile, might have adopted this narrowly Austrian perspective. Almost certainly it was not Nelson but the long-standing Austrian tradition of commemorating the defeat of the Turks in 1683 that prompted the theatricality of the work, specifically the menacing trumpet fanfares in the opening Kyrie and in the Benedictus. In 1798 Princess Marie Hermenegild's name day was celebrated on 9 September, the moveable feast of the Most Holy Name of Mary; this was also the day when it was customary to celebrate the defeat of the Turks. Haydn probably had this dual celebration in mind – a parallel situation to 1796 when the feast day of St Bernard coincided with the name day – but since he did not finish the mass until 31 August there was insufficient time to copy the parts and rehearse the work. Instead, the mass was performed a fortnight later, on 23 September, not in the customary venue of the Bergkirche but in the more spacious, if rather sparse, parish church, the Martinkirche. Meanwhile, as a good Catholic, the princess would have celebrated her name day on 9 September, but there is no record of the musical content of that service.

By the end of October Haydn was back in Vienna. There was no major work on the stocks and the composer was able to spend a comparatively relaxed winter living in Gumpendorf. His brother Michael Haydn, whom he had not seen for twenty-seven years, was in Vienna and for about ten days they were in daily contact, rekindling a friendship that was to grow even stronger over the next few years. At a special celebratory lunch in Gumpendorf Haydn booked a wind ensemble, a Harmonie, to provide musical entertainment, much to the alarm of Jako who cried out 'What's that?'

The abandoned plan of a public performance of *The Creation* in the Burgtheater was revived and the theatre was booked for 19 March which, by accident rather than by design, marked the end point of a short season of performances of Haydn's music in Vienna, in private and in public. His compositions, including a mass, were included in at least two concerts in the music room of Prince Lobkowitz's palace near the Burgtheater, there were two private performances of *The Creation* in the Schwarzenberg palace, on 2 and 4 March (the other work presented by Swieten that year was Handel's *Messiah*, spread over two evenings) and the vocal version of *The Seven Last Words* was played at the two charity concerts of the Tonkünstler-Societät, on 17 and 18 March. The inevitable sense of anticipation was further enhanced by the unusual wording of the poster for the concert. As well as the expected particulars of date, venue, work, composer, starting time, prices and that the text was available at the box office, there was the lengthy, rather convoluted request that approval of Haydn's achievement would be most appropriately marked by the absence of applause between numbers, 'otherwise the true connection between the single parts, from the uninterrupted succession of which should rise the effect of the whole, would be necessarily disturbed'.[13]

One member of the audience who recorded his memories of the concert was the ten-year-old Swedish violinist and composer, Johan Fredrik Berwald (1787–1861), who was visiting Vienna with his father.[14]

Paul Wranitzky arranged to get us tickets for this musical celebration. As early as four o-clock in the afternoon, our temporary servant came and said that we should hasten to the theatre, because it was besieged by a large number of people even though the concert was not due to start until seven o'clock . . . The whole went off wonderfully. Between the main parts of the work, tumultuous applause; during each part, however, it was as still as the grave. When it was over there were calls 'Father Haydn to the front! Father Haydn to the front'. Finally the old man came forward and was greeted with a tumultuous *Applaudissement* and with cries, 'Long live Father Haydn! Long live music!' which ended the celebration. Their imperial majesties were all present and joined in the 'bravo' calls. Among the persons of rank I noticed several princely persons driven out by the French, also the Grand Duke of Tuscany and his wife, the Duke of Parma with the daughter of Louis XVI, and so on.

The Berwalds had been invited to visit Haydn at his home in Gumpendorf. The mood there the next day could not have been more different. Haydn was due home shortly and the two whiled away the time talking to 'Frau Doctor', seated on a bench surrounded by cats and dogs: no, she had not been with her husband to London – 'I'll never leave my dear Vienna' – and neither had she heard *The Creation*, 'People say it's supposed to be good, I wouldn't know.' Berwald completed his account with the Viennese tittle-tattle that the unhappy marriage was the reason why Haydn composed so much.[15]

As if living up to this image, after the first public performance of *The Creation* Haydn immersed himself in a remorseless schedule of work: ambitious plans for the publication of the oratorio, the composition of *The Seasons* to capitalize on the success of *The Creation*, a new mass for the name-day celebrations in September 1799 and collaboration with the Leipzig firm of Breitkopf & Härtel on a series of initiatives that were designed to shape an artistic legacy. Over the next two years, until the first performances of *The Seasons* in May 1801, Haydn drove himself hard in the manner that he had known for forty years but, as he approached the age of seventy, energy was not always the equal of ambition, he complained more frequently about the burden of work and there was a dawning realization that fashioning a legacy meant accepting old age.

Appropriately, it was during this last phase of sustained and relentless creativity that his wife died, of crippling arthritis on 20 March 1800, the day after Haydn's name day. Her will disbursed money, jewellery, clothing and various keepsakes (including a splinter of the True Cross) to blood relatives, servants and friends, and then made her husband the residual legatee. She died in Baden and was buried there. A couple of months later Haydn felt obliged to write to Luigia Polzelli, assuring her that if he were to marry again, she would be the bride, and that, whatever happened, she would be granted a lifetime pension of 300 gulden in his will. They, too, had long drifted apart. Luigia went on to marry a singer, Luigi Franchi, and Haydn in his final will duly reduced the pension to 150 gulden.

Haydn's plans for the publication of The Creation were on a scale and an ambition unprecedented in the history of music. Manuscript rather than printed distribution of large-scale works such as operas and oratorios was the norm throughout Europe. For Haydn The Creation had always been a work that built on national traditions rather than merely relying on them and the challenge of matching, even surpassing Handel that motivated Haydn and Swieten may have played some part in the publication plans for the oratorio. Both would have known of the monumental edition of Handel's music that was published in London under the general direction of Samuel Arnold between 1787 and 1797, The Works of Handel, In Score, Correct, Uniform and Complete, in which that composer's oratorios gained a permanent, immutable legacy. With The Creation Haydn and Swieten added a further dimension, the wish to publish the work in two languages, German and English. When they conceived the idea, they knew that there was not a music publisher in Vienna or in London that could cope with this vision, a realization that served only to further the ambition and to the inevitable decision that it ought be published by the composer himself.

Most of the hard work fell on Haydn. The services of Artaria were engaged to prepare the engraved plates, 303 in number; some compromises had to be made to the appearance of single pages, with trombones and the contrabassoon relegated to an appendix. Haydn also paid for the paper, imported from northern Italy. The expenses were to be recouped by seeking subscriptions, to be paid not in advance but on receipt of the score. The price was a modest one for a work of this scale, 3 ducats (13 gulden 30 kreutzer) in Austria and

Germany, 30 shillings in England and 20 roubles in Russia; for instance a set of six quartets typically cost 4 or 5 gulden in Vienna, 10/6 in London. Eventually 507 copies were ordered by 409 subscribers, whose names appeared in the preliminary pages of the score; this would have brought in close to 7,000 gulden, a good profit on total costs of 2,500 gulden.

Haydn's house in Gumpendorf was turned into a busy office. He sought subscriptions in a variety of ways: advertising in newspapers, personal letters, through the secretary of the Tonkünstler-Societät, Paul Wranitzky, contacting Burney and Salomon in London, who willingly sought further subscribers as did the musician Johann Dengler in Moscow and Breitkopf & Härtel in Leipzig; the scores themselves were distributed from Artaria's office in the Kohlmarkt. Haydn was overwhelmed by the response, telling Breitkopf & Härtel with considerable pride, 'perhaps no work has ever been published with as many different subscribers as this one'.[16] Publication was first intended for the autumn of 1799, was postponed to the turn of the year and finally occurred on 26 February 1800.

The printed score was an impressive demonstration of Haydn's standing, something that he had sensed for the last few years but not fully comprehended. The bilingual title page described him as 'Doctor of Music and Kapellmeister in the service of Prince Esterházy'; the subscription list that follows revealed the social as well as geographical extent of his fame (see Figure 12). It is headed by members of the imperial family in Vienna, some of whom had known Haydn for several decades, the Empress Marie Therese, Elector Maximilian Franz (now living in Vienna rather than Bonn), the Archduke and Archduchess of Tuscany, Archduke Joseph (the Palatine of Hungary), Archduke Ferdinand and Prince Albert of Sachsen Teschen. Next came the British Royal Family, the King, the Queen, the Prince of Wales, the Princess of Wales, the Duchess of York and five royal princesses, followed by German royalty from Gotha, Darmstadt, Weimar and Stuttgart. The main list is spaciously printed in double columns in alphabetical order with an indication of any multiple copies that had been ordered. Count

VERZEICHNISS der SUBSCRIBENTEN.

Ihre Majeſtät die Kayſerinn Königinn

Seine Churfürſtliche Durchlaucht von Cölln

Ihre Königl. Hoheiten { der Erzherzog Grofsherzog und
die Erzherzoginn Grofsherzoginn von Toscana

Seine Königl. Hoheit der Erzherzog Joseph Palatinus von Hungarn

S. K. H. der Erzherzog Ferdinand

S. K. H. der Herzog Albert von Sachſen - Teschen.

Seine Majeſtät der König von England

Ihre Majeſtät die Königinn von England

S. K. H. der Prinz von Wallis

I. K. H. die Prinzeſsinn von Wallis

I. K. H. die Herzoginn von Yorck

I.I. K.K. H.H. { Auguſta
Elizabeth
Maria
Sophia
Amalia } Prinzeſsinnen von England

Seine Durchlaucht der Erbprinz von Sachsen - Gotha

S. D. der Prinz Friedrich von Sachsen - Gotha

S. D. der Prinz Georg von Hefsen - Darmstadt

Ihre Durchlaucht die Herzoginn Amalia von Sachsen - Weymar

I. D. die Herzoginn Francisca von Wirtemberg

Die K. K. Hofbibliothek.

A.	
Abrams Miſs	Annwsmith, Daniel
Abrams. Miſs Theodoſia	Apony, Graf v. . . . . . 2 Ex.
Adams. J. B.	Arembcrg, Herzog v.
Albertazzi.	Arnold D'.
Aldefeld.	Artaria & comp. . . . . 2 Ex.
Alderson. Miſs	Atherton, Eſquire
Alsop. T.	Atwood.
Amade. Graf Franz v.	Auersberg. Fürſt Carl von . . . 2 Ex.
Anderson. Miſs.	Aylward D'.
	Ayrton, D'.

12. Subscription list in the published score of The Creation (1800).

Harrach ordered one copy as did Count Lichnowsky, Prince Galitzin and the blind pianist, composer and teacher Maria Theresia von Paradies; Count Joseph Erdödy purchased two copies, Baron Swieten and Count Fries four each, Prince Lobkowitz and Princess Esterházy and Prince Schwarzenberg six each while Princess Schwarzenberg purchased a further three for the family. From Britain single orders were received from the Right Honourable Lady Bruce, Charles Burney, John Hunter junior (probably on behalf of his mother Anne Hunter), Madame Mara, Thomas Twining and Charles Wesley (the son); Salomon ordered twelve while the single largest order from any individual, sixteen, came from a certain Miss Griffith, 16 Portland Place, London.

By the end of the year these subscription copies prompted several performances in the two printed languages: in German in Bayreuth, Braunschweig, Breslau, Brünn (Brno), Buda, Dresden, Innsbruck, Kremsmünster, Leipzig, Linz, Prague and Salzburg, and in English in London, Oxford and Worcester. For the next decade it was a work that dominated musical culture throughout Europe. Haydn himself sanctioned further translations, into French and Italian, glanced at one in Swedish, and may or may not have known of versions in Czech, Danish and Russian.

Already, at the time of the first public performance of The Creation in March 1799, it was known that Swieten and Haydn were working on a second oratorio, The Seasons. This time Swieten was the instigator of the project and again the impulse was to unite the heritages of Austria and Britain. He turned to the epic poem The Seasons by James Thomson, a work of over 5,000 words from which he cleverly culled a text for Haydn of some 650 lines, written in German and drawing on an existing translation by B.H. Brockes. The measured tread of the four seasons provided a similar simplicity of structure to that given by the seven days in The Creation and the mix of recitative, aria and chorus is similar, though the chorus is more consistently a participant, rather than an observer, in The Seasons. Swieten again presented his handwritten libretto with some annotations in the margin on how the text should be set. Haydn was never as enthusiastic about this second collaboration and had particular and repeated reservations about the amount of word painting that he felt obliged to include. For the time being, in the summer of 1799, the composer was able to put such concerns to one side as he concentrated on composing a new mass for the customary

September name-day celebrations in Eisenstadt, the work that later became known as the 'Theresienmesse' because of the mistaken belief that it had been specifically composed for Empress Marie Therese; she was merely presented with a manuscript copy by Haydn.

Almost certainly the mass was performed on Sunday 8 September. Just over a fortnight later Haydn was expressing his doubt about the new oratorio to the German music lexicographer Ernst Ludwig Gerber.[17]

> Since this subject cannot be as sublime as that of The Creation, comparison between the two will show a distinct difference. Despite this, and with the help of Providence, I shall press on, and when this new work is completed I shall retire, because of the weakened state of my nerves.

As he pressed on with some reluctance on the new oratorio, a new aspect of Haydn's international reputation began to occupy more and more of his time, the relationship with the ambitious firm of Breitkopf & Härtel. Under the guidance of two successive generations of the family in the eighteenth century Breitkopf had established itself as the leading publisher of music in Germany; like many other publishers of the time it also acted as a music shop, selling manuscript copies and music printed by other firms. Breitkopf had first written to Haydn in 1789 when he gave them the two-movement piano sonata in C (Hob. XVI:48), subsequently published as part of a series entitled Musicalisches Pot-Pourri, miscellaneous piano pieces by a variety of composers. Haydn commitments over the next few years to Artaria, Bland, and Longman and Broderip meant that he ignored several requests from Breitkopf for new music. From 1796 onwards, however, it was a firm that no composer could afford to ignore. In that year it was purchased by Gottfried Christoph Härtel who, along with money, injected the business with unprecedented energy and ambition, laying the foundation of an enterprise that was to become one of the most potent commercial forces in music in the nineteenth and twentieth centuries. As well as publishing individual works (or sets of works) in the traditional manner, it very soon sought particular authority as the provider of multi-volume serial editions of music by particular composers, textually accurate and cleanly printed, a notable contribution to the increasing interest in the historical legacy of composers and to the incipient dominance of Germany (or what could be appropriated by Germany) in that process. First, the firm targeted Mozart's music. They approached Constanze Mozart and with her cooperation began to issue an *Oeuvres complettes* that was divided into three broad areas, keyboard works, scores of operas, cantatas, church music and the like, and performance parts for symphonies, concertos, quintets, quartets etc. The firm asked Constanze to persuade Haydn to deal with the firm, but she declined; a direct approach offering to publish *The Creation* was also unsuccessful. A fruitful partnership between publisher and composer was established only with the arrival of Georg August Griesinger in Vienna in 1799.

Born in Stuttgart in 1769, Griesinger studied theology at the University of Tübingen and as a young man earned a living as a tutor to various sons of the aristocracy in Germany and Switzerland. In the spring of 1799 he was appointed tutor to the nine-year-old son of Count Hilmar Adolph von Schönfeld, the Saxon ambassador in Vienna. Soon Griesinger began to undertake diplomatic duties on behalf of the Saxon legation in Vienna, the beginning of a diplomatic career in the city that was to last over forty years. His keen interest in music soon led him to become the eyes and ears of Breitkopf & Härtel in Vienna, becoming acquainted with leading composers and patrons in the city, advising the firm and negotiating on its behalf. Visiting Haydn was a priority and after several aborted visits to Gumpendorf Griesinger finally met him on 25 May 1799, reporting enthusiastically back to Breitkopf & Härtel.[18] Haydn apologized for not replying to the many letters sent by the firm ('he hoped that you will forgive a man of 67 for whom every moment is precious'), liked the idea of a complete edition of his piano music but did not have the time to compose new sonatas, pointed out that new instrumental works were already promised to Longman, Broderip and Clementi in London, and thanked

Breitkopf & Härtel for the complimentary copies of the first volumes of the Mozart *Oeuvres complettes*. 'That, my respected friend, is the content of my conversation with Haydn; he is a cheerful, still well preserved man and is for all his colleagues a model of modesty and simplicity.'

Like Silverstolpe, Griesinger soon gained the trust of Haydn and became one of his closest friends in the last ten years of his life. By the end of the year Breitkopf & Härtel had issued the first of twelve volumes of keyboard sonatas, keyboard trios and songs under the general title of *Oeuvres Complettes de Joseph Haydn*. In response to the firm's request for a suitable portrait of Haydn to be engraved on the title page of the series, the composer had suggested the Guttenbrunn portrait of him as a young man (reproduced on the cover of this biography). Griesinger reported that Haydn's wife thought it a good resemblance, also that it had been painted by her former lover; when she took the portrait with her to Baden the idea of using it on the title page of the complete edition was abandoned and another, inferior engraving of an older looking Haydn, by Vincenz Georg Kininger, was substituted.

Before the first volume appeared Griesinger had secured Haydn's cooperation on a more unlikely project, a series of volumes devoted to his masses. Griesinger reported Haydn's remark, 'I am rather proud of my masses',[19] but the idea of a publisher in Protestant Germany issuing Catholic liturgical music in full scores was particularly bold. Five of the six late masses plus the composer's longest mass, the first Missa Cellensis, were published between 1802 and 1808, encouraging performances in concert halls as well as churches. Using Haydn's status as the greatest living composer Breitkopf & Härtel willingly promoted the distinctive religious fervour of the music and the composer's view that it was a key part of his legacy.

In all of Haydn's masses there prevails not the gloomy godliness and the ever present penitential piety that we find in the masses of the great masses of former times, especially in Italy; rather a cheerful, reconciled devotion, a softer melancholy, and a happy, self-knowing realization of heavenly goodness.[20]

The next stage in Breitkopf & Härtel's plan was an edition of the complete symphonies of Haydn. To set this in motion the firm forwarded a list of such works, 123 in number, compiled from a variety of sources. Haydn whittled the number down to 108, though he did manage to include four symphonies twice and three works that were actually by other composers (Michael Haydn, Hofmann and Vanhal). In the end the complexities of the project meant that it was abandoned, a situation that was never rectified in the subsequent history of the firm.

One genre that did not feature in Breitkopf & Härtel's plans was the string quartet. Here, it had been anticipated by Haydn's former pupil and friend, Ignaz Pleyel, who had successfully established a publishing business in Paris that flourished despite the difficulties of trading in the Napoleonic period. Compiling a complete collection of quartets was easier than symphonies since all but one of them (the op. 42 quartet in D minor) had already been published in Paris over the previous thirty years by a variety of firms; they were also fewer in number and with an unchanging format for the printer, four parts. Anxious to gather the approval of Haydn, Pleyel sent him a list of the contents, eighty quartets at this stage (up to and including the op. 76 quartets). The composer was even more casual about authorizing this collection than he had been in the case of the symphonies for Breitkopf & Härtel, sanctioning a set of six quartets originally published by Bailleux in Paris in 1777 under his name; in fact the true author was Roman Hofstetter, a Benedictine monk in the monastery of Amorbach in Bavaria. Pleyel's collection of quartets, including the spurious op. 3, was published in four volumes, with an engraving of the composer and, unusually, with a choice of paper quality. A total of 130 people subscribed to the enterprise and the whole was dedicated to 'Premier Consul Bonaparte'.

Orderly and authoritative publication of music was not the only means by which Breitkopf & Härtel sought to increase the understanding of music and the status of composers. In the autumn of 1798 the firm inaugurated a new music journal, the *Allgemeine musikalische*

Zeitung. It was not the first German musical journal but it was to be the most durable and for Viennese readers it provided the only regular account of musical life in the city. It appeared every week and offered articles on composers, surveys of musical life both contemporary and historical, anecdotes, reviews of publications and concerts in German-speaking Europe, lists of new publications plus the occasional music supplement. Haydn was a subscriber. In the second issue he would have read with interest a whole series of allegedly authentic anecdotes about Mozart. Modern scholarship has doubted the veracity of many of these. Haydn, however, would have been touched by the remark attributed to Mozart: 'It was from Haydn that I first learnt how to write quartets.'[21]

By June 1799 Griesinger had secured Haydn's interest in providing an account of his life – 'the idea did not seem to displease him'[22] – and he began to formulate plans that led eventually to the biography that appeared in instalments in the *Allgemeine musikalische Zeitung* in the months after Haydn's death in 1809 and then as a single volume published by Breitkopf & Härtel the following year. At first, Griesinger was rather disheartened about the project, reporting to the publishers that it was difficult to find anybody who could provide material about Haydn other than the composer himself. Haydn was an old man, for his time a very old man, and many of the people who had known him in his youth and middle age had died, three Esterházy princes, Leopold Dichtler, Dittersdorf, Eleonore Jäger, Maria Anna von Genzinger and Mozart, to name only a few; others, like Bland, Burney, Salomon and Rebecca Schroeter, were resident in London while Pleyel was in Paris and Polzelli in Italy. His oldest surviving friend was Luigi Tomasini, still a colleague at the Esterházy court. His name occurs only once in the biography (a passing reference to his place of burial in the Bergkirche), which suggests that Griesinger decided fairly early on in the project not to seek out any remaining living testimony but to rely almost exclusively on the composer for his material.

Most of 1800 was taken up with the composition of *The Seasons*, written with fitful rather than consuming energy. A bout of illness in early summer (described as a rheumatic fever of the head) delayed progress and prompted a period of depression; Haydn even contemplated never finishing the work and, in a particularly low-spirited mood, the inevitability of death. As the oratorio moved towards completion Haydn's mood picked up. He was in Eisenstadt in September for the name-day celebrations, enlivened that year by the four-day visit of Nelson, his mistress Emma Hamilton, her mother (Mrs Cadogan) and the poet Ellis Cornelia Knight. For Haydn this was a stimulating, if brief reminder of his time in London. Emma Hamilton, whose corpulence shocked contemporary commentators (Silverstolpe thought her 'the fattest woman I've ever laid eyes on'),[23] was a gifted singer and she, like many ladies before her, was charmed by Haydn. They performed 'Arianna a Naxos' together, Johann Elssler was instructed to prepare a manuscript copy of 'The Spirit's Song' as a gift and he wrote a new work for her to perform, another cantata for voice and piano, setting some verses by Ellis Cornelia Knight, 'The Battle of the Nile'. The man himself, Lord Nelson of the Nile, was rather aloof but accepted a used quill from the composer and gave him a watch in return. A few weeks later Haydn was required to accompany the Esterházy court on a rare visit to Eszterháza, which the Kapellmeister found disagreeable rather than nostalgic, telling Griesinger on his return to Vienna that the sharp wind had made him unwell.

The two performances of *The Creation* that were given at the Christmas concerts of the Tonkünstler-Societät were to be directed by Haydn, but he passed the duty on to Paul Wranitzky. On 16 January 1801 he did direct the work – 'with youthful fire' according to Griesinger[24] – in a charity concert in the Redoutensaal to raise money for soldiers wounded in the recent brutal campaigns in Bavaria and Italy. *The Seasons* was now complete and Swieten's Gesellschaft der associerten Kavaliere began preparing for the private performances in the Schwarzenberg palace. Haydn's indifferent health (especially headaches) and frequent lack of energy were a concern and at one stage it was thought that the performances would be better postponed until the following year. While Haydn recognized that 'youthful fire' was now something that could only occasionally be captured, the lure of that potential experience, coupled with the old sense of duty and the new sense of a legacy, stiffened the composer's resolve one more time. While Elssler, Swieten and others prepared for the first performances of *The Seasons* he directed two performances of the choral version of *The Seven Last Words* on successive nights for the Easter concerts of the Tonkünstler-Societät. Three performances of *The Seasons* were given in the Schwarzenberg palace, on 24 April, 27 April and 1 May, all directed by the composer. Unbelievably, between the first and second performances, on 25 April, he directed a private performance of *The Creation* at the imperial court in which the empress sang the soprano part.

Griesinger himself undertook to write the report for the *Allgemeine musikalische Zeitung* on the three performances of *The Seasons*:[25] 'Silent devotion, astonishment and loud enthusiasm relieved one another with the listeners: for the most powerful penetration of colossal ideas, the immeasurable quantity of happy thoughts surprised and overpowered even the most daring of imaginations.' Comparison with *The Creation* inevitably characterized the views of other commentators, sometimes prompted by knowledge of Haydn's own views of the relative merits of the two works: it was too similar to the earlier oratorio, there was too much word painting and it was too long. Already by the time of the first public performance in the Redoutensaal on 29 May there was an emerging view that *The Seasons* was not the equal of *The Creation*; the hall was about two-thirds full for the performance, respectful rather than ardent.

Haydn had already decided that he would not repeat the tiring exercise of publishing the oratorio himself, though he was still anxious that it should be distributed to as wide a European audience as possible. In this he had the eager support of Breitkopf & Hartel. At first composer and publisher hoped to present the score as a trilingual one, German, English and French. In the end Breitkopf prepared two versions of the score, one in German and English, the other in German and French.

Shortly after the first public performance of The Seasons Haydn moved to Eisenstadt for the summer. He seems to have rested for a couple of months and then repeated the stressful experience of 1799, writing a new mass (the 'Schöpfungsmesse') for the September name-day celebrations in a matter of weeks rather than months. At the same time he was contemplating yet another oratorio, the third in five years. Rather than Swieten, who also was increasingly prone to illness, Empress Marie Therese was the instigator. She was a devotee of music who liked to participate as a willing, if not particularly capable soprano in private performances of operas and church music in the imperial court. The empress had already received one work from Haydn, the wonderfully athletic Te Deum in C, a work that recaptures the brazen excitement of Habsburg church and state ceremonial that the composer remembered from his youth. There was something old-fashioned too about the subject matter of the proposed oratorio, The Last Judgement, more related to Baroque religiosity than the Enlightenment values of The Creation and The Seasons. At the same time, and for the first time in his life, Haydn was anxious that the text should have real literary merit. In September 1801 the Allgemeine musikalische Zeitung published a short poem in praise of The Creation by the popular German poet, Christoph Martin Wieland (1733–1813); prompted by this tribute Haydn tried to interest Wieland in the project. For over a year Griesinger kept Breitkopf & Härtel informed but in the end nothing came of it.

While Haydn's interest in the aborted oratorio was a genuine one, other requests for new works were turned down with little consideration, a cantata to celebrate the signing of the Treaty of Lunéville (1801), a sonatine for piano and harp for the Edinburgh publisher George Thomson, a chorus for a play by Kotzebue and a new symphony for the Concert des Amateurs in Paris. He was approaching seventy and had served the Esterházy court for forty years and while Haydn's standing was now more akin to that of the illustrious Goethe at Weimar than a Kapellmeister who provided music and performances as required, in some ways the job had not changed at all in those years; in

September 1801, for instance, Haydn was curtly reminded by the prince that 'members of the Chormusik – without exception – must appear at all times with their uniforms clean and neat, and with powdered wigs'.[26] Alongside these occasional displays of petty authority the prince, and especially the princess, demonstrated increasing care for their ageing Kapellmeister and began to implement the idea that he should have a formal deputy, a repeat of the process that had first introduced Haydn to the court. The first choice was Haydn's brother Michael, who was formally offered the post of Vice Kapellmeister during a visit to Vienna in the autumn of 1801. He had worked at the Salzburg court for nearly as long as Haydn had worked at the Esterházy court, thirty-eight years, but the French occupation of the city the previous year had made his position a precarious one. His unrivalled experience as a composer of church music would have made him particularly suited to the Esterházy court and the prince tried to lure him with a promise of a salary that was more than twice the size of the one he had in Salzburg. But Michael Haydn was unsure and when Salzburg came under the direct rule of the Habsburg family, in the person of the musically sensitive Archduke Ferdinand, he decided to remain in the environment that he knew. The court now turned to a particularly conscientious member of the Esterházy musical retinue, Johann Nepomuk Fuchs (1766–1839). He had first joined the court at the age of twenty-two, in 1784, when he became piano teacher to the newly married Princess Marie Hermenegild and later played the violin in the orchestra. Along with most of the other musicians he lost his position when Prince Nicolaus I died. Subsequently, Prince Anton and then Prince Nicolaus engaged him as a piano teacher. As early as 1801 he was helping Haydn with some of the routine administrative duties. A year later, on 14 August 1802, he was formally appointed Vice Kapell-meister, an appointment that reflected his abilities as an administrator but which seems to have encouraged a new ambition as a composer in those areas favoured by the court, church music and opera.

For what was to be his last mass for the name day of Princess Marie Hermenegild, his last major work as Esterházy Kapellmeister and his last major work altogether, Haydn allowed himself ample time, beginning the 'Harmoniemesse' in Vienna in April 1802. He found the required concentration draining and even admitted to the prince, without any of the old irony, that he was 'labouring wearily on the new mass',[27] an implicit indication that both he and the prince had accepted the wisdom of appointing a Vice Kapellmeister. The name-day celebrations of 1802 were to be the last of many occasions stretching across forty years in which Haydn's music featured in festivities surrounding a visit by a member of the imperial royal family or a leading aristocrat to the Esterházy court.

The principal guest in 1802 was Count Louis Starhemberg (1762–1833), an old friend of Prince Nicolaus, and a career diplomat for the Habsburg court. From 1793 he had been the Austrian ambassador at the court of St James in London, where he would certainly have been aware of Haydn's popularity, even if there is no record of them having met in the city. For fifteen years he successfully nurtured the warm relationship between Austria and Britain during a period of continual warfare, becoming, like Haydn, a committed Anglophile; his country residence in Twickenham housed a large library of English literature, from Shakespeare to fashionable Gothic novels. On summer holiday in Austria in 1802, he was invited to attend the name-day celebrations in Eisenstadt and recorded his impressions in a diary.[28]

Starhemberg and the other guests arrived at seven in the evening, on Tuesday 7 September. After an excellent meal in the palace he retired to his room but did not sleep very well because the bedclothes were too short. On the following day, the actual name day, a procession of carriages took the family and their guests to the Bergkirche where a 'fine and excellent new mass by the famous Haydn' was given; the composer, 'who is still in the service of the prince', directed. After the service the guests returned to the palace, where the princess formally received numerous personal congratulations. A lavish dinner was served, accompanied by music. The prince proposed a toast to the princess, signalled by trumpet fanfares and the distant sound of cannon fire. Further toasts were offered, including one to Count Starhemberg and one to Haydn who, the count noted with a practised eye to protocol, sat at the same table as the prince and princess. After dinner there was a ball, opening formally with a minuet danced by members of the Esterházy family but continuing with more fashionable waltzes. Following a supper break the ball resumed and did not finish until two in the morning, though the count retired at midnight. The following morning the guests were woken by the sound of horns, summoning them to a hunt. In the afternoon there was a concert directed by Haydn including, rather unusually, movements from the 'Harmoniemesse'. After supper Starhemberg left for Vienna, arriving at four in the morning.

Haydn was never comfortable in the company of aristocracy and royalty, yet he had always appreciated their gestures of support and their recognition of his achievements. With the appointment of a deputy and this recent genuine demonstration of affection by the Esterházy family, he was in a reflective mood, no longer willing to fight against old age, but doing his best to accommodate it sensibly. He had received a letter from Bergen in north Germany, informing him of the impact that *The Creation* had made in the town. As always, Haydn was flattered and in his reply mused on the compulsive nature of his creativity.[29]

> Often, when struggling against the obstacles of every sort that oppose my labours: often, when the powers of mind and body weakened, and it was difficult for me to continue in the course I had entered upon, a secret voice whispered to me: 'There are so few happy and contented people here below; grief and sorrow are always their lot; perhaps your labours will at once be a source from which the careworn, or the man burdened with affairs, can derive a few moments of rest and refreshment.' This was, indeed, a powerful reason to press onwards, and this is why I now look back with cheerful satisfaction on the labours extended on this art, to which I have now devoted so many long years of uninterrupted effort and exertion.

7 'Gone is all my strength'

For Haydn, the winter of 1802–3 was characterized by bouts of ambition and energy that then gave way to illness. On two consecutive nights, 22 and 23 December, he directed a performance of *The Seasons* for the Tonkünstler-Societät in the Burgtheater and three days later, on 26 December, a performance of *The Creation* in the Redoutensaal to raise money for the hospital in the district of St Marx: three performances, plus associated rehearsals, of two large-scale works in two different venues across five days. Within a month he was complaining to his brother Michael about 'continual nervous weakness that makes me quite incapable of doing anything';[1] by March it was rheumatic fever which made him prefer working at the clavichord rather than at any of the three pianos he owned. He toyed with the idea, proposed by Griesinger, of writing a short choral work in praise of music, *Polyhymnia*, but nothing came of it. Since 1799 Haydn had provided the Edinburgh publisher, George Thomson, with a steady supply of settings of British folksongs, lucrative work at one guinea per setting that did not require sustained concentration. Even so he had begun to ask pupils to do the work for him, Sigismund Neukomm, and later Frédéric Kalkbrenner, but even that covert subcontracting was becoming a chore and by 1804 he stopped altogether.

More challenging, and deeply frustrating, was the inability to finish a string quartet in D minor. This was to have formed part of a set of six commissioned by Prince Lobkowitz in 1799. Two had been completed,

13. Sketches for the first movement of Haydn's last quartet (c.1802).

presented to the prince and then published as a pair, op. 77, by Artaria
in the autumn of 1802. A slow movement and a minuet of a third
quartet had been composed, movements that demonstrate the composer at his most ambitious, even unyielding. That perennial fascination with the cutting edge of musical style prompted Haydn to refer
to the work as his 'favoured child',[2] a child he could no longer rear.
He sketched material for the two outer movements but lacked the
concentration to work them into fully grown musical structures (see
Figure 13). For three years he persisted, often a quarter of an hour at a
time, finally informing Griesinger in August 1805 that he had to admit
defeat. Griesinger, who now enjoyed the complete trust of the composer, forwarded the autograph manuscript of the two completed
movements to Breitkopf & Härtel in Leipzig: 'Here, my friend, follows
Haydn's swansong.'[3] Composer, agent and publisher agreed that
when the two movements were published they should be followed by a
quotation of the opening soprano line of a part song by Haydn, one

that set a text by one of his favourite poets, Ludwig Gleim (1719–1803): 'Hin ist alle meine Kraft, Alt und schwach bin ich' (Gone is all my strength, Old and weak am I). For about a year Haydn had been using this quotation in a more whimsical manner, printed on his visiting card and freely distributed to visitors who were unsettled by the mixture of sadness and self-deprecation. In that sense he had not lost his strength.

Kapellmeister Haydn made his last visit to Eisenstadt in the summer of 1803. Although he was still expected to attend to some administrative duties, the conscientious Johann Fuchs was assuming more and more responsibility. He directed all the church-music performances in August and September, including works by Haydn. Over the previous four years the number of musicians employed at the Esterházy court had increased steadily to over forty. From 1804 onwards, in a way that would have elicited Haydn's approval as well as some surprise, the numbers increased even further, reaching a peak of nearly 100 in 1808. The most unexpected element of this increase was the establishment of an entirely new musical body, a Knabenchor, a boy's choir, to sing at the church services at the court and to nurture future members of the musical retinue. Haydn himself had been a choirboy; he had also spent decades as Esterházy Kapellmeister struggling to keep the church-music establishment afloat and must have viewed this development with self-satisfaction as well as ironic detachment.

In the same year, 1804, a major new appointment was made by Prince Nicolaus, Johann Nepomuk Hummel (1778–1837). Born in Pressburg, he had studied with Mozart in the 1780s and subsequently pursued a career as a pianist-composer that took him to Prague, northern Germany, Copenhagen, Edinburgh and London. In London in 1792 he and Haydn became firm friends, acknowledged many years later by the dedication of a piano sonata in E flat (op. 13) to the older composer. With the exception of Haydn, Hummel in his mid-twenties was the most distinguished musician at court. He was given the title of Konzertmeister, the third in the pecking order after Haydn and Fuchs, though within a year his salary was the highest of any of them. While Haydn was supportive of both Fuchs and Hummel, the working relationship of the two colleagues at court was a difficult one. The loyal and dutiful Fuchs could not get on with the ambitious, often cavalier Hummel. Nevertheless musical life flourished, with Fuchs and Hummel supplying new church music and the season of operas becoming ever more extensive, including works by Mozart, Anton Polzelli and Seyfried, as well as by the two resident composers. As in Vienna, the new fashion was for operatic works in German rather than Italian.

It was not only musical life at court that was changing apace. During his last visit in 1803 Haydn stayed at the palace itself where he would have noticed the extensive building work going on around him. The palace was substantially altered according to the fashionable Classical style: the moat was filled in, a balcony built above the main entrance, a colonnade built on the garden side and the four onion domes of the corner towers dismantled and replaced with a canopy roof. The gardens, too, were transformed in the manner of Capability Brown, with wandering pathways, copses, lakes, pools, temples and grottos, all set in a carefully manufactured natural landscape. To pump water around this new landscape an English steam engine had been purchased by the prince in 1803, the first in the Austro-Hungarian territories. Given Haydn's fondness for all things English and all things mechanical the steam engine, in particular, would have fascinated him.

Eisenstadt, the palace, the Bergkirche, the musicians' quarters together with the rewards and travails of court life were soon the stuff of memory. From October 1803 to May 1809 Haydn lived in the comfort of his house in Gumpendorf. He was not alone in the house. Ernestine Loder, the granddaughter of his sister Anna Maria, had a room in the house and faithfully cared for her great-uncle. During the day they were joined by Johann Elssler (increasingly acting more as a secretary, adviser and friend, rather than a copyist), a housekeeper (Theresia Mayer), a cook (Anna Kremnitzer), a kitchen maid (Theresia Schaller) and a general maid (Antonia Wierländer). The small courtyard at the back of the house caught the afternoon sun and local children were invited to play there. Haydn occasionally played cards, became rather obsessive about household accounts and read more extensively than had been possible earlier in his career. He received the *Allgemeine musikalische Zeitung*, which kept him up to date on musical developments throughout German-speaking Europe and, more sporadically, elsewhere. His interest in German literature tended towards the old-fashioned and sentimental rather than the progressive and epic; Goethe and Schiller, for instance, were not represented in his library while the elegant, simple, sometimes pious poetry of Christian Fürchtegott Gellert (1715–69) was always favoured. His interest in the natural world was served by several multi-volume encyclopedias and by books on agriculture, astronomy, geography, history, horticulture, medicine and meteorology. From the 1780s he had collected engravings and his collection included several that would have reminded him of his visits to London: Cramer, Dussek, Pleyel, Salomon, a boxing match and 'Sabrina releasing the Lady from the Enchanted Maid'; since the visits these had been supplemented by engravings of Nelson and a 'Plan of the Battle of Aboukir'. He also owned drawings or plaster casts of Cherubini, Gyrowetz, Michael Haydn and Mozart, together with four porcelain or wax busts of himself and a reproduction of the monument that had been erected in his honour in Rohrau in 1793. More eccentric, some of the walls in the house were decorated with the autograph manuscripts of forty of Haydn's canons, a talking point for several visitors, one that could be relied upon to prompt the wry response that he could not afford wallpaper.

While Haydn was still physically active he often hired a coach to take him into the inner city; as arteriosclerosis set in, his painfully swollen legs meant that he became more confined. Some sources suggest that it was a lonely existence, relieved by visits from familiar acquaintances, such as Princess Esterházy and Griesinger or younger musicians who had come to pay homage such as Cherubini, Pleyel, Anton Reicha, Tomaschek and Weber; while there is no record of Beethoven visiting Haydn in Gumpendorf it would be inappropriate to deduce from the absence of evidence that he was necessarily indifferent to the older composer and that he deliberately chose not to visit him. More than one person noted a certain practised routine to the visits. Haydn had always been particular about his appearance and he now dressed rather elegantly in expensive clothes, an aged dandy; he wore a signet ring and sat in a chair holding a walking cane; next to him was a small table on which rested his gloves and hat. He particularly liked to reminiscence about his time in England, wished to be remembered to all the ladies, cried readily when talking of Mozart and invariably asked for his collection of newspapers cuttings, medals and other honours to be brought in.

Individuals wholly unknown to Haydn were also cordially received. In November 1806, for instance, a young art student in Vienna named Franz Pforr (1788–1812), later to become well known as one of the Nazarene painters, went with two friends to Gumpendorf, a visit almost certainly facilitated by one of Pforr's teachers, Albert Christoph Dies. In a letter back to a friend in Frankfurt Pforr spoke of being received kindly but feeling rather awestruck. He also quoted Haydn directly on the relative merits of The Creation and The Seasons: '"The Creation" said he "is my best work, the subject, of course, sublime, for there speak angels and God himself; The Seasons is long and not nearly as good, the subject is deficient, always love, wine, barrows and grapes," and here he smiled "what is that?"'[4]

For some years there had been the occasional perplexed comment by people who met the composer that there was a disjunction between the man and his music, that the former did not live up to the latter. Even Griesinger's letters to Breitkopf & Härtel hint at this apparent paradox. With reference to his lack of discrimination when it came to choosing texts he blamed the composer's 'unscientific education'; at the same time he would not allow his personality to be belittled, 'Haydn is modest, but not stupidly humble'.[5] As the composer's physical and mental powers declined, those who habitually called him 'Papa' or 'Vater' out of reverence and affection inevitably embraced a third element, condescension.

Haydn's last public appearance in Vienna as a conductor of his music occurred a few months after his last visit to Eisenstadt, on 26 December 1803, when once more he gave his services to raise money for the hospital in St Marx in a concert in the Redoutensaal, this time a performance of the choral version of *The Seven Last Words*. Since several members of the imperial court were present the occasion was reported in the *Wiener Zeitung*:[6] 'J. Haydn who, despite his great age and weak health, took it upon himself to conduct the whole music, gave through this kindness new evidence that he is as great a friend of man as he is an artist.' Emperor Franz donated 1,000 gulden and the total money raised after expenses came to 3,650 gulden. In a letter written to George Thomson the following autumn Haydn reflected on the many charity concerts in which he had participated over recent years, claiming that the Tonkünstler-Societät alone had accumulated 40,000 gulden from performances of *The Creation* and *The Seasons*. The city of Vienna acknowledged Haydn's services with two awards, a citizen's medal (the 'Salvator Medal') in May 1803 and honorary citizenship in April 1804. Haydn was long accustomed to receiving awards from throughout Europe, from Amsterdam, Laibach (Ljubljana), Modena, Oxford, Paris, Stockholm and Venice, but these two awards from Vienna were especially cherished. With them the composer of 'Gott erhalte Franz den Kaiser' and the conductor of over twenty charity concerts in six years was, finally, acknowledged as a true Viennese. There was another aspect that appealed to Haydn. Rather than a welcome act of patronage by a prince or a tribute from musical peers, these two rewards came from the Viennese authorities acting on behalf of their citizens; the composer's response reflected that unshakeable belief in the interdependence of community and religion: 'vox populi, vox Dei', the voice of the people is the voice of God.

Encouraged as much by his own sense of a legacy as by the desire of Breitkopf & Härtel and Pleyel to present his music in 'complete' editions, Haydn instructed Elssler to compile a thematic catalogue of his music, relying on a variety of existing catalogues and, more uncertainly, the composer's memory. The lengthy, informal title of the catalogue is also a frank indication of its limitations: 'Catalogue of those compositions that I remember approximately to have composed between my 18th and 73rd years'. As well as the musical incipit of each work Haydn and Elssler numbered each item, 118 symphonies, 125 baryton trios, 83 quartets, 43 songs and so on, but did not provide any dates. While Haydn's own autograph manuscripts usually indicated the year of composition the composer owned only a small proportion of his output and it was left to later scholars to match entries in the catalogue with extant dated sources. It was also left to scholars to add works that escaped Haydn's trawl and to weed out a few that he did not compose. For all its bibliographical weaknesses the catalogue is an impressive display of a lifetime of creativity, over 100 pages containing over 1,000 items, and has guided scholarship ever since. Three copies were written out in Elssler's professional musical hand. The first, which was discovered only in 2007,[7] was presented to Pleyel, the second given to Breitkopf & Härtel and the third was retained by the composer with the expectation that it would be acquired by the Esterházy family after his death.

As the three versions of the catalogue neared completion a new figure entered Haydn's life, someone who was anxious to record his impressions of the composer. Albert Christoph Dies (1755–1822) was a landscape painter, a professor at the imperial academy in Vienna. From 1805 onwards he was commissioned to paint the new English gardens at the Esterházy palace and it was this connection with Haydn's patron as well as the particular urging of a friend, Anton Grassi, who had prepared two busts of the composer, that led painter and composer to form a trusting relationship. Between April 1805 and August 1806 Dies regularly visited Haydn in Gumpendorf, recording his visits in the form of a diary. A patient and diplomatic man, he noted the composer's changing moods and his particular susceptibility to the weather. Some visits were entirely futile, others saw Haydn anxious to recount his many tales. The visits and subsequent accounts were meant to move systematically through Haydn's life and, in this, Dies was largely successful. By the summer of 1806 he was up to date and the later, fewer visits, to August 1808, ensured that he kept abreast of Haydn's increasing frailty. Nevertheless Dies was always willing to adapt his broad, chronological plan in order to record any new information that Haydn happened to divulge about an earlier period. This diary-cum-biography was described by Dies as a collection of 'isolated vignettes', a deliberately different approach from that of Griesinger. The intended readership was different too. While Griesinger was aiming at the readership of the *Allgemeine musikalische Zeitung*, the discriminating musical reader with a clear sense of history, Dies was aiming at a more local readership, those people who had known the composer, or knew someone who did, and who would respond to its familiar, garrulous tone; it was published in Vienna in 1810 and dedicated to Prince Nicolaus. Unlike the Griesinger biography it was never reprinted in the nineteenth century.

Though different in outlook the biographical endeavours of Griesinger and Dies focus narrowly on the man, his personality and the particular events of his life. Neither author refers to contemporary events outside Haydn's life, including the increasingly oppressive effect of the Napoleonic Wars on Viennese life in the first decade of the nineteenth century. By 1805 Austria had been at war with France for thirteen years, during which it had been forced to abandon its wider European role in order to concentrate on defending its core territories, buttressed by the cultivation of nationalism and the implementation of censorship. In the previous year, 1804, Franz had given himself a new title, Emperor of Austria, one that confirmed the new Habsburg identity. Now the war took a serious turn for the worst. In the autumn of 1805 Napoleon's troops marched eastwards from Bavaria along the Danube with ruthless efficiency. Emperor Franz, his family, and a good deal of the Habsburg family treasure were hurriedly removed from Vienna. A peaceful surrender was negotiated and the French entered the city on 12 November. Napoleon established his head-quarters at Schönbrunn, barely two miles from Haydn's house in Gumpendorf, while his generals occupied many of the aristocratic palaces in the inner city. For sixty-seven days Vienna was an occupied city. Neither Griesinger nor Dies mentions the invasion: Griesinger had moved to the Bohemian countryside while Dies carried on visiting Haydn, encouraging him to talk about Salomon and the London visits. Haydn would have consoled himself by playing 'Gott erhalte Franz den Kaiser', his 'prayer' as he sometimes called it, and may have surprised himself by devising an alternative bass line, a musical challenge he was still, on occasions, able to savour.

The invasion exacerbated the financial difficulties of the country and the plight of its poorest citizens. Inflation had been rising steadily since the turn of the century, particularly affecting food and rented accommodation, and the currency was unstable; by the end of 1806 food prices were more than double what they had been ten years earlier. At the turn of the century Kapellmeister Haydn had often been called upon to sanction small adjustments to the salaries of musicians at the Esterházy court to reflect the increasing cost of living; at the beginning of 1806 they all received substantial increases in salary. Later in the year, during one of her visits to Haydn, Princess Esterházy learnt that the nominal Kapellmeister had been forced to dip into his savings in order to meet rising costs. The princess returned the following day with a letter from the prince.[8]

Dear *Kapellmeister* Haydn!
My dear wife, the Princess Maria, told me of your wish to receive from me six-hundred gulden annually, in addition to your regular emoluments; she added that the realization of this would be a great source of comfort and consolation to you. It is with great pleasure that I hasten to use this opportunity to show my esteem and friendship for you, and herewith inform you of my guarantee that you shall receive the sum of three hundred gulden biannually.'

Financial comfort could not stop the inexorable progress of infirmity, cruelly diminishing the man. Haydn was more or less housebound from 1806, one of his pianos was removed that summer and the tedium of daily existence was relieved only by cherished reminders of the past, a gift of tea from Silverstolpe, a letter from a former pupil in

St Petersburg, or a visit from Constanze Mozart. A couple of difficult journeys were made to the Servite church in Rossau where, over half a century earlier as a young man, he had briefly contemplated joining the order to escape from daily hunger. The church contained a chapel dedicated to the thirteenth-century Servite monk, Peregrine, in which pilgrims prayed for relief from pain of the lower limbs. Haydn's instinctive Catholic belief had not changed in over fifty years and on two successive annual feast days, 1 May in 1807 and 1808, he was carried into the church in order to pray in the chapel of St Peregrine.

Haydn the musician would have been buoyed up during the winter of 1807–8 by a new venture in the musical life of Vienna, a subscription concert series that ran from November to March, usually termed the Liebhaber Concerte, intended to promote high-quality performances of orchestral and vocal music. The first of the twenty concerts was given in the Mehlgrube but then transferred to the large hall in the university. Mozart was the best-represented composer across the season, with fourteen performances of various overtures, concertos and symphonies; Beethoven, too, figured prominently, eleven performances of similar works that he had composed up to that time. Haydn had fewer performances, six in all, mainly of the 'London' symphonies but his revered status was made clear in the last concert, on 27 March 1808, which was devoted to a performance of *The Creation*. In the broad history of music in the city this concert series articulated characteristics that were not to become a permanent part of the Viennese tradition until the 1820s, the primacy of Haydn, Mozart and Beethoven and the centrality of the symphony. Only in one way did the Liebhaber Concerte fail to anticipate the future: while Haydn's *Creation* reflected the general esteem in which that composer was held, as well as the particular part the work had played in Viennese life of the previous ten years, by the 1820s Beethoven, not Haydn, was the pivotal figure in the history of music in the city.

Haydn had been invited to the concert on 27 March, a few days before his seventy-sixth birthday, turning the performance of a much loved work into a theatre of homage, and since it was a Sunday and midday rather than a weekday evening, one that also merged the praising of Haydn with that of God and the natural world that characterizes the oratorio. Prince Esterházy sent a carriage to Gumpendorf to fetch the composer, a journey of some twenty minutes; he was greeted by Beethoven, Gyrowetz, Hummel and Salieri; Heinrich von Collin presented him with a three-verse poem in high rhetoric; and the audience, punctuated by fanfares from trumpets and timpani, called out 'Vivat' and 'Long live Haydn'. He was seated next to Princess Esterházy who, fearing that the composer might be feeling a draught, placed her shawl on his legs, a gesture that was followed by other ladies who surrounded him with their shawls. Under Salieri's direction the performance used the Italian translation by Carpani; when it reached 'E la luce fu' (And there was light) there was thunderous applause and Haydn raised his hands to heaven in a gesture of thanksgiving. Thinking that the whole occasion might be too much for him, he decided to leave at the end of Part 1, carried in his armchair through the wide doorway towards the grand central staircase and to the sound of unending applause.

The public adulation of Viennese society was joined a few weeks later by the particular adulation of Esterházy musicians. Now numbering over ninety, they had been dispatched in eleven carriages to Vienna to participate in a performance of a mass by Hummel and a vespers setting by Fuchs as part of a canonization service in the Ursulin cloister in the Johannesgasse, in the inner city, on 22 May. Hummel and the Knabenchor visited Haydn in Gumpendorf, as did other groups of musicians. Kapellmeister Haydn, 'Papa Haydn', 'Vater Haydn', would have been pleased to see former colleagues such as Sebastien Binder (trumpet), Michael Ernst (violin), Josepha Hammer (alto), Jacob Hyrtl (oboe), Barbara Pilhofer (soprano) and Anton Polzelli (violin). Only in one respect would he have been dejected; his oldest colleague and friend, Luigi Tomasini, had died a few weeks earlier, on 25 April, at the age of sixty-six.

Austria in the last winter of Haydn's life was a bellicose country to the point of folly. Sensing that Napoleon was vulnerable following his unsuccessful campaign in the Iberian Peninsular, the government whipped up nationalist expectations that it could defeat Napoleon in Germany and regain some of the former Habsburg territories. It hoped to secure the cooperation of other countries but failed, and by the spring of 1809 it was in the disastrous position of being both committed to war and standing alone. The last months of Haydn's life were played out against this background of national fervour, a fervour promoted, as always, by 'Gott erhalte Franz den Kaiser' and enhanced by a couple of opportunistic performances of the 'Military' symphony in the Burgtheater.

Haydn's doctor now visited him at least twice a day and his apothecary bills were considerable. In a final compassionate gesture Prince Nicolaus agreed to pay all the expenses incurred in 1808 and to underwrite all future ones. Haydn had first prepared a will in 1801 but in February 1809 he revised it, mainly to reflect the fact that many former beneficiaries had died in the interim. It is a lengthy, considered document of fifty clauses that reflects the personal concerns of a sensitive man who had achieved fame and fortune. Money was left for services and prayers in Gumpendorf, Eisenstadt, Müllendorf, St Georgen – two villages near Eisenstadt – and Rohrau. The Barmherzige Brüder and the Franciscan monks in Eisenstadt received donations, as did a school fund in Vienna, the poor of the St Marx district and a hospital fund in Eisenstadt. Surviving nieces and their children were remembered, especially Ernestine Loder who received a total of 1,000 gulden, plus her bed, sheets, bureau, a mirror and 'the relic of the True Cross', and a nephew, Mathias Frölich, a blacksmith in Fischamend (a village on the Danube between Vienna and Hainburg) was made the residual legatee. Only one Esterházy musician is mentioned, Barbara Hilhofer, but the assistant wine steward at the court is remembered as is a cashier and former valet in the Harrach household. The Harrach family was given money to maintain the composer's monument in the castle gardens in Rohrau. Luigia Polzelli's legal position was made clear: a lifelong income of 150 gulden but no further claims. Two lace makers in the Wieden district and a blind beggar in Eisenstadt received bequests while Philipp Schimpel, choirmaster in Hainburg, and his wife received 100 gulden plus a portrait of her father, Mathias Franck, 'my first master in music'. Finally, all the servants and maids who worked for Haydn were remembered with Johann Elssler, 'my true and faithful servant', receiving the largest single amount, 6,000 gulden plus some of the composer's best clothes, a coat and waistcoat, a pair of knee breeches, an overcoat and a hat. A few weeks before Haydn's death the will was read in front of the servants and some witnesses.

The remaining two months of Haydn's life coincided with the humiliation of Austria at the hands of Napoleon. Haydn's oldest piano, the one he had cheekily instructed Artaria to pay for in 1788, was sold on 1 April, Austria declared war on France on 9 April, the imperial family and the Esterházy family fled eastwards to Pest and Haydn continued his habit of playing 'Gott erhalte' on the clavichord, an assured demonstration of hope rather than of defiance. By 10 May the French forces were on the outskirts of Vienna and Gumpendorf was caught in the crossfire between the advancing troops and the inner city. A cannon ball fell in the courtyard and, despite being visibly shaken, Haydn offered words of comfort to his servants: 'Children don't be afraid, for where Haydn is, nothing can happen.'[9]

On 12 May the city surrendered and, in an incident that showed the transcendent appeal of the composer's music, he was visited a few days later by a French army captain who proceeded to pay his respects by singing the aria from Part 2 of The Creation that describes God's ultimate act of creation, mankind: 'Mit Würd' und Hoheit angethan' (In native worth and honour clad). The national anthem was played for the last time on 26 May and on the following day Haydn was confined to his bed. Over the following four days he became weaker and weaker, but remained calm. Surrounded by Ernestine Loder, his servants and a neighbour he died at 12.40 on the morning of 31 May.

Images of Haydn: 1809

Georg August Griesinger, *Biographische Notizen über Joseph Haydn* (1810), translation (amended) from V. Gotwals, *Haydn. Two Contemporary Portraits* (Madison, 1968), pp. 7–8.

Griesinger had paid his last visit to Haydn on 3 May 1809. He was to spend the following months in Störmthal, near Leipzig, where the Schönfeld family had its summer residence and had asked Johann Elssler to keep him informed about Haydn's irreversible decline. The martial law that was imposed on Vienna by the French occupation and the disruption to the postal services to the north of the city meant that it was nearly three weeks after Haydn's death before Griesinger heard the news. The plan to publish a biography of Haydn in instalments in the *Allgemeine musikalische Zeitung* was immediately put into action and the first instalment appeared on 12 July. The opening paragraphs were not a homely tribute but had the authority of a dispassionate observer, someone who was anxious to claim Haydn's status in the German-speaking world and his reputation far beyond that. Informed by personal knowledge and controlled by his training in the principles of rhetorical writing Griesinger began with a masterly exordium, one that was worthy of the composer himself.

> Joseph Haydn has ended his glorious career. By his death Germany again suffers a national loss; for Haydn was founder of an epoch in musical culture, and the sound of his harmonies, universally

understood, did more than all written matter together to promote the honour of German artistic talent in the remotest lands. Haydn's quartets and symphonies, his oratorios and church pieces, please alike on the Danube and on the Thames, on the Seine and on the Neva, and they are treasured and admired across the sea as in our own part of the world. Original and abundant ideas, deep feeling, fantasy wisely controlled by penetrating study of the art, skill in the development of an idea basically simple, calculation of effect by a clever distribution of light and shade, pouring forth of the slyest humour, an easy flow and free movement – these are the qualities that distinguish Haydn's earlier and latest works alike.

Haydn has laboured for more than half a century as a writer of music, and all his works together constitute a not inconsiderable library. He set down in the year 1805 the incipits of those compositions he could casually recall writing between his eighteenth and his seventy-third years. In this still incomplete catalogue are 118 symphonies, 83 quartets, 24 trios, 19 operas, 5 oratorios, 163 compositions for the baryton, 24 concertos for various instruments, 15 masses, 10 smaller church pieces, 44 clavier sonatas with and without accompanying instruments, 42 German and Italian songs, 39 canons, 13 three- and four-part choruses, harmonization and accompaniment for 365 old Scotch songs, and many more divertimenti, fantasias, capriccios, five-, six-, seven-, eight-, and nine-part compositions for sundry instruments.

A productiveness so unusual is astonishing. Even Haydn used to wonder about it, and to say that he knew no epitaph more suited to him than the three words *Vixi, scripsi, dixi* [I lived, I wrote, I spoke]. Nevertheless, he who had already accomplished so much said on his seventy-fourth birthday [1806] that his field was limitless; what could still happen in music was far greater than that which had already happened. Ideas often came to him whereby his art might still be carried much further, but his physical powers no longer permitted him to put them into execution.

Haydn has not outlived his fame; close to two generations have done homage to his works, and from this alone his worth as an artist must be judged. But may one not also be curious to learn of his individuality, the story of his development, his character, his manner of living, and the views of a man so widely celebrated, to whose muse every lover of music owes so many happy hours?

It is in that spirit that this biography, too, has been written.

Some of the English translations acknowledged below have been tacitly amended.

1 God and country

1 Gerhard von Breuning, *Memories of Beethoven. From the House of the Black-Robed Spaniards*, trans. Henry Mins, trans. and ed. Maynard Solomon (Cambridge, 1992), pp. 98–9.

2 Albert Christoph Dies, *Biographische Nachrichten von Joseph Haydn* (Vienna, 1810); modern edn (Berlin, 1962), p. 21; Vernon Gotwals (trans. and ed.), *Haydn. Two Contemporary Portraits* (Madison, 1968), p. 82.

3 Georg August Griesinger, *Biographische Notizen über Joseph Haydn* (Leipzig, 1810), p. 8; Gotwals, *Haydn*, p. 9.

4 Percy Scholes (ed.), *Dr. Burney's Musical Tours in Europe*; Vol. 2: *An Eighteenth-Century Musical Tour in Central Europe and the Netherlands* (London, 1959), p. 72.

5 *Ibid.*, p. 84.

6 *Ibid.*, p. 105.

7 Griesinger, *Biographische Notizen*, p. 10; Dies, *Biographische Nachrichten*, p. 28; Gotwals, *Haydn*, p. 10, p. 87.

8 Autobiographical sketch of 1776. Dénes Bartha (ed.), *Joseph Haydn: Gesammelte Briefe und Aufzeichnungen* (Kassel, 1976), p. 77; H.C. Robbins Landon, *Haydn: Chronicle and Works*; [vol. 2]: *Haydn at Eszterháza 1766–90* (London, 1978), p. 398.

9 Griesinger, *Biographische Notizen*, p. 14; Gotwals, *Haydn*, p. 12.

10 Griesinger, *Biographische Notizen*, p. 17; Gotwals, *Haydn*, p. 14.

11 Dies, *Biographische Nachrichten*, p. 45; Gotwals, *Haydn*, p. 99.
12 Griesinger, *Biographische Notizen*, p. 20; Gotwals, *Haydn*, p. 15.

2   Serving princes

1 Bartha, *Briefe*, pp. 41–4; H.C. Robbins Landon, *Haydn: Chronicle and Works*; [vol. 1]: *Haydn: The Early Years 1732–1765*, pp. 350–2.
2 Johann Mattheson, *Der vollkommene Capellmeister*, trans. E.C. Harriss (Ann Arbor, Mich., 1981), p. 864.
3 Robert Freeman, 'Robert Kimmerling: A Little-Known Haydn Pupil', *Haydn Yearbook*, 13 (1982), pp. 145–7.
4 Griesinger, *Biographische Notizen*, p. 13; Gotwals, *Haydn*, p. 12.
5 Bartha, *Briefe*, p. 52; Landon, *Haydn: The Early Years 1732–1765*, pp. 418–19.
6 Bartha, *Briefe*, p. 50; Landon, *Haydn: The Early Years 1732–65*, p. 420.
7 János Hárich, 'Documents from the Archives of János Hárich', *Haydn Yearbook*, 18 (1993), p. 72.
8 Rosemary Hughes (ed.), *A Mozart Pilgrimage. Being the Travel Diaries of Vincent and Mary Novello in the year 1829*, transcribed and compiled by Nerina Medici di Marignano (London, 1955), p. 196.
9 The Esterházy documents do not permit the string players to be identified with absolute certainly because many individuals were capable of playing more than one instrument. See Sonja Gerlach, 'Haydns Orchestermusiker von 1761 bis 1774', *Haydn-Studien*, 4 (1976), pp. 35–48.
10 6 April 1775, as quoted in Landon, *Haydn at Eszterháza 1766–1790*, p. 215.

3   Italian opera at Eszterháza

1 Bartha, *Briefe*, p. 135; Landon, *Haydn at Eszterháza*, p. 487.
2 Griesinger, *Biographische Notizen*, p. 21; Gotwals, *Haydn*, p. 15.

4   'My misfortune is that I live in the country'

1 Bartha, *Briefe*, pp. 95–7 ; Landon, *Haydn at Eszterháza*, pp. 446–7.
2 Bartha, *Briefe*, pp. 83–4; Landon, *Haydn at Eszterháza*, pp. 42–3.
3 Bartha, *Briefe*, p. 119; Landon, *Haydn at Eszterháza*, p. 465.

4 Bartha, *Briefe*, p. 96; Landon, *Haydn at Eszterháza*, p. 446.

5 Bartha, *Briefe*, p. 202; Landon, *Haydn at Eszterháza*, p. 718.

6 Bartha, *Briefe*, p. 109; Landon, *Haydn at Eszterháza*, p. 461.

7 Bartha, *Briefe*, p. 111; Landon, *Haydn at Eszterháza*, p. 462.

8 Bartha, *Briefe*, p. 119; Landon, *Haydn at Eszterháza*, p. 465.

9 Irmgard Leux-Henschen, *Joseph Martin Kraus in seinen Briefen* (Stockholm, 1978), p. 264; Landon, *Haydn at Eszterháza*, p. 478.

10 Bartha, *Briefe*, p. 195; Landon, *Haydn at Eszterháza*, p. 710.

11 Bartha, *Briefe*, p. 551; H.C. Robbins Landon, *Haydn: Chronicle and Works*; [vol. 3]: *Haydn in England 1791–1795* (London, 1976), p. 269.

12 Bartha, *Briefe*, pp. 86–7; Landon, *Haydn at Eszterháza*, p. 419.

13 Bartha, *Briefe*, p. 101; Landon, *Haydn at Eszterháza*, p. 449.

14 Michael Kelly, *Reminiscences* (London, 1826), vol. 1, p. 237.

15 Emily Anderson (ed.), *The Letters of Mozart and his Family* (London, 1938), vol. 3, p. 1321.

16 Otto Erich Deutsch, *Mozart. A Documentary Biography*, trans. Eric Blom, Peter Branscombe and Jeremy Noble (London, 1965), p. 250.

17 Joachim Hurwitz, 'Haydn and the Freemasons', *Haydn Yearbook*, 16 (1986), p. 95.

18 *Public Advertiser*, 14 May 1785.

19 Alvaro Ribeiro (ed.), *The Letters of Dr Charles Burney*; vol. 1: 1751–1784 (Oxford, 1991), p. 400.

20 Facsimile in Landon, *Haydn at Eszterháza*, pp. 496–7.

21 Landon, *Haydn at Eszterháza*, p. 597.

22 *The Times*, 31 January 1788.

23 Letter of 14 March 1790. Bartha, *Briefe*, p. 231; Landon, *Haydn at Eszterháza*, p. 739.

24 Bartha, *Briefe*, p. 228–9; Landon, *Haydn at Eszterháza*, p. 737.

25 Bartha, *Briefe*, p. 243; Landon, *Haydn at Eszterháza*, p. 745.

26 Dies, *Biographische Nachrichten*, p. 78; Gotwals, *Haydn*, p. 120.

5 London – Vienna – London

1 Ingrid Bodsch, 'Das kulturelle Leben in Bonn unter den letzten Kölner Kurfürsten Maximilian Franz von Österreich (1780/84–1794)', in Bodsch (ed.), *Joseph Haydn und Bonn. Katalog zur Ausstellung* (Bonn, 2001), pp. 61, 70–1, 186–7.

2 Bartha, *Briefe*, pp. 250–1; Landon, *Haydn in England*, p. 36.

3 '18th and 19th Century Newspaper Articles Regarding Haydn and Contemporaries', *Haydn Yearbook*, 21 (1997), pp. 78–9.

4 Letter of 8 January 1791. Bartha, *Briefe*, p. 251; Landon, *Haydn in England*, p. 36.

5 Landon, *Haydn in England*, p. 43.

6 *Ibid.*, p. 77.

7 Griesinger, *Biographische Notizen*, p. 40; Gotwals, *Haydn*, p. 25.

8 Bartha, *Briefe*, p. 259; Landon, *Haydn in England*, pp. 95–6.

9 Bartha, *Briefe*, pp. 260–1; Landon, *Haydn in England*, pp. 97–8.

10 Letter of 12 April 1792. Bartha, *Briefe*, p. 519; Landon, *Haydn in England*, p. 154.

11 Bartha, *Briefe*, pp. 486, 488, 513; Landon, *Haydn in England*, pp. 175–6.

12 28 June 1792. Bodsch, *Joseph Haydn und Bonn*, p. 188.

13 Letter of 29 June 1793. Bartha, *Briefe*, p. 295; Landon, *Haydn in England*, p. 220.

14 Ignaz de Luca, *Topographie von Wien* (Vienna, 1794); facsimile edn (Vienna, 2003), pp. 386–7.

15 Landon, *Haydn in England*, p. 233.

16 *Ibid.*, p. 234.

17 *Ibid.*, p. 241.

18 *Ibid.*, p. 241.

19 *Ibid.*, p. 251.

20 Bartha, *Briefe*, pp. 534–5; Landon, *Haydn in England*, pp. 262–3.

21 Bartha, *Briefe*, pp. 539–41; Landon, *Haydn in England*, pp. 266–7.

22 *Ibid.*, p. 280.

23 Bartha, *Briefe*, p. 553; Landon, *Haydn in England*, pp. 309.

24 *Ibid.*, p. 308.

25 Griesinger, *Biographische Notizen*, p. 59; Gotwals, *Haydn*, p. 34.

6 Viennese composer, European composer

1 Letter of 2 August 1794. E. Anderson (ed.), *The Letters of Beethoven* (London, 1961), vol. 1, p. 18.

2 H.C. Robbins Landon, *Haydn: Chronicle and Works*; [vol. 4]: *Haydn: The Years of 'The Creation' 1796–1800* (London, 1977), p. 241.

3 *Ibid.*, p. 249.

4 Bartha, *Briefe*, p. 313; Landon, *Haydn: The Years of 'The Creation'*, p. 246.

5 *Ibid.*, p. 112.

6 Bartha, *Briefe*, p. 335; Landon, *Haydn: The Years of 'The Creation'*, p. 483.

7 Neil Jenkins, 'The Text of Haydn's *The Creation*; New Sources and a Possible Librettist', *Haydn Society Journal*, 24/2 (2005), pp. 37–53.

8 Landon, *Haydn: The Years of 'The Creation'*, p. 116.

9 Griesinger, *Biographische Notizen*, p. 101; Gotwals, *Haydn*, pp. 54–5.

10 C.-G. Stellan Mörner, 'Haydniana aus Schweden um 1800', *Haydn-Studien*, 2 (1969), p. 26–7; Landon, *Haydn: The Years of 'The Creation'*, pp. 252, 266.

11 *Ibid.*, p. 316.

12 *Ibid.*, p. 320.

13 Georg Feder, *Joseph Haydn. Die Schöpfung* (Kassel, 1999), p. 144; Landon, *Haydn: The Years of 'The Creation'*, p. 453.

14 Mörner, 'Haydniana', pp. 5–6; Landon, *Haydn: The Years of 'The Creation'*, p. 455.

15 Mörner, 'Haydniana', p. 6; Landon, *Haydn: The Years of 'The Creation'*, p. 456.

16 Bartha, *Briefe*, p. 341; Landon, *Haydn: The Years of 'The Creation'*, p. 496.

17 Bartha, *Briefe*, p. 339; Landon, *Haydn: The Years of 'The Creation'*, p. 487.

18 Otto Biba (ed.), *'Eben komme ich von Haydn...'. Georg August Griesingers Korrespondenz mit Joseph Haydns Verleger Breitkopf & Härtel 1799–1819* (Zurich, 1987), p. 26.

19 *Ibid.*, p. 36.

20 Advertisement in *Allgemeine musikalische Zeitung*, 10 March 1802; H. C. Robbins Landon, *Haydn; Chronicle and Works*; [vol. 5]: *Haydn: The Late Years 1801–1809* (London, 1977), p. 223.

21 Maynard Solomon, 'The Rochlitz Anecdotes: Issues of Authenticity in Early Mozart Biography', in Cliff Eisen (ed.), *Mozart Studies* (Oxford, 1991), p. 16.

22 Biba, *'Eben komme ich von Haydn...'*, p. 31.

23 Landon, *Haydn: The Years of 'The Creation'*, p. 560.

24 Biba, *'Eben komme ich von Haydn...'*, p. 53.

25 Landon, *Haydn: The Late Years*, p. 43.

26 Bartha, *Briefe*, p. 380; Landon, *Haydn: The Late Years*, p. 79.

27 Bartha, *Briefe*, p. 404; Landon, *Haydn: The Late Years*, p. 227.

28 Summarized in G. Heilingsetzer, '"Der wahre Sitz eines Souverains." Ein Besuch in der Esterházy-Residenz Eisenstadt (1802)', in Jakob Perschy (ed.), *Die Fürsten Esterházy. Magnaten, Diplomaten & Mäzene*, exhibition catalogue (Eisenstadt, 1995), pp. 190–8.

29 Bartha, *Briefe*, p. 410; Landon, *Haydn: The Late Years*, p. 233.

7 'Gone is all my strength'

1 Bartha, *Briefe*, p. 419; Landon, *Haydn: The Late Years*, p. 252.

2 Biba, '*Eben komme ich von Haydn...*', p. 227.

3 *Ibid.*, p. 247.

4 www.bela1996.de/art/pforr/pforr-02 (accessed 15 March 2008).

5 Biba, '*Eben komme ich von Haydn...*', p. 126.

6 Landon, *Haydn: The Late Years*, p. 273.

7 Sotheby's Music Sale, London, 23 May 2007; catalogue, pp. 53–7.

8 Bartha, *Briefe*, p. 462; Landon, *Haydn: The Late Years*, pp. 348–9.

9 Johann Elssler's account of the last three weeks of Haydn's life; Landon, *Haydn: The Late Years*, pp. 385–6.

'The Acta Musicalia of the Esterházy Archives', nos. 1–35, Haydn Yearbook, 13 (1983), pp. 5–96; nos. 36–100, Haydn Yearbook, 14 (1984), pp. 9–128; nos. 101–52, Haydn Yearbook, 15 (1985), pp. 93–180; nos. 153–74, Haydn Yearbook, 16 (1986), pp. 99–207; nos. 175–200, Haydn Yearbook, 17 (1992), pp. 1–84; nos. 201–79, Haydn Yearbook, 18 (1993), pp. 115–96.

Anderson, Emily (ed.). The Letters of Beethoven (London, 1961).

The Letters of Mozart and his Family (London, 1938).

Bardi, Terézia. 'Newly Found Inventories of Esterházy Sceneries', Haydn-Studien, 9 (2006), pp. 94–106.

Bartha, Dénes (ed.). Joseph Haydn: Gesammelte Briefe und Aufzeichnungen (Kassel, 1976).

Bartha, Dénes and László Somfai. Haydn als Opernkapellmeister (Budapest, 1960).

Biba, Otto. 'Beethoven und die "Liebhaber Concerte" in Wien im Winter 1807/8', Beiträge '76–78: Beethoven Kolloquium 1977: Dokumentation und Aufführungspraxis, ed. Rudolf Klein (Kassel, 1978), pp. 82–93.

'Beobachtungen zur Österreichischen Musikszene des 18. Jahrhunderts', Österreichische Musik – Musik in Österreich. Beiträge zur Musikgeschichte Mitteleuropas, ed. Elisabeth Theresia Hilscher, Wiener Veröffentlichungen zur Musikwissenschaft, 34 (Tutzing, 1998), pp. 213–30.

'Eben komme ich von Haydn ...'. *Georg August Griesingers Korrespondenz mit Joseph Haydns Verleger Breitkopf & Härtel 1799–1819* (Zurich, 1987).

'Nachrichten zur Musikpflege in der gräflichen Familie Harrach', *Haydn Yearbook*, 10 (1978), pp. 36–44.

Bodsch, Ingrid (ed.). *Joseph Haydn und Bonn. Katalog zur Ausstellung* (Bonn, 2001).

Breuning, Gerhard von. *Memories of Beethoven. From the House of the Black-Robed Spaniards*, trans. Henry Mins, trans. and ed. Maynard Solomon (Cambridge, 1992).

Brown, A. Peter. 'Marianna Martines' Autobiography as a New Source for Haydn's Biography During the 1750's', *Haydn-Studien*, 6 (1986), pp. 68–70.

Performing Haydn's The Creation (Bloomington, Ind., 1986).

Burney, Charles. *A General History of Music, from the Earliest Ages to the Present Period* (1789), ed. Frank Mercer, 2 vols. (New York, 1957).

Clark, Caryl (ed.). *The Cambridge Companion to Haydn* (Cambridge, 2005).

'Fabricating Magic: Costuming Salieri's Armida', *Early Music*, 31 (2003), pp. 451–61.

Cooper, Barry. *Beethoven* (Oxford, 2000).

Csendes, Peter, and Ferdinand Opil (eds.). *Wien, Geschichte einer Stadt:* vol. 2, *Die frühneuzeitliche Residenz (16. bis 18. Jahrhundert)*, ed. Karl Vocelka and Anita Traninger (Vienna, 2003); vol. 3, *Von 1790 bis zur Gegenwart* (Vienna, 2006).

DeNora, Tia. *Beethoven and the Construction of Genius: Musical Politics in Vienna 1792–1803* (Berkeley, 1995).

Deutsch, Otto Erich. *Mozart. A Documentary Biography*, trans. Eric Blom, Peter Branscombe and Jeremy Noble (London, 1965).

Dies, Albert Christoph. *Biographische Nachrichten von Joseph Haydn* (Vienna, 1810); modern edn (Berlin, 1962).

Dittersdorf, Carl Ditters von. *Lebensbeschreibung. Seinem Sohne in die Feder diktirt*, ed. Norbert Miller (Munich, 1967); trans. A. D. Coleridge, *The Autobiography of Karl von Dittersdorf, Dictated to his Son* (London, 1896).

Edge, Dexter. 'New Sources for Haydn's Early Biography', unpublished paper read at the annual meeting of the American Musicological Society, 1993.

Review of Mary Sue Morrow, *Concert Life in Haydn's Vienna: Aspects of a Developing Musical and Social Institution* (Stuyvesant, NY, 1989), *Haydn Yearbook*, 16 (1992), pp. 108–66.

Eisen, Cliff. 'The Mozarts' Salzburg Music Library', in Cliff Eisen (ed.), *Mozart Studies*, 2 (Oxford, 1997), pp. 85–138.

Eybl, Martin. 'Franz Bernhard Ritter von Keeß – Sammler, Mäzen und Organisator', *Österreichische Musik – Musik in Österreich. Beiträge zur Musikgeschichte Mitteleuropas*, ed. Elisabeth Theresia Hilscher, Wiener Veröffentlichungen zur Musikwissenschaft, 34 (Tutzing, 1998), pp. 239–50.

Feder, Georg. 'Joseph Haydn', *Die Musik in Geschichte und Gegenwart*, 2nd. edn, Ludwig Finscher (ed.), Personenteil, vol. 8 (2002), cols. 901–1094.

Joseph Haydn. Die Schöpfung (Kassel, 1999).

Fisher, Stephen C. 'A Group of Haydn Copies for the Court of Spain: Fresh Sources, Rediscovered Works, and New Riddles', *Haydn-Studien*, 4 (1978), pp. 65–84.

Freeman, Robert. 'Robert Kimmerling: A Little-Known Haydn Pupil', *Haydn Yearbook*, 13 (1983), pp. 143–79.

Gates-Coon, Rebecca. *The Landed Estates of the Esterházy Princes. Hungary during the Reforms of Maria Theresia and Joseph II* (Baltimore, 1994).

Gerlach, Sonja. 'Haydns "chronologische" Sinfonienliste für Breitkopf & Härtel', *Haydn-Studien*, 6 (1988), pp. 116–29.

'Haydns Orchestermusiker von 1761 bis 1774', *Haydn-Studien*, 4 (1976), pp. 35–48.

'Johann Tost, Geiger und Großhandlungsgremialist', *Haydn-Studien*, 7 (1988), pp. 344–65.

Gotwals, Vernon (trans. and ed.). *Haydn: Two Contemporary Portraits*, trans. of Griesinger, *Biographische Notizen* and Dies, *Biographische Nachrichten* (Madison, 1963).

Griesinger, Georg August. *Biographische Notizen über Joseph Haydn* (Leipzig, 1810).

Hárich, János. 'Das fürstlich Esterházy'sche Fideikommiß', *Haydn Yearbook*, 4 (1968), pp. 5–35.

'Das Repertoire des Opernkapellmeisters Joseph Haydn in Eszterháza (1780–1790)', *Haydn Yearbook*, 1 (1962), pp. 9–109.

'Documents from the Archives of János Hárich', *Haydn Yearbook*, 18 (1993), pp. 1–109; 19 (1994), pp. 1–359.

'Inventare der Esterházy-Hofkapelle in Eisenstadt', *Haydn Yearbook*, 9 (1975), pp. 5–125.

Harrison, Bernard. *Haydn. The 'Paris' Symphonies* (Cambridge, 1998).

Heartz, Daniel. *Haydn, Mozart and the Viennese School 1740–1780* (New York, 1995).

Horányi, Mátyás. *The Magnificence of Eszterháza* (Budapest, 1962).

Hughes, Rosemary (ed.). *A Mozart Pilgrimage. Being the Travel Diaries of Vincent and Mary Novello in the year 1829*, transcribed and compiled by Nerina Medici di Marignano (London, 1955).

Hurwitz, Joachim. 'Haydn and the Freemasons', *Haydn Yearbook*, 16 (1986), pp. 5–98.

Ingrao, Charles. *The Habsburg Monarchy 1618–1815* (Cambridge, 1994).

Jahn, Michael. *Die Musikhandschriften des Domarchivs St. Stephan in Wien*, Veröffentlichungen des rism-österreich A/1 (Vienna, 2005).

Jenkins, Neil. 'The Text of Haydn's *The Creation*; New Sources and a Possible Librettist', *Haydn Society Journal*, 24/2 (2005), whole issue.

Jolán, Bak. *Fertöd. Esterházy Kastély*, 2nd edn (Eszterháza, 2003).

Jones, David Wyn. *The Life of Beethoven* (Cambridge, 1998).

(ed.). *Oxford Composer Companions. Haydn* (Oxford, 2002).

Kálmán, Varga. *Maria Theresia in Esterház* (Budapest, 2000).

Kelly, Michael. *Reminiscences* (London, 1826).

Lamkin, Kathleen. *Esterházy Musicians 1790 to 1809. Considered from New Sources in the Castle Forchtenstein Archives*, Eisenstädter Haydn-Berichte, 6 (Tutzing, 2007).

Landon, H.C. Robbins. *The Collected Correspondence and London Notebooks of Joseph Haydn* (London, 1959).

'An Englishman in Vienna and Eisenstadt Castle in 1748 and 1749', *Haydn Yearbook*, 18 (1993), pp. 197–212.

'Four New Haydn Letters', *Haydn Yearbook*, 13 (1983), pp. 213–19.

Haydn: Chronicle and Works. [Vol. 1], *Haydn: The Early Years 1732–1765* (London, 1980).

Haydn: Chronicle and Works. [Vol. 2], *Haydn at Eszterháza* (London, 1978).

Haydn: Chronicle and Works. [Vol. 3], *Haydn in England 1791–1795* (London, 1976).

Haydn: Chronicle and Works. [Vol. 4], *Haydn: The Years of the 'The Creation' 1796–1800* (London, 1977).

Haydn: Chronicle and Works. [Vol. 5], *Haydn: The Late Years 1801–1809* (London, 1977).

Haydn: A Documentary Study (New York, 1981).

'A Letter from Dr. Burney to Longman, Clementi & Co', *Haydn Yearbook*, 17 (1992), pp. 170–4.

'More Haydn Letters in Autograph', *Haydn Yearbook*, 14 (1984), pp. 200–5.

'New Haydn Letter', *Haydn Yearbook*, 15 (1985), pp. 214–18.

Larsen, Jens Peter (ed.). *Three Haydn Catalogues*, 2nd edn (New York, 1979).

Leux-Henschen, Irmgard. *Joseph Martin Kraus in seinen Briefen* (Stockholm, 1978).

Lister, Warwick. 'The First Performance of Haydn's "Paris" Symphonies', *Eighteenth-Century Music*, 1 (2004), pp. 289–300.

Luca, Ignaz de. *Das gelehrte Oesterreich* (Vienna, 1778).

Topographie von Wien (Vienna, 1794); facsimile edn (Vienna, 2003).

McGrann, Jeremiah W. 'Of Saints, Namedays, and Turks: Some Background on Haydn's Masses Written for Prince Nikolaus II Esterházy', *Journal of Musicological Research*, 17 (1998), pp. 195–210.

McVeigh Simon. *Concert Life in London from Mozart to Haydn* (Cambridge, 1993).

'The Professional Concert and Rival Subscription Series in London, 1783–1793', *Royal Musical Association Research Chronicle*, 22 (1989), pp. 1–135.

Mathew, Nicholas. 'Heroic Haydn, the Occasional Work and 'Modern' Political Music', *Eighteenth-Century Music*, 4 (2007), pp. 7–25.

Mattheson, Johann. *Der vollkommene Capellmeister*, trans. E. C. Harriss (Ann Arbor, Mich., 1981).

Matthews, Betty. 'Haydn's Visit to Hampshire and the Isle of Wight, Described from Contemporary Sources', *Haydn Yearbook*, 3 (1965), pp. 111–21.

Michtner, Otto. *Das alte Burgtheater als Opernbühne vor der Einführung des deutschen Singspiels (1778) bis zum Tod Kaiser Leopolds II. (1792)* (Vienna, 1970).

Moore, Julia. 'Beethoven and Inflation', *Beethoven Forum*, 1 (1992), pp. 191–223.

Mörner, C.-G. Stellan. 'Haydniana aus Schweden um 1800', *Haydn-Studien*, 2 (1969), pp. 1–33.

Morrow, Mary Sue. *Concert Life in Haydn's Vienna: Aspects of a Developing Musical and Social Institution* (Stuyvesant, NY, 1989).

Mraz, Gerda, Gottfried Mraz and Gerald Schlag (eds.). *Joseph Haydn und seine Zeit*, exhibition catalogue (Eisenstadt, 1972).

Olleson, Philip. 'The London Roman Catholic Embassy Chapels and their Music in the Eighteenth and Early Nineteenth Centuries', in David Wyn Jones (ed.), *Music in Eighteenth-Century Britain* (Aldershot, 2000), pp. 101–18.

Oppermann, Annette. 'Schreibraum und Denkraum – Joseph Haydns Skizzen zur "Schöpfung"', *Die Musikforschung*, 56 (2003), pp. 375–81.

Pandi, Marianne, and Fritz Schmidt. 'Musik zur Zeit Haydns und Beethovens in der Preßburger Zeitung', *Haydn Yearbook*, 8 (1971), pp. 165–265.

Pauly, Reinhard G. 'The Reforms of Church Music under Joseph II', *Musical Quarterly*, 43 (1957), pp. 372–82.

Perger, Richard. *Das Palais Esterházy in der Wallnerstraße zu Wien* (Vienna, 1994).

Perschy, Jakob (ed.). *Die Fürsten Esterházy. Magnaten, Diplomaten &*
Mäzene exhibition catalogue (Eisenstadt, 1995).

Pforr, Franz. Letters to Johann David Passavant, www.bela1996.de/
art/pforr/pforr-02

Price, Curtis, Judith Milhous and Robert D. Hume. *Italian Opera in*
Late Eighteenth-Century London. Vol. 1, *The King's Theatre, Haymarket*
1778–1791 (Oxford, 1995).

Radant, Else. 'The Diaries of Joseph Carl Rosenbaum 1770–1829',
Haydn Yearbook, 5 (1968), whole issue.

Ribeiro, Alvaro (ed.). *The Letters of Dr Charles Burney*. Vol. 1, 1751–1784
(Oxford, 1991).

Rice, John A. *Empress Marie Therese and Music at the Viennese Court*
1792–1807 (Cambridge, 2003).

Ridgewell, Rupert. 'Music Printing in Mozart's Vienna: The Artaria
Press, 1778–1794', *Fontes Artis Musicae*, 48 (2001), pp. 217–36.

Riedel, F.W. *Kirchenmusik am Hofe Karls VI. (1711–1740). Untersuchungen*
zum Verhältnis von Zeremoniell und musikalischem Stil im Barock-
zeitalter, (Munich, 1977).

Riepe, Juliane. 'Eine neue Quelle zum Repertoire der Bonner
Hofkapelle im späten 18. Jahrhundert', *Archiv für Musik-*
wissenschaft, 60 (2003), pp. 97–114.

Scholes, Percy A. *An Eighteenth-Century Musical Tour in Central Europe*
and the Netherlands. Dr Burney's Musical Tours in Europe, vol. 2
(London, 1959).

Schönfeld, Johann Ferdinand von. *Jahrbuch der Tonkunst von Wien und*
Prag (Vienna, 1796); facsimile edn (Munich, 1976). Partial trans.
in Elaine Sisman (ed.), *Haydn and His World* (Princeton, 1997),
pp. 289–320.

Schroeder, David P. *Haydn and the Enlightenment. The Late Symphonies*
and their Audience (Oxford, 1990).

Scott, Marion M. 'Haydn Stayed Here!', *Music and Letters*, 32 (1951),
pp. 38–44.

Scull, Tony. 'More Light on Haydn's "English Widow"', *Music and*
Letters, 78 (1997), pp. 45–55.

Seifert, Herbert. 'Die Verbindungen der Familie Erdödy zur Musik', *Haydn Yearbook*, 10 (1978), pp. 151–63.

Sisman, Elaine (ed.). *Haydn and His World* (Princeton, 1997).

Solomon, Maynard. 'The Rochlitz Anecdotes: Issues of Authenticity in Early Mozart Biography', in Cliff Eisen (ed.), *Mozart Studies* (Oxford, 1991), pp. 1–59.

Somfai, László. *Joseph Haydn. His Life in Contemporary Pictures* (London, 1969).

Spink, Ian. 'Haydn at St Paul's – 1791 or 1792?', *Early Music*, 33 (2005), pp. 273–80.

Steblin, Rita. 'Haydns Orgeldienst in "der damaligen Gräfl. Haugwitzischen Kapelle".' *Wiener Geschichtsblätter*, 55 (2000), pp. 124–34.

Szerző, Katalin. 'Neue Dokumente zur Esterházy-Sammlung', *Haydn-Studien*, 9 (2006), pp. 82–93.

Tank, Ulrich. 'Die Dokumente der Esterhazy-Archive zur Fürstlichen Hofkapelle in der Zeit 1761 bis 1770', *Haydn-Studien*, 4 (1980), pp. 129–333.

Weber, William. 'Musical Culture and the Capital City: The Epoch of the *beau monde* in London, 1700–1870', in Susan Wollenberg and Simon McVeigh (eds.), *Concert Life in Eighteenth-Century Britain* (Aldershot, 2004), pp. 71–89.

Webster, James, and Georg Feder. *The New Grove Haydn* (London, 2002).

Woodfield, Ian. 'John Bland: London Retailer of the Music of Haydn and Mozart', *Music and Letters*, 81 (2000), pp. 210–44.

Salomon and the Burneys. Private Patronage and a Public Career, Royal Music Association Monographs, 12 (Aldershot, 2003).

CPSIA information can be obtained
at www.ICGtesting.com
Printed in the USA
LVHW022302100423
744030LV00015B/878

9 781107 610811